LIFE HISTORY RESEARCH IN
Psychopathology

VOLUME 2

Life History Research in Psychopathology

VOLUME 2

MERRILL ROFF, LEE N. ROBINS, AND MAX POLLACK, EDITORS

The University of Minnesota Press, Minneapolis

© Copyright 1972 by the University of Minnesota. "Models of Etiology for the Study of Children at Risk for Schizophrenia" by Norman Garmezy © Copyright 1971 by the University of Minnesota. "Ex–Problem Drinkers" by Genevieve Knupfer © Copyright 1971 by the University of Minnesota. All rights reserved. Printed in the United States of America at the Lund Press, Minneapolis. Published in the United Kingdom and India by the Oxford University Press, London and Delhi, and in Canada by the Copp Clark Publishing Co. Limited, Toronto

Library of Congress Catalog Card Number: 77-98098
ISBN 0-8166-0637-4

"Psychopathy: Heredity and Environment" by Fini Schulsinger has been reprinted by permission from the *International Journal of Mental Health*, 1, No. 1 (Spring–Summer 1972), 190–206, published by International Arts & Sciences Press, Inc., White Plains, New York 10603.

Preface

THIS is the second volume in a series on Life History Research in Psychopathology. Like the first, this volume combines papers originally presented at two conferences on Life History Research in Psychopathology. The third conference was held at the Hillside Hospital, Glen Oaks, New York, in conjunction with the dedication of the Leon Lowenstein Research Building. The fourth conference, which was funded in part by the National Institute of Mental Health (Grant MA 18737) was held at Washington University in St. Louis.

These conferences began in response to the growing interest in longitudinal research in many different fields of study. At the third conference the conferees established themselves as an organization, the Society for Life History Research in Psychopathology, with membership open to researchers with a major commitment to longitudinal investigation no matter what their discipline or training. Life history research has attracted the efforts of research workers from many disciplines, including genetics, psychology, psychiatry, sociology, social work, and law.

Since the participants do come from different disciplines and different backgrounds, and are interested in communicating with those of different professional expertise and orientation, contributors have attempted to describe their activities in such a way that they would be comprehensible to persons with different backgrounds. Insofar as this has been achieved, the papers are comprehensible and of interest not only to other specialists in the same area but also to research workers and advanced graduate students in other areas.

The research programs described have received financial support from various agencies, and detailed acknowledgments are made by the different authors. It may be noted here that almost every research program represented has received at least part of its support from the National Institute of Mental Health, for at least part of its duration.

Life History Research in Psychopathology

Space does not permit the acknowledgment of the assistance the different authors have received from school systems, hospitals, child guidance centers, community clinics, and other cooperating organizations. The research programs described here would not have been possible without this help. We hope that this collection of papers will give these helping organizations an increasingly clearer idea of what these different programs were about.

Similarly, space does not permit mention of all the assistants without whose help this wide range of research programs would not have been possible. There is some indication that many of them have acquired a taste for longitudinal or follow-up work. It is hoped that their experiences in connection with these projects will lead them to similarly fruitful research as they advance professionally.

The assistance we have received from the University of Minnesota Press has been so supportive both qualitatively and quantitatively, that specific mention of them cannot be avoided.

M. R.
L. R.
M. P.

Table of Contents

INTRODUCTION   3

Section 1. Beginning in Childhood

MODELS OF ETIOLOGY FOR THE STUDY OF CHILDREN AT RISK FOR SCHIZOPHRENIA BY NORMAN GARMEZY   9

DIFFERENCES IN OUTCOME WITH EARLY INTERVENTION IN CHILDREN WITH BEHAVIOR DISORDERS BY STELLA CHESS AND ALEXANDER THOMAS   35

A COMPARISON OF THE SCHOOL RECORDS OF PERSONALITY DISORDERS, SCHIZOPHRENICS, AND THEIR SIBS BY MARGARET G. WOERNER, MAX POLLACK, CAROL ROGALSKI, YVETTE POLLACK, AND DONALD F. KLEIN   47

Section 2. Juvenile Delinquency

THE PSYCHOMETRIC PREDICTION OF DELINQUENCY BY ROBERT D. WIRT, ANNA C. HAMPTON, AND PHILIP D. SEAT   66

A TWO-FACTOR APPROACH TO JUVENILE DELINQUENCY AND THE LATER HISTORIES OF JUVENILE DELINQUENTS BY MERRILL ROFF   77

Section 3. Psychopathology among Different Family Members

PSYCHOPATHY: HEREDITY AND ENVIRONMENT BY FINI SCHULSINGER   102

THE HALF-SIBLING APPROACH IN A GENETIC STUDY OF ALCOHOLISM BY MARC SCHUCKIT, DONALD W. GOODWIN, AND GEORGE WINOKUR   120

FAMILY DIFFERENCES IN ILLNESS AND PERSONALITY
IN AFFECTIVE DISORDER BY REMI J. CADORET   128

Section 4. New Ways of Studying Life Histories

AN ACTUARIAL EVALUATION OF THE CAUSES AND
CONSEQUENCES OF DEVIANT BEHAVIOR IN YOUNG
BLACK MEN BY LEE N. ROBINS   137

THE ROLE OF PSYCHIATRIC CASE REGISTERS IN THE
LONGITUDINAL STUDY OF PSYCHOPATHOLOGY
BY HAROUTUN M. BABIGIAN   155

SOCIAL CLASS AND THE RELATION OF REMOTE
TO RECENT STRESSORS BY BARBARA SNELL DOHRENWEND
AND BRUCE P. DOHRENWEND   170

THE CONGENITAL BACKGROUND TO BEHAVIOR
DISTURBANCE BY D. H. STOTT   186

Section 5. Maladjustment over Time at the Adult Level

A THIRTY-YEAR FOLLOW-UP OF SOMATIC SYMPTOMS
UNDER EMOTIONAL STRESS BY GEORGE E. VAILLANT
AND CHARLES C. MC ARTHUR   199

THE COMMUNICATION OF SUICIDAL INTENT IN
PSYCHIATRIC ILLNESS: A FOLLOW-UP BY RICHARD W.
HUDGENS, ELI ROBINS, JON TEK LUM, AND CHARLES H.
MERIDETH   211

SIMPLE AND HEBEPHRENIC SCHIZOPHRENIA: A
FOLLOW-UP STUDY BY RODRIGO A. MUNOZ, GARY KULAK,
SUSAN MARTEN, AND VICENTE B. TUASON   228

LIFETIME PATTERNS OF NARCOTIC ADDICTION
BY JOHN A. O'DONNELL   236

EX–PROBLEM DRINKERS BY GENEVIEVE KNUPFER   256

LIST OF CONTRIBUTORS AND PARTICIPANTS   281

INDEX   285

LIFE HISTORY RESEARCH IN
Psychopathology

VOLUME 2

1 Introduction

LIFE HISTORY research is defined most broadly as the study of events occurring at two or more different age levels and of the relations among these, whether the technique for study be retrospective, prospective, or the matching of earlier and later records. It can encompass short-term or long-term changes, from the effect of child-rearing on first-grade school success to its effect on adult psychiatric health. At the other end of the age scale, it would include studies of characteristics of persons over sixty in relation to the subsequent onset of senility or death. Although the description of the expected natural course of psychopathology is within its province, one of the special interests of life history research is in attempting to distinguish factors which seem to be "causal" from those which are merely correlated. It can, of course, concern itself with normal as well as deviant development. In the present set of volumes, attention is focused primarily on deviance, its antecedents and its later history, because (a) deviance presents pressing practical problems and (b) information is often collected more systematically about individuals showing various kinds of deviance than about "normal" persons.

Like the history of a nation, the history of an individual is unique. As contrasted with the histories of nations, however, the histories of persons offer an approximation to replication because of the great numbers of persons, the shortness of their life-spans, and the constraints of biology on the possible varieties of outcomes for them. Thus, through we can never hope to predict human outcomes totally, we can hope to generalize about the probabilities of sequences of events for persons, if not for nations. The convergences among the findings reported in these volumes are testimony to the fact that human histories are predictable in a statistical sense.

The emphasis in the conferences at which these papers were originally presented has been on research programs and their strategies, rather than on reports of isolated findings. Thus, papers in the present volume and in Volume 1 often present an overview of the work of investigators over a number of years. The research problems reported reflect the diversity of disciplines represented by its authors. The psychopathology studied in the current volume includes not only disorders that come to the attention of psychiatrists, but also crime, heavy drinking, subjective symptoms of stress, marital instability, and drug abuse. This broad definition of psychopathology has enabled the conferences and the volumes resulting from them to give specialists in one area of human behavior an opportunity to share the insights of persons from different disciplines and with different interests. Not only can research strategies be transferred effectively across disciplines, but our confidence in findings is greatly increased when we find them to be stable across the widely differing populations to which various disciplines have access.

Discussions following the presentations are included (except in a few cases where they were lost through recording difficulties). Sometimes the comments provided immediate support and corroboration by other investigators. Sometimes requests for elaboration brought further explanation from the author which added importantly to his paper. Occasionally there was sharp disagreement.

The papers themselves fell into five general sections. The first section includes studies of childhood characteristics that portend later psychopathology. The second section includes studies of predictors of juvenile delinquency, and of the relations between various aspects of juvenile delinquency and subsequent adult adjustment. The third section includes studies of psychopathology among different members of the same families. Persons who have parents or siblings known to have a psychiatric disorder are among the subjects of these studies. Unusual family arrangements through which these people were brought up apart from the affected family members provide an opportunity to disentangle the effects of nature from the effects of nurture. Where upbringing was not apart from the affected members, results were tested for their consistency with genetic hypotheses.

The fourth division, New Ways of Studying Life Histories, reports ingenious methods of examining data to tease out relationships not apparent at a casual glance. This section also contains a study of the planned development of psychiatric case registers for the inescapably essential purpose of obtaining information through research. There is a strong current trend toward recognition of possible or probable congenital factors in psychopathology. Research on the contribution of heredity to the devel-

INTRODUCTION

opment of intelligence by psychologists from thirty to forty years ago indicated some of the difficulties inherent in such work; answers cannot be expected to appear quickly. The sampling problem in these earlier studies was also easier to deal with since everyone has some intelligence level, whereas the number of adults with severe psychopathology is relatively small for any particular category. One paper on stressor events acts as something of a counterbalance to an overemphasis on genetic factors by concentrating on the cumulative effect of stressful occurrences in the lives of persons at different class levels.

The fifth division contains follow-up studies within the adult period. Probably less attention has been paid to the middle adult years as an age period than to any other part of the life-span. In the course of the discussion one person advanced the proposition that "there is as broad a shift between ages 18 and 47 as there is between ages 3 and 15." Whether or not this is overstated, or to what psychological characteristics it would apply, may be subject to disagreement, but we believe that the data necessary to give an adequate answer, positive or negative to this, are not yet available. One thing is clear from studies of maladjustment at the adult level — it is essential to consider them over some period of time, that is, over some years, if meaningful statements are to be made about the prediction of the course of the difficulty and the evaluation of any attempts at therapy. Evaluations of treatment on periods of inadequate duration are apt to be misleading. The problems of narcotic addiction and problem drinking are not chronic, static conditions, but change over substantial periods of time as indicated in the papers in this last section.

The formal institutional affiliations of the contributors are listed on pages 283–284, but some further information about them may serve to identify them more informally. In cases of multiple authorship, not all authors are described.

NORMAN GARMEZY, whose overview of the general problem of vulnerable children opens the book, is probably as familiar with all the work being done on predisposition to schizophrenia as anyone in the country. He is the co-author of a well-known earlier study of the antecedents of schizophrenia, and is at present engaged in an intensive study of the children of schizophrenic mothers.

STELLA CHESS and ALEXANDER THOMAS are a husband/wife team whose work has included the book *Temperament and Behavior Disorders in Children*. As contrasted with some earlier psychiatric approaches, particularly those dominated by Freud, they tend to consider

Life History Research in Psychopathology

the temperament of persons as a fact or a given, whether or not it can be fully explained. They have emphasized the potential importance of differences in temperament between parent and child as a source of conflict and eventual maladjustment.

MARGARET WOERNER, MAX POLLACK, and DONALD KLEIN are two psychologists and a psychiatrist from Hillside Hospital, a psychiatric research hospital in New York City, who described earlier work on other phases of this same research project in Volume 1. Through cooperation with the public school system in that area, they have been able to obtain information recorded during childhood for some individuals who were part of the patient population under study at Hillside.

ROBERT WIRT is director of clinical training in psychology and director of the clinical child psychology program at the University of Minnesota. His earlier work in delinquency and related areas includes a monograph with Peter Briggs on the MMPI scores of juvenile delinquents. He has also cooperated actively with Minnesota probation personnel in evaluating some of their rehabilitation programs.

MERRILL ROFF has been working for many years on a program of studying childhood or adolescent antecedents (from information recorded during childhood or adolescence) in relation to adult adjustment level and adult psychopathology of various kinds. A second large-scale project, in partnership with S. B. Sells, involved the appraisal of peer status of a very large sample of elementary school children in two states. His paper in the present book reports research results both for early delinquency (in connection with grade school samples) and young adult outcomes for a large population of males who had exhibited delinquency during the juvenile period.

FINI SCHULSINGER is one of the leading psychiatrists in Denmark. The Danish system of records is at least as good as that of any country in the world. It is thus possible to do certain kinds of research there which cannot be done as well in most other places. He is the co-director, with Sarnoff Mednick, of a large-scale, long-term study of children at high risk for schizophrenia.

MARC SCHUCKIT is a young psychiatrist who has been doing research in alcoholism with Drs. WINOKUR and GOODWIN since completing medical school. He is now finishing his residency in preparation for a career in academic psychiatry.

REMI CADORET is a physiologist turned psychiatrist. A student of

ESP in his pre-psychiatric days, he now specializes in research in the genetics of depression.

LEE ROBINS is a sociologist who for many years has enjoyed the collaboration of psychiatrists in long-term follow-up studies of child guidance clinic patients and schoolchildren. Her paper here is based on a follow-up study of 235 black schoolboys into their early thirties.

HAROUTUN BABIGIAN has been involved in the development of what is probably the most comprehensive psychiatric case register in this country, the register for Monroe County, New York. In its first ten years, this powerful instrument has provided data for various studies, and will, with the passage of time, offer a unique opportunity for life history studies of various kinds.

BARBARA DOHRENWEND and BRUCE DOHRENWEND are a married team who have collaborated in a series of studies on stressful life situations which may contribute to the development of psychopathology. One comprehensive description of their work is given in their book *Social Status and Psychological Disorder: A Causal Inquiry*.

D. H. STOTT has been concerned with life history factors for many years. Among his earlier contributions are the Bristol Social Adjustment Guides (with E. G. Sykes), based on British children, and the book *Studies of Troublesome Children*, also based on a sample of British origin.

GEORGE VAILLANT has a standing commitment to life history work. Among his major contributions are follow-up studies of schizophrenia and schizophrenic remission and a twelve-year follow-up of New York narcotic addicts.

RICHARD HUDGENS is a psychiatrist who has been interested in adolescence and transcultural comparisons, as well as in suicide. The study he presents here is a follow-up of a sample originally studied by ELI ROBINS, who is head of the Department of Psychiatry at Washington University and a pioneer in the study of psychiatric correlates of suicide.

RODRIGO MUNOZ, while on the psychiatric staff of the Malcolm Bliss Mental Health Center, St. Louis, became interested in that almost featureless diagnostic category "simple schizophrenia." His paper tests the validity of this category by seeing whether at follow-up patients still have the same symptom picture. Dr. Munoz has also been following emergency room psychiatric patients to find out whether they are still alive and, if so, what their psychiatric status is a year after they sought care.

JOHN O'DONNELL has been connected for many years with the United States Public Health Service Hospital at Lexington, Kentucky. He edited (with John C. Ball) a book on narcotic addiction and has also written a monograph on a follow-up study of former patients of the hospital, which is one of two such institutions in this country.

GENEVIEVE KNUPFER began as a sociologist and then took medical and psychiatric training, so that she is one of the few people qualified both in sociology and psychiatry. She has been intensively engaged in a study of problem drinkers or alcoholics.

In comparison with the papers of Volume 1, these cover a wider range of problems, age levels, and methods. The complexities of human beings and their stabilities and changes are impressive, whereas the amount of prospective life history research is still relatively small. The result is a wide gulf between what we know and what we would like to know, and much of the work is genuinely exploratory in nature. There are points of both agreement and disagreement in the papers included; this will be apparent to the careful reader. It would be highly undesirable to attempt to impose any single theoretical pattern on all the work described below. In the present state of the art it is wisest for each set of workers to follow where their own data lead, without too much concern for its agreement or disagreement with other work which may be done on other kinds of samples in different ways. In fact, there are indications that many of our findings have a substantial cross-populational robustness. When we obtain similar results with disparate methods, it leads us to believe that our findings are not so method-bound as might appear from the consideration of the work of any one person or set of persons. The teasing out of similarities which may appear among different workers, using different methods, directed toward the solution of different problems, is a fascinating procedure which will not be attempted here. We are, however, reaching a point where the beginnings of a synthesis of work from diverse problems and settings can be made.

NORMAN GARMEZY] *Models of Etiology for the Study of Children at Risk for Schizophrenia*

IN HIS exciting volume, *The Genetics of Psychopathology* (1971), David Rosenthal poses a centuries-old problem. "Men," he writes, "have always stood awestruck when gazing at the face of madness. By definition, madness involves behavior that is irrational or senseless . . . yet men have always tried to understand and explain it, to comprehend the strange or crazy behavior of other humans."

Just as untutored men have been confounded by the tangible signs of madness, so too have men of science puzzled over the origins of such incomprehensible actions. From man's earliest view of madness as rooted in evil and in demoniacal possession, science has slowly progressed toward a more rational accounting, tracing its way from religion through philosophy to biology, with the hope of finding in the various organs of man the solution to the mystery of psychosis. For some, the search has come to rest in brain and chromosome; others, dissatisfied with a biology of being, have sought their paths of understanding in the role played by family, society, and culture.

These two viewpoints — the biological tradition of nineteenth-century Germanic psychiatry and the psychological tradition provided by the great insights of Freud and the major psychoanalytic theorists who followed him into the twentieth century — long stood apart. Thus, early efforts to generate a sophisticated orientation to etiological factors in mental disorder suffered from the vices of narrowness and parochialism.

Today, issues of causation in psychopathology seem to be undergoing a marked revival, sparked by a growing acceptance of the view that

NOTE: The final preparation of this paper was supported by USPHS Contract No. PH 43-68-1313, Research Career Award MH-K6-14,914, and a grant from the Supreme Council 33° A. A. Scottish Rite, Northern Masonic Jurisdiction USA (Schizophrenia Research Program).

the question of etiology is not a narrow one of biogenesis *versus* psychogenesis, or a constitutional anlage as *opposed* to a predisposing environmental stressor, but rather that a rational theory of the origins of disordered man requires a unification of viewpoints. Psychopathology, whether the focus be schizophrenia or other forms of behavior pathology, implicates individual differences in innate trait dispositions that are joined to deviant social learning histories arising out of psychological forces within the family and society.

And yet, psychiatry, so enamored of the press of childhood in evaluating adult deviance, has been slow to apply this genetic-developmental orientation to disordered children. Historically, the reasons for this neglect seem clear. Child guidance clinics in America were born of therapeutic hope; the early formulations of a genetic viewpoint in adult psychiatry more often reflected therapeutic despair. A New England social conscience that dictated the mode of moral treatment in mental institutions of the nineteenth century with its attendant high rates of patient discharge was slowly converted (abetted by the immigration into New England of large numbers of lower-class Irish citizens) into a view of mental disorder as powerfully genetic in origin and, presumably, irreversible. The existence of the custodial mental institution was thus justified (Dain, 1964).

But the child guidance movement would have none of that. The treatment of disturbed children arose out of two sources that were antithetical to a genetic-biological orientation. One base was to be found in psychoanalysis — a movement that discounted the irreversibility of emotional disorder. The demonstration by Freud in 1909 that a powerful generalizing phobia could be understood, contained, and successfully treated resulted in a mode of therapeutic intervention that has sustained child psychiatry for six decades. Freud's liberation of Little Hans from the tyranny of his *wiwimacher* proved to be more than a just exchange; for Hans, in turn, freed psychiatry from its view that children were mini-adults and that childhood behavior disorders were of relatively little consequence. It was the Freudian Revolution that made evident that psychogenic components were not mere shadowy influences in psychopathology; substantively they deserved equal, if separate, standing with biogenetic factors. Although neurotic Hans came to serve as the prototype for childhood phobias and their treatment, acceptance of dynamic forces in childhood disorders did not come easily. It is interesting to note that even in 1909 an American psychologist saw fit to review Freud's classic study of Little Hans with this observation of the antecedents of the boy's phobia: "Acquaintances of Freud, working under his direction, have studied a remarkable case of sexual precocity of a boy who at the age of three began to be interested above all things in the *wiwimacher* (Hans' name for his penis) and was eagerly concerned as to whether chairs, animals, men and women etc. possessed this part, and could not be withheld from incessant interest and conversation on the topic. The child was plainly hereditarily *belastet* (tainted), but was cured by hypnotic treatment modified in form to be applicable to children" (Walters, 1909). The account, as one can see, bears the mark of several improvisations; but the gratuitous introduction of hereditary tainting reflects an earlier psychophobia every bit as powerful as the biophobias of some mental health workers today.

Such simplistic views are simply not consonant with the nature of severe psychopathology in children. Unless childhood is to be viewed as completely discontinuous with adulthood (a view that child psychiatrists and developmental psychologists would reject out of hand), either an exclusively biological or an exclusively psychological orientation to childhood (or adult) disorder can only undermine efforts to understand etiology and prognosis or to develop a rational basis for intervention.

The second source that led to the rejection of a genetic view of disordered childhood was to be found in sociology. Child treatment in America initially had powerful sociological roots, and these origins often dictated the clinic intake patterns for the first three decades of this century. It was Healy, with his interest in delinquency, to whom American child psychiatry must look for its paternity. When Mrs. W. F. Dummer, a Chicago philanthropist, enjoined Dr. William Healy to study the work that was being done in 1909 on the causes and prevention of delinquency, she did more than spark a movement. She sponsored a tract, *The Individual Delinquent* (Healy, 1915), that focused on the pervasive socioeconomic roots of delinquency and by so doing retrieved that field from the hapless mire of such genetically toned concepts as "moral imbecility," "degeneracy," and "defective mentality." Emphasis on the innate gave way to the environmental; psychological causation as the basis for the intrapsychic conflicts stressed by psychoanalytic theory was broadened to incorporate culture and role; and the concept of punishment to inhibit antisocial acts was converted to an emphasis on the need for psychological and sociological change as the prerequisite to altering patterns of delinquency. When Aichhorn (1935) finally published his *Wayward Youth* years later, following upon his training in the Vienna Psychoanalytic Institute, the study of the origins of delinquency made the final crossover from biology through sociology to dynamic psychology. It is not surprising, then, given these historical antecedents, that the study of delinquency has been characterized by numerous investigative efforts to uncover the complex sources for such behavior, whereas the search for the etiology of schizophrenia — to choose one critical example — has, until recently, been a far more speculative enterprise than an empirical one. Thus, debate regarding the antecedents of schizophrenia has flourished in the absence of solid data, and the nature of diathesis and stress (assuming both to coexist) has remained more often the object of verbal exchange rather than experimental test for many psychiatrists and psychologists.

Methods for Studying Vulnerability

As an area for experimental study, delinquency has had advantages over schizophrenia other than its historical origins. Since the study of delinquency focuses on the years of childhood and adolescence, the investigator is temporally much closer to the presumed antecedents of such disordered behavior. This closeness to *observed* rather than to retrospectively reported aspects of early family neglect, cultural and economic deprivation, and social disorganization has provided a view of behavior that is more suggestive of cause and effect relationships. By contrast, the adult psychopathologies far removed from the early eventful and presumably significant years of childhood have required a total dependence upon retrospective case history data. More recently, the reliability and validity of data garnered in this manner have become a focus of debate among researchers espousing differing models of etiology. Studies of mothers' retrospections of the early years of the lives of normal children (Haggard, Brekstad, & Skard, 1960; Mednick & Shaffer, 1964; Robbins, 1963; Wenar, 1961; Yarrow et al., 1970) have made clear to the experimentally minded that one cannot rely with confidence on the veridicality of parental recall of early events in the life of a child. For parents of disturbed children, this problem is compounded by defensiveness, guilt, and motivated forgetting. Mednick and McNeil (1968) have provided an extensive review of the many difficulties that inhere in observations of adult schizophrenic patients and their families: problems of the effects of institutionalization, drug regimens, length of hospitalization, sampling bias, personality changes induced by illness, and modifications in family role relationships that are the result rather than the antecedent of a child's disordered behavior.

All these factors have been potent reasons for the retreat from the case method, with its dependence upon retrospection, for detailing the precursors of psychopathology in adulthood. Although strongly in agreement with this view, I feel it necessary to introduce at least the cautionary metaphoric note that premature disposal of this bathwater may insure the disappearance of the toddler in the tub as well. There is still a great amount to be learned from case history material in our search for the components of vulnerability to psychopathology. As we turn to alternate experimental and clinical strategies for the study of such precursor states, it is important that we not dismiss the case history as an outdated irrelevancy in these exciting times (Garmezy, in press). There is a tendency for quantitatively-minded investigators to demean studies in which $N = 1$ and to view studies of groups as reflections of the nomothetic precision of science and the case study as the idiographic and imprecise expression of the clinician. Psychological science would question the legitimacy of such a superficial distinction. Consider for a moment the scientific significance of Ebbinghaus's effort to understand the nature of memory through analysis of his learning of nonsense syllables or Stratton's effort to invert his perceptual world by man-made lenses and thus understand better our modes of adapting to the environment. Or consider the case of Galton, whose ideographic observations of his own verbal associative behavior provided a method that opened new vistas into cognitive processes. Because Galton's N was 1, are we less appreciative of his rich insight that man's thinking is akin to the ocean in which the conscious aspect of his reflections is like the waves that break upon a distant shore, and the unconscious component is analagous to the ocean's vast, deep, formless depths?

Do we retreat from Galton, whose genius produced a science of individual variation, because a prophetic metaphor written two decades before Freud was based upon self-study and reflection of his personal past? Are Ebbinghaus and Stratton less worthy of regard because their N's were so self-consciously small? Of course not! But there is a point to be made about the contributions of these classical studies. All three investigators were systematically studying ongoing processes. Precursor states to the phenomena under observation, except in Galton's case, were not central to the observations made by these luminous figures. To have used these same observations of current functioning to infer aspects of the past would have been an infinitely more difficult, if not an impossible, task. Yet this is what mental health workers face in their efforts to piece together from the present the nature of vulnerabilities rooted in the past.

Life History Research in Psychopathology

How can we accomplish this inordinately difficult task in the study of behavior disorder? How can we derive information about precursor states, antecedent events, and the signs of early vulnerability in those destined to become the disturbed members of our society? The study of the predisposition to schizophrenia can serve as an excellent example of the development of a progressive sophistication in the investigative methods used to search for answers to such questions (Garmezy, in press). Thus, a dependency upon life history data derived from retrospective clinical accounts has been augmented by the direct experimental observation of patients and parents. But one must again ask whether the study by Mishler and Waxler (1968), to cite one example of careful systematic research into the transactions of patient, parents, and siblings, could have been generated without the extensive data base on deviant family organization educed from multiple case histories and clinical reports of therapeutic exchanges with families (e.g., Lidz et al., 1965).

The distrust of what we learn of the past by inquiry in the present has turned some investigators to society's records in a search for more neutrally derived information. Thus, school records, teachers' assessments, court and child guidance files increasingly have become the digs for those seeking information about the early years of disordered adults (Ricks & Berry, 1970; Watt et al., 1970). Unfortunately, investigations based on such earlier records suffer from serious methodological shortcomings: biases inherent in child guidance clinic intake procedures; primitivity of case records written in an earlier and less sophisticated psychiatric era; the biasing role of subjective impression and theoretical allegiances of caseworkers, teachers, and others; the infrequency of relevant controls; the difficulty of generating a psychodynamically meaningful view of another human from the sparse and partial descriptions so characteristic of society's methods of recordkeeping and the contaminating effects of one observer's descriptions on other observers who subsequently add entries in any cumulative record.

Recognizing the limitations of such retrospective pursuits, whether through the medium of parental informants in the present or caseworker and teacher informants of the past, other researchers have turned to prospective, longitudinal studies. But long-term longitudinal research is arduous and time-consuming, although a hardy few (Mednick & Schulsinger, 1968, 1970) have chosen this difficult method. Other investigators have turned to a variant of the longitudinal study that telescopes time through the medium of the follow-up method. Typically, such studies have taken samples of children grown to adulthood who had been seen during their childhood in a clinic or hospital setting (Robins, 1966). The focus: What in the past can clarify the quality of contemporaneous adaptation? Typically, the evaluations occur at two points in time — childhood and adulthood — with interim contacts usually absent. But such methods of follow-up, too, despite the superior achievements of a project such as Robins's *Deviant Children Grown Up*, pose many difficulties. Intake procedures in the original settings may reflect the biasing presses of society; cases that provide evidence of satisfactory and continued contact may be atypical and unrepresentative of the original intake service; the ubiquitous problem of the mobility of Americans that makes the task of follow-up burdensome and arduous; and knowledge of early status may influence the researcher's judgment of the later competence qualities of his sample.

For these reasons, many investigators are now turning to new strategies of longitudinal and cross-sectional research using children who are at *high-risk* for the later development of psychopathology or who appear to be *vulnerable* to behavior pathology in adulthood. Within the area of schizophrenia, there are a number of such risk projects under way, including those of Mednick and Schulsinger in Denmark; Anthony in St. Louis; Rodnick, Goldstein, and Judd in Los Angeles; Erlenmeyer-Kimling, Ranier, and Mednick in New York; Sameroff and Zax in Rochester, N.Y.; Schachter in Pittsburgh; a large-scale investigation by 14 investigators in the Department of Psychiatry at the University of Rochester; McNeil, Cromwell, and Kai in Sweden; Marcus and Rosenthal in Jerusalem; Rutter's earlier study in England; Nerle and Weintraub in Long Island; our own in Minneapolis; and others. Obviously, a Zeitgeist is emerging. Similarly, other mental disorders are attracting investigators to do comparable studies, as is evident from the present volume and previous programs of the Conference on Life History Research in Psychopathology (Roff & Ricks, 1970).

I shall not detail the many studies that fall under the rubric of these different research procedures (i.e., case history, follow-up, follow-back, and follow-through). Nor shall I cite the pros and cons of each method. A preliminary statement related to these issues will shortly appear (Garmezy, in press), and an extended review of the empirical status of the field is nearing completion. In addition, a volume is now in preparation for the National Institute of Mental Health under the tentative title *Vulnerable Children: The Study of Preschizophrenia*. Therefore, in this paper, I shall focus largely on only one issue — the relationship of models of etiology to the selection for vulnerability, particularly with reference to the later onset of schizophrenia. Two other problems that are now of central concern to risk researchers, namely, the choice of control groups and variables to be studied, have been discussed elsewhere (Garmezy, 1970, 1971, in press).

Etiological Models for the Study of Risk

The selection of children who may be potentially vulnerable to psychopathology is largely determined by an investigator's preference for a specific etiological model. In the study of schizophrenia three dominant models have been advocated (although combinatorial models add to the numbers): the genogenic, the psychogenic, and the sociogenic. These have been more recently joined by a fourth model that stresses early deficiencies induced by pregnancy, birth, prenatal, and perinatal defects.

The Nature of Models. How can so many diverse models coexist with seeming indestructibility for a disorder as malignant and pervasive as schizophrenia? Maher (1966) described the situation uncommonly well when he noted that "hypothesis struggles with hypothesis in a conflict in which new contenders enter the field but the defeated never retire." The nature of models and the current status of psychopathology help to explain our dilemma.

A model is essentially an explanatory system, frequently drawn from one discipline and translated to another in an effort to facilitate the task of better describing events and relationships in the latter field. By coordinating terms with events in the physical world, an effective model can often serve as a tentative theoretical structure for integrating subsets of existent data and for predicting new relationships within a subject domain. It is thus a "working framework" for research; its effectiveness is unrelated to the polemical talents of its proponents but tends rather to be a function of the knowledge and insights it helps to generate and of its integrative and predictive value.

But these integrative qualities of models are, in part, related to the scientific status of the domain in which the model is applied. Unfortunately, the domain of psychopathology consists largely of descriptive phenomena that are couched in what Kaplan (1964) in *The Conduct of Inquiry* has termed the *literary style* (with its emphasis on persons, individuals, and events), the *academic style* (with its flavor of the verbal rather than the operational) or, in some instances, the *eristic style* (which is characterized by deduction, experimentation, and data collection). But the more advanced styles of the *symbolic*, the *postulational*, and the *formal*, in which rigorous and logical conceptualizations are accompanied by explicit rules for deriving propositions and testing them by equally rigorous mathematical proof, are not (and for now cannot be) the working modes of psychopathologists. Our scientific efforts are often primitive, our observations too frequently imprecise, or the phenomena we observe unreliable; even when reliability does exist, the data often allow for a choice of seemingly discrepant but apparently tenable interpretations. If you doubt this, then take on the relatively simple task of assigning to any empirical statement of schizophrenic performance an explanation based upon a biogenetic or a learning-environmental model. It is not surprising, therefore, that in the study of behavior pathology contradictory hypotheses readily coexist, proof is often a fragile verity, and disproof is a rare claimant of our scientific enterprise. We cannot suggest, then, in the present stage of our science, that only a single model will suffice or prove to be the one true portrait of reality. Such an assignment would be one made largely on faith and less in keeping with the data base of our discipline.*

For a model makes no claim to reality; at best, it is a vision of a theoretical structure that may, in time, prove to be viable. In Kaplan's words, we are dealing essentially with a metaphor in which a "similarity" rather than an "identity" is depicted; a model suggests what the phenomena that intrigue us can be *like* rather than what they truly *are*. Thus, even apparently incompatible models can coexist in psychopathology until their respective powers can be compared by the process of empirically testing the hypotheses each generates.

This may become one of the future valuable contributions that can be made by risk researchers. Diversity of formulation can, in this instance,

---

* This issue is relevant in describing children who may be predisposed to the later development of schizophrenia. Alternately, I have labeled them as *at risk* or as *vulnerable*. The term *at risk* has its roots in genetic theory, and genetics remains the most powerful and productive etiological statement available to us in the study of schizophrenia. But the term *vulnerable* is a more generic one and has the additional virtue of being neutral with regard to any one etiological model. If pressed to the wall, I would probably urge that we describe these children as *vulnerable* to later disorder, until we have a far more solid empirical foundation for a definitive statement of etiology.

Further, we know that the majority of children who are at risk will not develop schizophrenia, yet we have no alternative term to describe them. My own research (and personal) interest in those who, despite stress and adversity, maintain a set to strive toward competence and adaptation has led me to use the term *invulnerable* to describe these children. Their significance for the mental health movement is enormous and makes more incomprehensible our neglect of them in experimental and clinical research.

be a virtue. In Kaplan's words, "The dangers are not in working with models, but in working with too few, and those too much alike, and above all, in belittling any effort to work with anything else."

The Genetic Model. Mednick and Schulsinger deserve the credit for initiating the study of high-risk samples using schizophrenic mothers as the basis for selecting children who would be particularly prone to the later development of schizophrenia. Although the etiological model for this selection criterion is almost explicitly a genetic one, it is interesting to learn that Mednick's etiological position initially had a more neutral cast — if anything, he professed allegiance to a learning model. Selection for risk on the basis of mother's psychiatric status was designed initially to heighten the frequency of long-range negative outcomes in his proband group. By so doing, Mednick hoped to overcome one critical investigative problem, namely, the low base rate for schizophrenia that exists in our culture. This method of selection increases at least fivefold the likelihood of an ultimate schizophrenic process within Mednick and Schulsinger's experimental group over the anticipated probability for children selected at random from the Danish population. That such random selection would have been an unacceptable procedure is clearly evident from incidence statistics supplied by Yolles and Kramer (1969). Although their figures apply to the United States, such incidence data are not too dissimilar to those of Western Europe. If anything, data from the United States tend to show higher incidence rates for schizophrenia, thus enlarging the base rate problem for European risk researchers. Comparing age specific rates for high and low risk geographical areas, Yolles and Kramer concluded (pp. 78–79):

> If the age specific rates from the high risk area in Detroit applied to a cohort of births subjected throughout their lifetime to the mortality rates that existed in the United States during 1960, approximately six percent of all such children who would reach the age of 15 years would develop schizophrenia during their subsequent lifetime. If the rates from the low risk area applied, the corresponding probability would be two percent. In a population subjected to an estimated minimum incidence rate of 50 per 100,000 in all age groups and to the 1960 U.S. mortality rates, about three percent of the children reaching age 15 years would develop schizophrenia during their subsequent lifetime.

Since incidence and not prevalence statistics are most useful in longitudinal studies of high-risk children, this projected estimate of 3 per cent would pose insuperable problems for follow-through studies. Large-scale epidemiological studies would have to be undertaken; but such large *N*'s would be prohibitive for the types of intensive laboratory, naturalistic, and clinical studies that are required in research of this kind. Obviously some method of increasing the projected N for later breakdown is necessary if one hopes to use data collected in childhood to evaluate diathesis, situational, and stress factors that may predispose a child to the later development of schizophrenia. Subject selection based on the empirical probabilities generated by genetic studies provided Mednick and Schulsinger with the solution to the base rate problem. Thus, genetic susceptibility became one criterion for choosing vulnerable samples. The fact that other investigators have followed the procedure of selecting a cohort of schizophrenic mothers (and fathers, too, as in the case of Anthony's [1968] project), using as probands the children of such parents attests to the popularity and, one would hope, to the viability of the procedure.

One can, of course, extend the genetic model even further, heightening anticipated incidence rates by selecting offspring both of whose parents have been diagnosed schizophrenic. On the basis of five studies, the probability of ultimate schizophrenia in this truly high-risk group of children (Erlenmeyer-Kimling suggests labeling children who have only one parent schizophrenic as "intermediate" risk cases) becomes a conservative age-corrected risk for reported schizophrenia of approximately 35–45 per cent (Rosenthal, 1970).

Selecting such high-risk choices, of course, poses major logistical problems. Erlenmeyer-Kimling has faced this challenge in New York State, and at the 1968 meetings of the American Psychiatric Association she discussed the feasibility of finding sufficient numbers of children born to such dual mated pairs. Her observations on the search for this highly selected group are intriguing:

> Surprisingly, the frequency of fertile marriages between schizophrenic patients is not so low as has been thought. At least, it did not prove to be especially low in a survey which has recently been completed by my colleagues and myself on the marriage and fertility rates of schizophrenic patients admitted to State Hospitals in New York during 1934–1936 and 1954–1956. In the sample of admissions during 1954–1956, for example, we found that one in 73 white female patients and one in 94 white male patients was married to another schizophrenic patient. The rates are somewhat higher for non-white patients and markedly higher if the unmarried patients are first screened out and the search is confined to married patients. The ascertainment probability for an assortative mating case is, therefore, between two and five times greater than the probability of locating a schizophrenic monozygotic twin with surviving cotwin. Just as the ascertainment of monozygotic twins has been con-

sidered well worth the trouble, so, too, is the ascertainment of families containing two schizophrenic parents.

Having located 30 fertile assortative matings in her first survey, Erlenmeyer-Kimling then initiated a "casual search" for additional cases, enlisting the aid of professional personnel of the hospitals she and her colleagues had surveyed earlier with but a "minimum of effort." With rigorous selection criteria operative, she reports finding 32 additional families. These 62 families have had a total of 160 children, of which "145 survived to age 15 or older, or were alive and younger than 15 when her informal survey was conducted." Of these children, 111 were born before the hospitalization of the second parent, 76 of whom were under 10 years of age. Erlenmeyer-Kimling, therefore, is confident that her sample is young enough and large enough to support a developmental study of this selected and extreme high-risk group. Unfortunately, there is evidence that familial disorganization marked the lives of these children — only 22 per cent had remained continuously housed in the parental home in which either one or both parents resided; 16 per cent of the children were reared by relatives; 38 per cent had been placed in foster homes or under the care of social agencies; and for 24 per cent information was not available about their placement histories. Such burdensome logistics are simply part of the facts of life for high-risk researchers. It will be necessary for other investigators to appreciate that the precision of design that brings joy and happiness to the hearts of experimental brethren is often beyond the control of those who choose to research risk for severe psychopathology. Our own experience in Minneapolis with children born to mothers who have been diagnosed schizophrenic also reveals a high loss rate through placement of children outside the home. In Erlenmeyer-Kimling's words, "Fewer children will fall into a continuous home-reared group, and even those that do will probably experience serious upheavals from time to time as the parents are rehospitalized and released." Since family disorganization influences output measures of adaptation, the control of this factor must be an important element in the design of risk studies.

Projects such as Mednick and Schulsinger's, Anthony's, and Erlenmeyer-Kimling's are rooted in a genetics literature that has grown more powerful with the addition of sophisticated studies by Heston (1966), Gottesman and Shields (1971), and the Rosenthal-Kety-Wender-Weiner-Schulsinger adoptee studies that are being conducted in Denmark (Rosenthal & Kety, 1968). These studies, over the next decade, will be strengthened appreciably by the contributions of risk researchers who are operating within a genetic framework.

The Psychogenic Model. An alternate method of selecting for risk or vulnerability in children is to focus not on the severity of disorder in mothers and fathers, but rather to do so on the basis of manifest symptomatology in already severely disturbed children. Underlying this selection procedure is the assumption that such children also contribute heavily to the pool of adult psychopathology. Follow-up studies of child guidance clinic cases, as exemplified by Robins's (1966) *Deviant Children Grown Up*, constitute proof of the validity of that assumption. A sharpening of research of this sort, accompanied by longitudinal studies, is beginning to provide clues to those symptomatic forms of childhood disorder that may weigh more heavily in predicting later severe forms of behavior pathology.

The selection of groups of already disordered rather than potentially disordered children bears the heavy imprint of a psychogenic model of etiology. An example of such research is provided by a project on adolescent clinic cases that is being conducted by Rodnick, Goldstein, Judd, and their colleagues at UCLA. In an ultimate sense, their research is focused on the antecedents to schizophrenia. But it is interesting to contemplate the reasons they offer for discarding a strategy that would have incorporated detailed experimental studies of families containing an already schizophrenic offspring (Goldstein et al., 1968, pp. 233–234):

A number of considerations directed us away from this research strategy. The most important consideration was the impact of a schizophrenic child upon the pattern of family interaction. The initial data in the current project revealed that it was difficult to distinguish between deviant parental behaviors which were a *response* to the child's psychosis and deviant parental behaviors which might have created and/or shaped the psychotic reaction. Using . . . observational procedures . . . we were deeply impressed with how radically a psychotic adolescent could limit and distort the pattern of interaction with his parents. Therefore, it seemed more pertinent to search for familial determinents of schizophrenia utilizing a more oblique research strategy. This led to the decision at this time to *not* study families containing a schizophrenic child. We chose to study less extreme patterns of abnormal behavior, which may possess some continuity with more severe psychotic disturbance.

In this study, we have restricted our attention to adolescence, the age range immediately prior to the peak onset of schizophrenia. We have searched for subgroups of disturbed adolescents who demonstrated contrasting styles of coping with stress which would allow for meaningful comparisons between the groups. Some of these modes of coping can be seen as containing components of the coping patterns of the schizophrenic, such as *withdrawal* and *social iso-*

lation, while others, such as *acting out* and *passive aggression*, seem unrelated or at best only indirectly related to the manifest complex of behaviors which we call schizophrenia. If relationships could be found between specific family patterns and specific types of coping styles in the adolescent, and if these relationships were congruent with studies of families containing a schizophrenic offspring, then possibly our understanding of family dynamics in psychopathology could be advanced.

At this point the posited relations between the coping styles of their adolescent clinic cases and ultimate schizophrenic pathology are being evaluated by the UCLA group. But as a strategy for pulling a high-risk sample, it is of some interest to note that the incidence of schizophrenia in the UCLA study is not dissimilar to the anticipated probabilities suggested by genetically oriented studies for offspring in one-parent schizophrenic families. Thus, as a means of identifying high-risk and vulnerable children, the cohorts on which to focus initially in selection would appear to be either markedly disordered parents or else markedly disordered children.

The UCLA project exemplifies more than merely an alternate method for selecting a cohort; it suggests another view of the predisposition to schizophrenia, namely, one in which psychogenic components play a significant role. This does not necessarily imply the absence of genetic factors, but rather a variation in the weighting an investigator is willing to assign to psychological factors. In general, family researchers have been more prone to accentuate the contributions of such components to the manifestations of illness in a family member.

The UCLA project assigns the varieties of disordered behavior exhibited by adolescents to the status of an independent variable and views family interaction as the dependent variable. This orientation, too, represents a powerful investigative area in schizophrenia and immediately brings to mind the work of Lidz (1968; Lidz et al., 1965), Wynne and Singer (Wynne, 1968) and Jackson, Bateson, Weakland, Haley, and others (e.g., Jackson, 1967). The emphasis within such investigations has been upon disordered communication among family members with the family seen as a "social system"; central to the theoretical constructions of these investigators have been such concepts as the *double bind, pseudomutuality, marital schism* and *marital skew, family symbiosis, shared focal attention*, and the like.

In part, the adherents of views such as these look to communicative incompetencies as a significant antecedent to the manifestation of disorder and, in part, as a consequent of it. The downward extension of such research into vulnerable families has two purposes: it represents an effort to disentangle antecedent from consequent and seeks to analyze the interactions among the variables of family structure, communication patterns, and forms of symptom expression. This appears to be the direction taken not only by the UCLA investigators but also by Wynne (1969) and Singer. The latter two have stressed research into various forms of cognitive control principles (powerful response dispositions of an attentional, perceptual, and cognitive cast) to typify trait dispositions within vulnerable subjects. However, the model they espouse is given a more neutral cast. Thus Wynne (1968, p. 189) has written: "available evidence suggests that these response dispositions are to some extent stable, 'built-in' aspects of an individual's functioning, but there is no prejudgment as to *how* they were built in, whether on an innate, inherited basis or on the basis of recurrent and perhaps intense experiential factors."

Since the causal chain is unknown, flexibility in deciding the choice of independent and dependent variables in a disordered family communication-disordered child network is possible. For the UCLA group the independent variable is the latter (symptoms in children), the dependent variable, the former (family communication style). For Wynne and Singer the relationship is reversed. To return to Wynne (1969), "Parental communication deviances, a far more subtle measure than symptomatology, appear to be a far more consistent indicator of schizophrenic symptomatology in an offspring than does symptomatology of the parents. If these parental deviances predate the offsprings' symptomatology, they should constitute a good device for identifying the families of preschizophrenics before the diagnosis of schizophrenia has been made."

Thus, another mode for selecting a vulnerable population is suggested with the hope that, in time, the nature of the correlation between these two variables (family communication deviance and developmental psychopathology) will be clarified and the causal sequence suggested. In this respect the work of Helm Stierlin, who is studying families of adolescents who have been tagged for "underachievement" in a school system, approaches the strategy of the Rodnick-Goldstein-Judd team. Stierlin's adolescents are 15 years of age, and a short-term prospective study of at least five years duration is contemplated with the expectation that the range of later adaptations in these children will vary markedly. It is expected that in some of the children schizophrenia will occur within 5–8 years after the project has been initiated, thus providing an accelerated longitudinal approach to the problem of which children within this group are at high risk.

We can thus summarize two current orientations to vulnerability: the first is based upon genetic vulnerability as evidenced in a proband selection process in which the defining criterion for risk is manifest schizophrenia in a cohort of mothers or fathers. Genetic linkage is the explicit given and presumably provides the source of the diathesis in a diathesis-stress model of schizophrenia (Rosenthal, 1963).

The second method of selection assumes that vulnerability can arise in a more generalized familial disorganization without the explicit identifying signs of schizophrenia in a parent. Here the model can be genetic but more typically assumes a psychological cast in which perceived deviance is assigned its locus in faulty parent-child and parent-parent relationships. Fortunately, a sophisticated appreciation of communication networks, role structure, and transactional patterns has resulted in the dismissal of simple old-fashioned notions of dominance and conflict as concepts of central significance. The fact that the UCLA group finds evidence of a relationship within their clinic pool of pathologically disturbed family relationships and schizophrenia in disturbed adolescent children is supportive of this second strategy for subject selection. For these investigators the diathesis, if one exists, is less central in their research planning than the stressors that may potentiate severe psychopathology in the children born into such deviant families.

The Sociogenic Model. The study of family deviance moves closer toward a potential third source of vulnerability to schizophrenia, in which the basis for risk is derived from studies rooted in the sociology of mental disorder. Most striking (and reaffirmed in numerous studies) is the inverse correlation found to exist between prevalence rates of schizophrenia and social status. Such data having a long-term and substantial empirical base have provided support for sociogenic hypothesizing. One can think, as reported by Sandifer (1962), of Jarvis's report in 1856 that the "pauper" class in comparison with the "independent" class contributed sixty-four times the number of cases of insanity tabulated in Massachusetts. Or one can consider the classic study by Faris and Dunham (1939) of Chicago's residential patterns in relation to psychiatric admissions performed thirty years ago and since replicated by other investigators in other cities. All studies confirm that the highest rates for mental hospital admissions for schizophrenia are drawn from what we now euphemistically term the "inner city." Supportively, there are the findings of Hollingshead and Redlich (1958) based on a census of all psychiatric patients from New Haven, Connecticut, that in terms of both incidence and prevalence statistics the lowest social class is the heaviest contributor to psychotic disorders. Prevalence data reveal rates of 111 per 100,000 general population for Classes I and II (the highest social classes) combined, of 168 and 300 respectively in Classes III and IV, and 895 in Class V (the lowest social class). The incidence of newly diagnosed cases shows a comparable, if less striking, pattern with 28 new cases in a six-month period per 100,000 general population drawn from Classes I and II combined as compared with 73 in Class V. In this sociological area, as in most things schizophrenic, issues of etiology are obscured, and controversy persists regarding not the data but their interpretation. Formulations of genetic selection and downward drift have vied with explanations based upon the social stresses generated by slum environments and family disorganization within the lowest social class (Langner & Michael, 1963; Srole et al., 1962).

The current view has recently been summarized in this fashion: "Is low social status more a cause or is it more a consequence of psychiatric disorder? On the basis of research to date, it has been impossible to tell: for this relationship can be explained with equal plausibility as evidence of social causation, with the environmental pressures associated with low social status causing psychopathology; or by contrast, it can be explained as evidence of social selection with pre-existing psychiatric disorder leading to low social status. The latter interpretation is compatible with the position that genetic factors are more important than social environmental factors in etiology" (Dohrenwend et al., 1970, p. 197).

Whether one views this inverse relationship as reflecting the contributions of diathesis or stressor, this substantial body of data remains a challenge to investigators of high-risk and vulnerable children. There is now evidence that sociologically minded investigators (Dohrenwend & Dohrenwend, 1969) are also attempting to mount studies designed to provide answers to the question of the extent to which heredity or social environment accounts for the social status-psychopathology relationship. The strategy, essentially epidemiological, involves first the distinction of situation-generated as opposed to defect-generated symptoms followed by a comparison of the frequency distributions of such symptoms in advantaged and disadvantaged ethnic groups with social class controlled. The successful execution of such studies may provide additional methods for the selection of high-risk or vulnerable probands.

But the critical questions remain. How does social class contribute to schizophrenic pathology, and what role can risk research play in clarifying the relationship? The most cogent description of the multiple ways in which social class dynamics can affect the probability of people developing schizophrenia has been provided by Kohn (1968, p. 164):

> Social class indexes and is correlated with so many phenomena that might be relevant to the etiology of schizophrenia. Since it measures status, it implies a great deal about how the individual is treated by others — with respect or perhaps degradingly; since it is measured by occupational rank, it suggests much about the conditions that make up the individual's daily work, how closely supervised he is, whether he works primarily with things, with data, or with people; since it reflects the individual's educational level, it connotes a great deal about his style of thinking, his use or non-use of abstractions, even his perceptions of physical reality and certainly of social reality; furthermore, the individual's class position influences his social values and colors his evaluations of the world about him; it affects the family experiences he is likely to have had as a child and the ways he is likely to raise his own children; and it certainly matters greatly for the type and amount of stress he is likely to encounter in a lifetime. In short, social class pervades so much of life that it is difficult to guess which of its correlates are most relevant for understanding schizophrenia. Moreover, none of these phenomena is so highly correlated with class (nor class so highly correlated with schizophrenia) that any one of these facets is obviously more promising than the others.

More recently, Kohn (1969) has focused on the relationship between social class, occupation, values, and orientation. His study leads him to conclude that higher social class position is characterized by a heightened valuation of self-direction and increased confidence that one's decisions and actions are consequential. Persons occupying lower social class positions value conformity to external authority and see themselves "at the mercy of forces and people beyond one's control, often, beyond one's understanding." Resistance to change, distrust of others, rigid conservativism, low self-esteem, heightened anxiety, and self-depreciation are all the lot of men who occupy lower social class positions and represent the products of a limited education and "constricting" occupational experiences. Kohn (1969, pp. 199–200) suggests that this conformist orientational system — transmitted to children by parents — ill prepares the child to deal with the stresses of lower-class living.*

The crucial family processes are less a matter of role-allocation (domineering mothers, for example) than many past discussions have emphasized, and more a matter of how children are taught to perceive, to assess, and to

---

* Kohn's (1970) most recent formulation also accepts the evidence for a genetic mechanism in schizophrenia.

and breech presentations. Careful perusal of these data brought out an additional striking relationship within the Sick Group (and the entire high-risk group). There is a marked correspondence between PBC and the anomalous electrodermal behavior reported above. All the GSR differences between the Sick and Well Groups could be explained by PBC's in the Sick Group. In the Control Group and the low-risk group the PBC's were not strongly associated with these extreme GSR effects. This suggests that the PBC's trigger some characteristic which may be genetically predisposed. The PBC's seem to damage the modulatory control of the body's stress-response mechanisms. PBC's are associated with rapid response onset, poor habituation of the response, poor extinction of the conditioned electrodermal response, and very rapid recovery from the response. In terms of the theoretical orientation guiding this project this lack of modulation may be viewed as an important etiological factor in the development of mental illness, especially schizophrenia.

In a more recent and as yet unpublished report, Mednick and Schulsinger have indicated that for their Sick group a confounding variable may be maternal separation at an early age. Current investigation is being directed toward an examination of the effects of separation hitherto attributed to PBC's on mental health (poor), schizoidia, greater impulsivity, and labile autonomic responsivity.

Two high-risk projects now under way in the United States may provide further evidence of these relationships. In Rochester, Sameroff and Zax are studying various aspects of cognitive and psychophysiological functioning in children born to schizophrenic mothers; Joseph Schacter at the University of Pittsburgh is also engaged in an extensive study of early neonatal responsiveness. Although these programs of research reflect selection for risk on the basis of a genetic model, the variables to be studied may well provide data on the role of prenatal and postnatal deficiencies on vulnerability in childhood and beyond.

The Future of Risk Research

The problem of which variables to study with children who are at risk has not been resolved. One can take two views of this selection task. The first is a more narrow selection based upon rather circumscribed theoretical models. Mednick's research is a case in point, for his model of schizophrenia embraces the concepts of autonomic lability, habituation, speed of decay of the autonomic response, and stimulus generalization, all of which are significant components of the longitudinal study he and Schulsinger are conducting in Denmark. The second basis for selection is more amorphous. I am reminded of what Rosenthal et al. (1968) wrote in their report of their Danish adoptee study. Their choice of behaviors to study, given a two-day period for evaluation, was multidetermined. There were those variables that were selected because other investigators had had success with them; there were those traditional psychological test procedures that are inevitably included in any assessment study; and (I believe more significantly) there were those variables whose relevance was reflected in the consistency with which they had differentiated schizophrenic patients from other individuals. Such a procedure incorporates a plea made by Erlenmeyer-Kimling (1968) in the APA paper to which I have alluded earlier.

Finally, what should prospective studies measure, what are the variables most likely to provide solutions to the etiology of schizophrenia? The answer will, of course, depend upon the investigator's theoretical orientations and notions about the nature of the disease . . . my own inclination would be to draw on hypotheses concerned with sensory input overload, perceptual distortion and possible defects in the brain stem reticular activating system; other workers doing prospective studies on the children of schizophrenic parents, or about to begin them, or considering doing them in the future, will have their own ideas about the variables that will help us to understand gene-environment interaction. Now diversity in research is a good thing, but fractionation is not — and we have already had too much of that in research on schizophrenia. For this reason, I would like to plead here that if, as seems likely, developmental studies of high and intermediate-risk children are about to become the "in" thing to do, they be done with attention to two things: first that they be designed and carried out so that *multiple* working hypotheses can be tested, second that they include some measures which will be standardized across all studies being done on similar groups of subjects. At least for once in behavioral research, let us plan carefully in advance how to achieve some comparative data. After all, longitudinal studies represent the heaviest type of commitment possible in research, and, if this is to be the next round in the struggle with schizophrenia, we had best attempt to make it an especially good one.

This last plea for collaboration strikes a responsive chord in many investigators, for such prospective studies are logistically difficult and extremely time-consuming. So significant is the appeal that the staff of the Center for Studies of Schizophrenia of NIMH is currently weighing various proposals for fostering collaboration among those researchers now involved in risk studies.

A final question. Will these newly emerging studies of children who are particularly vulnerable to psychopathology provide us with a solution to the riddle of schizophrenia? I think it best that we not be overly optimistic on that score. Schizophrenia has confounded scientists for more than a century and is quite likely to continue to deny us solutions until there have been greater advances in the biological disciplines and far more systematic studies of the role of experience in development. But the data to be collected on children who are at risk will eventually have to be incorporated into the complex theory of etiology that this extraordinarily complex disorder demands. After a century of focusing solely on the adult patient, we are now turning to an evaluation of children who may, for a variety of reasons, be predisposed to disorder. As a result, behavioral predictions will be more difficult and subject to greater error. But there will be gains. Risk research, if it does nothing else, should induce a degree of humility in its investigators confronted with the extraordinarily difficult task of separating causation from correlation. It will bring out of the shadows of neglect the *invulnerable* child who survives despite adversity, forcing us to look at processes of coping and adapting rather than solely at those that reflect failure and incompetence. It will, hopefully, provide a new impetus to the search for modes of intervention and prevention which may, in time, benefit our half million mentally ill children, our four million youngsters under 14 years of age who are burdened with severe behavioral difficulties, and the 10 per cent of our preschool children in Head Start programs who, as a consequence of severe emotional distress, are already disabled by the time they are four years old.

REFERENCES

Aichhorn, A. *Wayward Youth.* New York: Viking Press, 1935.
Anthony, E. J. The developmental precursors of schizophrenia. In D. Rosenthal & S. S. Kety (Eds.), *The transmission of schizophrenia.* Oxford: Pergamon Press, 1968. Pp. 293–316.
Birch, H. G., & Gussow, J. D. *Disadvantaged children: Health, nutrition and school failure.* New York: Harcourt, 1970.
Dain, N. *Concepts of insanity in the United States, 1789–1865.* New Brunswick, N.J.: Rutgers University Press, 1964.
Dohrenwend, B. P., Chin-Shong, E. T., Egri, G., Mendelsohn, F. S., & Stokes, J. Measures of psychiatric disorder in contrasting class and ethnic groups: A preliminary report of on-going research. In E. H. Hare & J. K. Wing (Eds.), *Psychiatric epidemiology: An international symposium.* London: Oxford University Press, 1970. Pp. 159–202.
Dohrenwend, B. P., & Dohrenwend, B. S. *Social status and psychological disorder: A causal inquiry.* New York: Wiley, 1969.
Erlenmeyer-Kimling, L. Studies of the children of schizophrenic parents: Pointers for the analysis of gene-environment interaction. Paper presented at the meeting of the American Psychiatric Association, Boston, May 1968.
Faris, R. E. L., & Dunham, H. W. *Mental disorders in urban areas.* Chicago: University of Chicago Press, 1939.
Fontana, A. F. Familial etiology of schizophrenia: Is a scientific methodology possible? *Psychological Bulletin,* 1966, 66, 214–227.

Life History Research in Psychopathology

Freud, S. Analysis of a phobia in a five-year-old boy. In *Collected Papers*. Vol. 3. London: Hogarth Press & The Institute of Psycho-analysis, 1956.

Garmezy, N. Vulnerable children: Implications derived from studies of an internalizing-externalizing symptom dimension. In J. Zubin & A. M. Freedman (Eds.), *Psychopathology of adolescence*. New York: Grune & Stratton, 1970. Pp. 212–239.

———. Vulnerability research and the issue of primary prevention. *American Journal of Orthopsychiatry*, 1971, 41, 101–116.

———. Research strategies for the study of children who are at risk for schizophrenia. In M. M. Katz, R. Littlestone, L. Mosher, M. S. Roath, & A. H. Tuma (Eds.), *Schizophrenia: Implications of research findings for treatment and teaching*. In press.

Goldstein, M. J., Judd, L. L., Rodnick, E. H., Alkire, A., & Gould, E. A method for studying social influence and coping patterns within families of disturbed adolescents. *Journal of Nervous and Mental Disease*, 1968, 147, 233–251.

Gottesman, I. I., & Shields, J. *Schizophrenia and genetics*. New York: Academic Press, 1971.

Haggard, E. A., Brekstad, A., & Skard, A. On the reliability of the anamnestic interview. *Journal of Abnormal and Social Psychology*, 1960, 61, 311–318.

Harper, P. A., & Wiener, G. Sequelae of low birth weight. *Annual Review of Medicine*, 1965, 16, 405–420.

Healy, W. *The individual delinquent*. Boston: Little, Brown, 1915.

Heston, L. L. Psychiatric disorders in foster home reared children of schizophrenic mothers. *British Journal of Psychiatry*, 1966, 112, 819–825.

Hollingshead, A. B., & Redlich, F. C. *Social class and mental illness*. New York: Wiley, 1958.

Jackson, D. D. Schizophrenia the nosological nexus. In J. Romano (Ed.), *The origins of schizophrenia*. Amsterdam: Excerpta Medica, 1967. Pp. 111–120.

Kaplan, A. *The conduct of inquiry*. San Francisco: Chandler, 1964.

Kohn, M. L. Social class and schizophrenia: A critical review. In D. Rosenthal & S. S. Kety (Eds.), *The transmission of schizophrenia*. Oxford: Pergamon Press, 1968. Pp. 155–173.

———. *Class and conformity: A study of values*. Homewood, Ill.: Dorsey Press, 1969.

———. Class, family and schizophrenia: A reformulation. Paper read at the Seventh World Congress of Sociology, Varna, Bulgaria, September 1970.

Langner, T. S., & Michael, S. T. *Life stress and mental health*. New York: Free Press, 1963.

Lidz, T. The family, language and the transmission of schizophrenia. In D. Rosenthal & S. S. Kety (Eds.), *The transmission of schizophrenia*. Oxford: Pergamon Press, 1968. Pp. 175–184.

———, Fleck, S., & Cornelison, A. R. *Schizophrenia and the family*. New York: International Universities Press, 1965.

Maher, B. *Principles of psychopathology*. New York: McGraw-Hill, 1966.

Mednick, S. A. Breakdown in individuals at high risk for schizophrenia: Possible predispositional perinatal factors. *Mental Hygiene*, 1970, 54, 50–63.

——— & McNeil, T. F. Current methodology in research on the etiology of schizophrenia: Serious difficulties which suggest the use of the high-risk-group method. *Psychological Bulletin*, 1968, 70, 681–693.

Mednick, S. A., & Schulsinger, F. Some premorbid characteristics related to breakdown in children with schizophrenic mothers. In D. Rosenthal & S. S. Kety (Eds.), *The transmission of schizophrenia*. Oxford: Pergamon Press, 1968. Pp. 267–291.

———. Factors related to breakdown in children at high risk for schizophrenia. In M. Roff & D. F. Ricks (Eds.), *Life history research in psychopathology*. Vol. 1. Minneapolis: University of Minnesota Press, 1970. Pp. 51–93.

Mednick, S. A., & Shaffer, J. Mothers' retrospective reports in child rearing research. *American Journal of Orthopsychiatry*, 1964, 33, 457–461.

Mishler, E. G., & Waxler, N. E. *Interaction in families.* New York: Wiley, 1968.

Pasamanick, B., Constantinou, F. K., & Lilienfeld, A. M. Pregnancy experience and the development of childhood speech disorders: An epidemiologic study of the association with maternal and fetal factors. *American Journal of Diseases of Children*, 1956, 91, 113–118.

Pasamanick, B., & Kawi, A. A study of the association of prenatal and paranatal factors with the development of tics in children: A preliminary investigation. *Journal of Pediatrics*, 1956, 48, 596–601.

Pasamanick, B., & Knobloch, H. Brain damage & reproductive casualty. *American Journal of Orthopsychiatry*, 1960, 30, 298–305.

———. Epidemiologic studies on the complications of pregnancy and the birth process. In G. Kaplan (Ed.), *Prevention of mental disorders in children.* New York: Basic Books, 1961. Pp. 74–94.

——— & Lilienfeld, A. M. Socio-economic status and some precursors of neuropsychiatric disorders. *American Journal of Orthopsychiatry*, 1956, 26, 594–601.

Pasamanick, B., Rogers, M. E., & Lilienfeld, A. M. Pregnancy experience and the development of behavior disorder in children. *American Journal of Psychiatry*, 1956, 112, 613–618.

Pollin, W., & Stabenau, J. R. Biological, psychological & historical differences in a series of monozygotic twins discordant for schizophrenia. In D. Rosenthal & S. S. Kety (Eds.), *The transmission of schizophrenia.* Oxford: Pergamon Press, 1968. Pp. 317–332.

Ricks, D. F., & Berry, J. C. Family and symptom patterns that precede schizophrenia. In M. Roff & D. F. Ricks (Eds.), *Life history research in psychopathology.* Vol. 1. Minneapolis: University of Minnesota Press, 1970. Pp. 31–50.

Robbins, L. C. The accuracy of parental recall of aspects of child development and child rearing practices. *Journal of Abnormal and Social Psychology*, 1963, 66, 261–270.

Robins, L. N. *Deviant children grown up: A psychiatric and sociological study of sociopathic personality.* Baltimore: Williams & Wilkins, 1966.

Roff, M., & Ricks, D. F. (Eds.) *Life history research in psychopathology.* Vol. 1. Minneapolis: University of Minnesota Press, 1970.

Rosenthal, D. (Ed.) *The Genain quadruplets.* New York: Basic Books, 1963.

———. *Genetic theory and abnormal behavior.* New York: McGraw-Hill, 1970.

———. *The genetics of psychopathology.* New York: McGraw-Hill, 1971.

——— & Kety, S. S. (Eds.) *The transmission of schizophrenia.* Oxford: Pergamon Press, 1968.

Rosenthal, D., Wender, P. H., Kety, S. S., Schulsinger, F., Welner, J., & Ostergaard, L. Schizophrenics' offspring reared in adoptive homes. In D. Rosenthal & S. S. Kety (Eds.), *The transmission of schizophrenia.* Oxford: Pergamon Press, 1968. Pp. 377–391.

Sandifer, M. G. J. Social psychiatry one-hundred years ago. *American Journal of Psychiatry*, 1962, 118, 749–750.

Srole, L., Langner, T. S., Michael, S. T., Opler, M. K., & Rennie, T. A. C. *Mental health in the metropolis.* New York: McGraw-Hill, 1962.

Stabenau, J. R., & Pollin, W. Early characteristics of monozygotic twins discordant for schizophrenia. *Archives of General Psychiatry*, 1967, 17, 723–734.

Walters, T. Reviews. *American Journal of Psychology*, 1909, 20, 466.

Watt, N. F., Stolorow, R. D., Lubensky, A. W., & McClelland, D. C. School adjustment and behavior of children hospitalized for schizophrenia as adults. *American Journal of Orthopsychiatry*, 1970, 40, 637–657.

Wenar, C. The reliability of mothers' histories. *Child Development*, 1961, 32, 491–500.

Wynne, L. C. Methodologic and conceptual issues in the study of schizophrenics and their families. In D. Rosenthal & S. S. Kety (Eds.), *The transmission of schizophrenia*. Oxford: Pergamon Press, 1968. Pp. 185–199.

———. Strategies for sampling groups at high risk for the development of schizophrenia. Workshop position paper at NIMH-sponsored Conference on High Risk for Schizophrenia, June 1969.

Yarrow, M. R., Campbell, J. D., & Burton, R. V. Recollections of childhood: A study of the retrospective method. *Monographs of the Society for Research in Child Development*, 1970, 35 (5, Serial No. 138).

Yolles, S. F., & Kramer, M. Vital statistics. In L. Bellak & L. Loeb (Eds.), *The schizophrenic syndrome*. New York: Grune & Stratton, 1969. Pp. 66–113.

STELLA CHESS
ALEXANDER THOMAS

Differences in Outcome with Early Intervention in Children with Behavior Disorders

Since 1956, the New York Longitudinal Study has been following the behavioral development of a sample of 136 children from the earliest months of life onward. The children, ranging in age from nine to fifteen, come from 85 middle- and upper-middle–class families, of which 45 have one child enrolled in the study, 31 have two, 7 have three, and 2 have four. Only 5 of the original sample of 141 children (4 per cent) have been lost to the study because of shifts in residence.

Behavioral data have been gathered from a number of sources. Parents were interviewed at regular intervals regarding their child-care practices, characteristics of the child's behavior in routine functions of daily living, his responses to changes in these routines or in his environment, and his reactions to special situations. Teachers provided information about each child's initial adaptation to school and his overall functioning during the school year. The child's behavior in school was observed directly by a member of the study team at least once a year. Collection of these school data began with the child's first school experience — nursery school in most cases — and continued through the second grade. Currently, we are gathering additional school data on academic achievement levels and overall adaptation to educational demands.

The children took standard psychological tests (Stanford-Binet) at three and six years of age. During these tests, their play and problem-solving activities were noted. Currently, psychological testing (WISC) is again being administered.

NOTE: This research was supported in major part by U.S.P.H.S. Grant MH-3614 from the National Institute of Mental Health.

Life History Research in Psychopathology

The longitudinal study has sought to delineate each child's temperamental characteristics in the first few months of life, the patterns of consistency of these characteristics over time, and the influence of temperament, in interaction with environmental influences, on normal and deviant behavioral development.

We have used the term *temperament* as it has been employed by other workers, especially Guilford (1959) and Cattell (1950), to denote the behavioral style of the individual child — the how rather than the what (abilities and content) or why (motivations) of behavior. Temperament thus denotes the child's individual style of behavior in varying situations, independent of the content of any specific behavior. It is a phenomenological term and contains no inferences as to genetic, endocrine, somatologic, or environmental etiologies. We have subsumed temperamental attributes under nine categories: activity level, rhythmicity, adaptability, approach-withdrawal, intensity of reaction, quality of mood, sensory threshold, distractibility, and persistence and attention span.

Several constellations of temperamental characteristics have been identifiable in a number of the children. These include, first, the easy child, characterized by regularity in biological functions, positive approach responses to new stimuli, high adaptability to changes, and a preponderantly positive mood of mild or moderate intensity; second, the difficult child, characterized by irregularity in biological functions, predominantly negative withdrawal responses to new stimuli, nonadaptability or slow adaptability to change, frequent negative mood, and predominantly intense reactions; and third, the slow to warm up child, characterized by negative responses of mild intensity to new stimuli with slow adaptability after repeated contact. These temperamental characteristics and constellations have been rated by both quantitative scoring and qualitative analysis. Definitions of the categories, methods of scoring, and techniques of data analysis have been reported in previous publications (Hertzig, Birch, Thomas, & Mendez, 1968; Thomas, Chess, & Birch, 1968; Chess, Birch, Hertzig, & Korn, 1963).

A major reason for our interest in the study of temperament was a growing conviction over the years, based on our own clinical psychiatric experience and the observations of other workers, that the ontogenesis and evolution of behavior disorders could not be explained by considering intra- and extrafamilial influences alone. It became evident that different children responded differently to similar patterns of parental attitudes and child care, that there were marked individual differences among children in their susceptibility to specific stresses and pressures, and that in general there was no simple relation between environmental circumstances and their behavioral consequences. Such observations have led more and more investigators to focus on attributes of the individual that may significantly influence his idiosyncratic responsiveness to environmental events. In our case, this concern led to an interest in temperamental characteristics and the dynamics of the interaction of temperament and environment in the development of behavior disorders. Therefore, from the beginning of our longitudinal study we made every effort to identify and evaluate those children with deviant behavior quickly, to analyze the anterospective behavioral data in all cases diagnosed as behavior disorder, to advise the parents about remedial measures, and to follow carefully the subsequent course of the disorder. We took responsibility for intervening therapeutically for three reasons: First, we were concerned about the children's welfare and felt that our intimate knowledge of the families and the children's development put us in the best position to help them. Second, if we appeared unconcerned over the child's problem, this would certainly have created resentment in many parents and terminated or at least inhibited their involvement in the study. And third, if we had not intervened, the parents might have gone elsewhere to seek psychiatric help, and we should have had only second-hand knowledge of the kind of intervention and the reactions of the child and parents to the psychiatric procedures.

Of the 136 children, 42 were identified as showing behavior disorders. This determination was not made merely because the parent or school expressed concern about a symptom, but only after careful diagnostic procedures confirmed the presence of symptoms and established a significant degree of behavior disturbance. In each case a clinical diagnosis was made — reactive behavior disorder, neurotic behavior disorder, or brain damage with secondary behavior disorder. No cases of childhood schizophrenia or mental retardation with behavior disorder were diagnosed in the 42 cases. (One child did have mild mental retardation without behavior disorder and was not included in the 42 clinical cases.) We also rated the severity of disorder — mild, moderate, moderately severe, and severe. The 42 clinical cases are 31 per cent of the total study population, a figure which approximates those found in other prevalence studies. (Two additional cases identified in the past few years are not included in the present report because of their short follow-up period). These data are cumulative, and the actual prevalence of behavior problems at any point of time in our population was, of course, lower than this cumulative figure of 31 per cent. The latest of the 42 cases was identified in June 1966, ten years after the beginning of the longitudinal study.

Age at onset of symptoms ranged from 24 months to 8 years 8 months. The time between onset of symptoms and the clinical diagnosis of behavior disorders ranged from 1 to 48 months. Of the 42 cases, 14 came to psychiatric evaluation within 3 months after the onset of symptoms, but the great majority, 65 per cent of the boys and 75 per cent of the girls, came to attention within one year after the onset of symptoms. Diagnoses of mild or moderate reactive behavior disorders were made for 36 children, severe reactive disorders for 4 children, and moderately severe neurotic behavior disorder for 1 child. The most seriously disturbed child, who required long periods of residential treatment, was diagnosed as having organic brain damage with secondary and elaborated behavior disorder.

A number of quantitative comparisons between the clinical cases and the remainder of the sample were done, using t tests and analyses of variance. In the clinical case we also culled the anterospective data from early infancy onward bearing on temperament, intrafamilial influences, and the sequences of symptom appearance and development. It was possible in each of the 42 cases to trace the ontogenesis of the behavioral disturbances in terms of the interaction of temperament and environment. Analysis of the case histories makes it clear that temperament alone does not produce behavioral disturbance. Some children with a temperamental structure closely similar to that of the clinical cases can be found in the normally functioning group. Rather, it appears that both behavioral disturbance and behavioral normality are the result of the interaction between the child with a given temperamental pattern and significant features of his developmental environment. Influential among these environmental features are intrafamilial as well as extrafamilial circumstances such as school and peer group. We found that the most stressful environmental demands and expectations are those related to the child's temperamental characteristics. Thus, parental approaches that may intensify such stressful demands to the point of symptom formation in some children may not do so in others of different temperament.

The clinical evaluation of the child's behavior problem and the initial recommendations for management were formulated by Chess, the study's child psychiatrist. In every case, the child's temperamental characteristics contributed to an understanding of the origins of the disorder and to the formulation of a treatment plan. In all but one of the 42 cases, the initial therapeutic recommendation was for parent guidance — that is, a program of altered parental functioning designed to modify stress that is harmful for an individual child. The cause of the excessive stress was formulated in terms of the poorness of fit or dissonance between environmental demands and the child's capacities or characteristics. To help identify the kind of dissonance contributing to a child's behavioral disorder, the anterospective longitudinal data and the clinical findings were analyzed. We then suggested a program of altered parental functioning calculated to eliminate the child-environment dissonance. Whenever appropriate, other ameliorative measures were recommended, such as a change in living arrangements at home, advice to the school, a change to another school, or remedial tutoring. The basic emphasis was on change in parental behavior and overtly expressed attitudes, not on underlying conflicts, defenses, or anxieties. The goal was to change specific aspects of the parents' actual functioning with their child, rather than to delineate or directly attempt to change covert attitudes that, presumably, might be related to overt behavior and attitudes.

The systematic use of parent guidance as the initial therapeutic procedure made it possible to study its effectiveness and to determine how often parent guidance proves adequate without recourse to time-consuming and expensive direct psychotherapy with parents, child, or both. In those cases where parent guidance proved unsuccessful, we were able to estimate the reasons. In one case, it was clear on initial evaluation that parent guidance would not be adequate. The child, aged 63 months, had a moderately severe neurotic behavior disorder. Our data indicated a history of parental practices and attitudes markedly unfavorable for this child and her temperamental pattern. It was also clear these approaches would not be easily amenable to change. Since the prognosis for treatment by parent guidance alone was so poor, we recommended direct psychotherapy for the child right at the start.

Psychotherapy was eventually instituted in six other children. In four of these cases, psychotherapy was recommended because of the failure of parent guidance; in one case, the parents themselves decided to arrange for psychotherapy, despite the advice that they give the guidance procedure more time; and in another case, the consequences of the child's temperamental reactions in school and with peers were so unfavorable that he had to gain an understanding of his maladaptive functioning before change could occur. Where psychotherapy was instituted it was done by therapists not connected with the study. Follow-up reports were received from these therapists. As indicated above, one child was hospitalized. Residential treatment was recommended for one other case, but refused by the parents.

FOLLOW-UP

Regular communication has been maintained with the children having behavior disorders, their parents, and their schools. The last follow-up in all cases has been within the past six months; the period of follow-up, which of course reflects the time at which the disorder was initially diagnosed, varies from 4 to 11 years. Ratings of degree of improvement or increased impairment were made on the basis of the data from the last follow-up. The top of Table 1 indicates the current outcome in terms of improvement or worsening of symptoms since the initial evaluation. A substantial number of cases, 14 out of 42, show recovery, and 19 others either moderate or marked improvement. Only 9 cases (21 per cent) show worsening of symptoms. There is no significant correlation between outcome and initial severity of symptoms.

The bottom of Table 1 relates outcome to the temperamental char-

Table 1. Changes in Severity of Symptoms and Temperamental Pattern between Initial Diagnosis and Follow-Up[a]

State	Recovered	Markedly Improved	Moderately Improved	Slightly Worse	Moderately Worse	Markedly Worse	Total
Severity of Initial Symptoms							
Mild	9	5	4	1	3	2	24
Moderate	4	2	4		1	1	12
Moderately severe	1	2	1		1		5
Severe		1					1
Total	14	10	9	1	5	3	
Temperamental Pattern							
Difficult	3	1	3		2	1	10
Easy	5	2	1	1	1		10
Slow to warm up	4	1	3		1		9
Persistent	1	3	1				5
Distractible and nonpersistent		2				2	4
Low activity	1		1				2
High activity					1		1
Other		1					1
Total	14	10	9	1	5	3	

[a] No Ss fell into the categories "slightly improved" and "unchanged."

acteristic or constellation which in qualitative analysis appeared most prominent in the child's functioning at the time of initial psychiatric diagnosis. As can be seen, there is no striking correlation between temperamental type and outcome. The findings suggest that difficult children with behavioral disturbances have as good a prognosis as the easy children. However, these children's greater vulnerability to stress is shown in several ways. Children with the cluster of temperamental characteristics typifying the difficult child compose approximately 4 per cent (4 cases) of the group without behavior problems but 23 per cent (10 cases) of the group with behavior problems. Although 59 per cent of the total clinical sample had mild symptoms on initial psychiatric evaluation, only 20 per cent of the difficult children were in the mild category. This was true in the absence of any significant differences between these children and the total group in age at onset of symptoms or age at psychiatric referral for evaluation. Finally, five of the seven cases for which not only parent guidance but also psychotherapy was required were difficult children. In other words, these youngsters appear to be more vulnerable to the development of behavioral disturbance and to present more severe symptoms when they become disturbed. They are also more likely to require psychotherapy. However, the overall prognosis in treatment need not be less favorable for these than for the other children.

Though the total number of cases with distractibility and nonpersistence is too small to draw any firm conclusions, it is of interest that 2 out of the 4 had outcomes in the "markedly worse" category. Only 1 other child — 1 difficult child out of 10 — had this outcome. Parent guidance was least successful in changing parental atitudes and behavior with this type of child. The parents in the study sample as a whole attached great importance to educational achievement for both sexes and to success in professional careers or business for the males. For such goals, persistence ("stick-to-it-iveness") is considered desirable and even essential. It is therefore harder for these parents to accept the validity and normality of the temperamental qualities of relative nonpersistence and easy distractibility in their children, especially in boys. In a few cases, this attitude was expressed openly in the parent guidance sessions with such remarks about the offspring as "He lacks character." It is worth noting that all four children with nonpersistence and easy distractibility were boys. The parents of this group had special difficulty in accepting the individuality of their child's temperamental pattern. This may have contributed significantly to the failure of parent guidance.

The high rate of recovery and improvement in this group of 42 children who developed behavior disorders in the early years of childhood is, of course, of great interest. Since the children are now only approaching or entering adolescence, no statement can be made about the long-term outcome. We plan to follow the sample at least through adolescence and into early adult life and to correlate long-term outcome with various antecedent variables (temperament, early development, intra- and extrafamilial environment, etc.). What can be emphasized at this point is the flexibility in development shown by these children. As emphasized by Kanner (1960), Robins (1966), and others, symptoms of behavioral dysfunction in early life do not necessarily indicate deep-seated disturbances that will have a continuous pathogenic influence on development. Where dysfunction does persist, symptoms and their significance may change at different age-stage levels of development or with changes in environmental demands and stresses.

Even where specific temperamental characteristics continue to have a significant influence on a child's development, this influence may show wide variation over time, depending on the consistencies or shifts in other psychological patterns or environmental influences with which temperament interacts. The three case vignettes presented below illustrate such differences in development and outcome over time. In the first case parental guidance was markedly successful, and recovery ensued. In the second case the parents also cooperated well in carrying through the guidance program, but the child was subjected periodically to environmental stresses outside the home. He was exceptionally vulnerable to these stresses because of his temperamental characteristics, so his developmental course was a highly fluctuating one. In the third case the parent guidance program was entirely unsuccessful, and a destructive mother-child interaction continued to play a strongly unhealthy role in the child's development.

Case 1. Dorothy, now 13 years old, functions well according to her parents, school, and our clinical judgment. Until recently, both parents had to make a constant effort to be content with Dorothy's temperamental individuality. Plodding, slow to react, she gave responses in low key. Her quickly reacting, highly expressive parents had for years found it hard to interpret her wants, though they could respond with certainty to Dorothy's two younger sisters, who expressed their desires and opinions unmistakably. Dorothy was dead pan when pleased, whined when discontented. In the preschool period, she had usually been pushed aside by all members of this fast-moving family. Her major temperamental characteristics were low motor activity level, low intensity level, high persistence, and slow adaptability. In addition, Dorothy's intelligence was average, whereas both sisters had superior intellectual capacity. Her language development had initially been slow enough to be classified as a developmental lag. But Dorothy also displayed down-to-earth common sense and practicality, and these qualities became more and more apparent as she grew older.

The first step in guidance was to interpret Dorothy to her parents, to help them see that the absence of demonstrativeness did not mean inability to feel joy, that whining when an excursion came to an end meant that the child had enjoyed the experience. Although periodic reviews and reinforcements of this type of interpretation were necessary, the parents did genuinely begin to tune themselves into Dorothy's style. They tried to keep the younger sisters from elbowing her aside by their faster and clearer overt reactions.

Although schoolwork has always been a struggle and examinations have caused anxiety, Dorothy has set her own goals, takes responsibility for studying, and accepts the test anxiety as something she must live with. Though she is in a less demanding school than either sister, it is a school with respectable expectations, and Dorothy's grades are B's and A's. Just as she had requested to be permitted to go on to third grade rather than repeat second so as to ease the pressure of study when changing schools, promising not to feel badly if she had to be put back (it was not necessary) she is now asking to be given an opportunity to try out for a more demanding school, promising to be content with the outcome.

At initial referral the descriptive terms used by Dorothy's parents included "truculent, narrow range of expressiveness, cannot follow simple commands." The current description of her includes "terribly proud, a companionable person, from a disturbed little girl she is at peace with herself, a totally responsive human being." The parents say that it used to be an effort to act toward Dorothy in certain ways different from their spontaneous reactions, but now they can be themselves. Dorothy still goes about things in her own quiet and slow way, but her parents now genuinely admire her clear facing of issues and have become truly convinced that any handicap occasioned by her slow pace of doing things is effectively offset by her persistence.

Case 2. Richard represents an exercise in roller-coaster adaptation, and in each change of circumstance the temperamental qualities noted in early infancy have continued to contribute an active influence. Very persistent once he became engaged in an activity, Richard had intensely negative reactions when pulled away from task involvement. He was basically a friendly, positive youngster but in the first-grade classroom he became frustrated when the teacher scheduled what were for him overfrequent changes in activity. The result was a series of tantrums in class. Though at first triggered when Richard was interrupted in an activity, the tantrums themselves soon became almost his dominant activity. Yet when he was brought to the principal's office, the child happily spent extended periods of time in paperwork or helpful chores.

The tantrums ended when a change in schools and scheduling permitted uninterrupted hours of study on a single subject at a time. His teachers considered Richard exceptionally well adjusted until the fourth grade. An explosive episode then resulted in his expulsion. He had prepared a poster for a contest, genuinely unaware that since he had not been selected as a participant, his teacher considered him insubordinate. When she tore up his completed poster in anger, he flung his book at her. The school officials regarded this as an assault on a teacher, and Richard was expelled. Although a favorable new school placement was made, the psychiatric discussion with Richard at this time revealed the beginning of protective denial. Said the boy, now age 8, "I don't want to talk about it, it makes me feel bad. That's just the way I am. Every once in a while I just do something terrible and talking isn't going to stop me." Nevertheless we talked about other things. About six months later his self-esteem had been substantially restored and eventually we were able to discuss the possibilities of personal control of his persistence and some selection by himself of times and places for applying it. School adaptation, after a shaky initial period during which Richard provoked a number of confrontations, became first good then excellent. Peer relationships were also good.

There was a change of schools in eighth grade. Just preceding this, Richard's father died, and his brother was drafted and sent to Vietnam. At school, Richard's academic functioning varied sharply with the teacher. He did high level work in one course, but in two others he refused to study and to hand in assignments. The relationship with his mother, previously good, became hostile. Richard would not get up in time for school. In the psychiatric sessions, he never introduced or acknowledged such problems, although he was ready to discourse pleasantly on other topics. He repeated eighth grade, again failed two subjects in the same manner. Toward the end of the year the mechanism of denial was relaxed and Richard began to explore his own contribution to the school problems. Because he liked the academic atmosphere and had many friends, he asked for a chance to stay. He applied himself successfully to summer school with the persistence which now became a strength. A trip abroad with his mother restored their former relationship. Despite a hair length and style which evoked negative reactions from strangers, the cruise members remarked to his mother on his maturity, helpfulness, and thoroughness in familiarizing himself with the political and monetary facts of each country before arrival. His current situation is again extremely positive. All teachers consider him a pleasure both in terms of attitude and work output; his social relationships are good; he and his mother remain on good terms, with Richard taking responsibility for getting work done and getting to school on time; the psychiatric sessions are productive. Whatever the impetus given to the negative situation by the outside stress, Richard's persistence in creating confrontations determined the negative feedback by teachers and his own acting out of his personal prophecy of disaster. Once he realized that he would be the loser in his persistent vendettas, and once he turned his full attention to remedying the situation, his persistence could be a positive quality.

Case 3. Roy, now 14, is currently classified as having a neurotic character disorder. Despite early identification of the problem and attempts to alter parental handling, the behavior disorder has become progressively more generalized and more fixated. Initial complaints at age 6 years 4 months were the child's refusal to carry out parental requests and his tendency to give up easily with new endeavors, both features starting at age 4 years. The temperamental characteristics of particular importance in his disorder were high distractibility and initial withdrawal from the new, both evident from early infancy; of equal importance were the parental interpretations and reactions. The mother was convinced that Roy's forgetfulness was specifically aimed at making life harder for her, and she had no patience to let him warm up to a new situation at his own pace. A compulsive personality despite years of psychiatric treatment, she could not permit her boy to experiment with self-servicing in young childhood because it might mean mess and delay. She was prone to scold and pressure when he failed to measure up to her impossible standards. The father, initially involved in activity with Roy, had gradually withdrawn from the daily battle.

Forgetfulness at age 6 had become negativism toward the mother by age 7, and by age 9 there was a continuous battle between mother and son over daily routines, with protective lying. Generalization of negativism to teachers and schoolwork had also occurred. A tic had been added to document the stress. Weekly guidance sessions with the mother for six months when Roy was age 10 made clear once more that her attitude and behavior could not be modified.

With increasing academic problems in this boy of superior intelligence, direct psychotherapy was recommended and Roy dutifully brought his body to the psychiatrist's office weekly for a period of almost two years. Denial and avoidance were prominent. He was a classical exponent of the "High D" syndrome. If he got a D on a test, his remark was that it was a high D, everyone else also got a low mark, the teacher wasn't good, and so on. When re-interviewed by one of the authors at age 14 Roy was pleasant and vague. Noninvolvement was the key to his replies. Thus, his temperamental style and its incompatibility with that of his mother not only created the behavior disorder but also gave the boy an effective style of protection from her merciless attacks, which he treated as the prototype of general attitudes and expectations.

As we have followed the development of the children in our sample, we have been impressed over and over again by the depth of understanding of the psychiatric and other behavioral data obtained at any one age made possible by the availability of the anterospective longitudinal data. It is indeed fascinating to uncover the richness of interplay of organismic and environmental factors and to trace the varieties of combinations of consistency and change over time. We look forward with special interest to the findings as our study population goes through the adolescent period.

REFERENCES

Cattell, R. B. *Personality: A systematic and factual study.* New York: McGraw-Hill, 1950.

Guilford, J. P. *Personality.* New York: McGraw-Hill, 1959.

Hertzig, M., Birch, H. G., Thomas, A., & Mendez, O. A. Class and ethnic differences in the responsiveness of preschool children to cognitive demands. *Monographs of the Society for Research in Child Development,* 1968, 33, (1, Serial No. 117).

Kanner, L. Do behavioral symptoms always indicate psychopathology? *Journal of Child Psychology and Psychiatry,* 1960, 1, 17–25.

Robins, L. N. *Deviant children grown up: A psychiatric and sociological study of the sociopathic personality.* Baltimore: Williams & Wilkins, 1966.

Thomas, A., Chess, S., & Birch, H. G. *Temperament and behavior disorders in children.* New York: New York University Press, 1968.

———, Hertzig, M. E., & Korn, S. *Behavioral individuality in early childhood.* New York: New York University Press, 1963.

MARGARET G. WOERNER
MAX POLLACK
CAROL ROGALSKI
YVETTE POLLACK
DONALD F. KLEIN ⎦ *A Comparison of the School Records of Personality Disorders, Schizophrenics, and Their Sibs*

THE now considerable body of literature dealing with the behavioral antecedents of schizophrenia has been recently reviewed in detail (Offord & Cross, 1969) and its methodology scrutinized (Mednick & McNeil, 1968). Personality disorders of the antisocial type have also been studied developmentally (Robins, 1966), but little attention has been paid to other subgroups of the personality disorders. The study of such groups is important not only in its own right, but also as a clinical control for work seeking developmental clues related specifically to the etiology of schizophrenia, as distinct from other varieties of psychopathology afflicting the same age groups.

The present investigation represents a continuation of our attempt to determine whether specific variables or patterns of childhood deviance can be identified and related to adult psychiatric status. The purpose of this study has been to investigate two questions: First, are the childhood (premorbid) personality characteristics of adolescent and young adult psychiatric patients significantly different from those of their psychiatrically normal biological sibs? Second, are there specific childhood patterns related to the two major functional disorders of this age group — namely, schizophrenia and the personality disorders?

In terms of the first question we have considered the sibs as a normal comparison group, having the advantage of better control than unrelated normals for factors such as socioeconomic status, home environment, and genetic makeup. Since Hillside Hospital maintains close communication with patients' families, we were in a position to have in-person study of the sibs.

Our previous work was retrospective and indicated that significant differences in certain childhood characteristics between patients and sibs were reported by mothers (Pollack, Woerner, Goodman, & Greenberg, 1966). In the present study we have attempted to improve the reliability of our information on childhood variables by employing school records as a data source.

This study can be described, in terms of design, as a "follow-back" investigation; it begins with a sample of identified psychiatric disorders, and searches back to material recorded in childhood, before the onset of illness. The use of school records, rather than child guidance clinic records (which several previous investigations have used as a childhood data source) has the advantage of not limiting the samples to patients who were sufficiently deviant as children to have been brought to the attention of a clinic. School records share with clinic records the disadvantage that the material has been recorded by many different observers, often in different formats, and the investigator is limited to the information that is available.

The fruitfulness of using school records to study the premorbid intelligence test performance of schizophrenics has been demonstrated by Lane and Albee (1970). Pollack, Woerner, and Klein (1970) confirmed their findings of lower IQ's for pre-schizophrenics compared with their siblings but found similar patterns for patients diagnosed as personality disorders.

A few investigations (Bower, Schellhammer, Daily, & Bower, 1960; Warnken & Seiss, 1965; Watt, Stolorow, Lubensky, & McClelland, 1970) have employed school records to study the premorbid personality characteristics of hospitalized schizophrenics compared with normal controls, but we know of no previous studies which have used this technique for studying patients diagnosed as personality disorders.

METHOD

Subjects. The subjects for this study were drawn from a larger series of hospitalized psychiatric patients and their siblings described in detail elsewhere (Pollack, Woerner, Goldberg, & Klein, 1968; Pollack, Woerner, & Klein, 1970). The sample reported on here includes those from the larger series for whom we were able to obtain school records with adequate information on the personality variables: 15 male and 18 female schizophrenic patients, and 21 male and 24 female personality disorder patients. Almost all of the personality disorder patients had diagnoses of either Hysterical, Emotionally Unstable, or Passive Aggressive Personality. In addition, five male patients were diagnosed Antisocial Personality and one as Inadequate Personality; one male and one female were diagnosed Paranoid Personality. Patients with severe alcohol problems, drug addiction, or severe acting out or aggressive behavior were not represented in this sample; they are excluded by the hospital admissions policy.

The normal sib comparison groups included 13 brothers and 14 sisters of schizophrenics, and 12 brothers and 20 sisters of personality disorders. (The fact that there were more patients than sibs reflects the selection of only normal sibs for these comparisons.) Normal sibs were those judged free of current symptomatology beyond a mild degree, with no history of psychiatric treatment or impairment of function which would have warranted treatment.

The mean age of the patients was 20 years at the time of study; the mean age of the sibs was 19. All subjects were white, and their families were primarily in the middle socioeconomic class.

Obtaining School Records. A list of names and dates of all schools attended by each subject was obtained from the parents as part of the routine data collection procedures. In addition, the parent (or subject himself for those age 21 or over) signed releases authorizing us to examine school records and confidential files. Permission was obtained from the office of the superintendent of the New York City (NYC) Public School system, as well as from all the parochial and suburban systems involved, for our staff to visit the schools and abstract information from the cumulative records and confidential files. For subjects who had attended schools beyond feasible traveling distance, records were solicited by mail. Since the majority of our subjects had been educated in the NYC public school system, and the cumulative records are stored in the school last attended, visits to the NYC high schools produced most of the data.

Graduate student assistants visited the schools and abstracted information from the records onto prepared forms with space for written comments to be copied verbatim. The assistants, of necessity, knew the names of the subjects, but did not know whether they were patients or sibs.

Coding School Record Information. The NYC cumulative record format for the elementary grades in use during the years in which the majority of our subjects attended school contained systematic information in terms of annual teacher ratings on fifteen items (two- or three-choice scales) relating to personality and adjustment. In addition, space was provided to record interviews with pupils or parents (usually in relation to problem behavior), special reports from other agencies, outstanding abilities, disabilities and problems, special interests, clubs, and recreational activities. The health records also contained material relevant to personality: symptoms and problems which included nervous habits and symptoms of "emotional disturbance" as well as space for notes regarding problems (often behavior problems) referred for special attention. The junior high school format was similar except that the annual teacher ratings were confined to seven items.

This format served as the basis for our coding scheme. However, in order to be able to incorporate information from records of other school systems, categories were developed within which we could include as much information as possible from all of the records despite variations in the recording system. In effect, our method was to cull from the records all notations of behavior deviance or problems (problem-statements) indicated either by written comments or negative teacher rating scale choices. We classified these problem statements as belonging to one of four categories: (a) Group Adjustment, (b) Work Habits, (c) Conduct, and (d) Personal Adjustment. For each category, ratings of 1 (no problem) to 4 (severe problem) were made, based upon the number and severity of the problem statements recorded. Separate ratings were made for elementary school (kindergarten through sixth grade) and junior high school (seventh and eighth grades).

In addition, within three of the four areas (Work Habits, Conduct, and Personal Adjustment) some problem statements were coded separately on a yes-no basis; yes indicated the presence of this statement at least once in the elementary *or* junior high school record.

The problem-statements included under each of the four areas are listed below; the starred items are those coded separately.

a. Group Adjustment
    Does not get along with others
    Usually nonconforming (to group control)
    Works and plays well with others (poor or unsatisfactory rating)
    Works constructively with group (poor or unsatisfactory rating)
    Respects rights of others (poor or unsatisfactory rating)
    Shows poor sportsmanship
    Does not cooperate with group
b. Work Habits
    * Usually not dependable, evades responsibility, unreliable

* Lazy, needs prodding, does not try his best, effort poor or unsatisfactory
  Rarely attends to work
  Does not complete work on time
  Is generally careless, does not work neatly
c. Conduct
  * Overaggressive, fights frequently; bully
  * Frequent temper outbursts, unstable; lacks self-control
  * Hyperactive
  Disruptive in class, loud
  Rude, talks back, sarcastic, disagreeable, or surly
  Steals
  Does not observe rules, disobedient, does not follow directions, uncooperative
  Destructive, does not take care of property
d. Personal Adjustment
  * Shy, withdrawn, does not participate, has no friends
  * Lacks confidence, needs frequent encouragement, insecure, oversensitive
  * Requires inordinate amount of attention, cries easily, whines
  * Worries about accomplishments, overconscientious, tense, anxious, self-conscious
  * Frequently seems unhappy, disturbed child
  * Usually lethargic, underactive
  * Parent-child relationship seems disturbed
  Does not assert himself
  * Has nervous habits, "nervous child"
  * Tics, twitches, eye-blinking, tremors
  * Nail-biting
  * Excess use of lavatory
  Fears, phobias
  Thumb-sucking, nose-picking
  * Any nervous habits or notation of nervous child

Interests and Extracurricular Activities. Interests and extracurricular activities, written in on the records in spaces provided for "special interests," "school clubs," and "recreational activities" were categorized for coding into two major groups: individual interests/hobbies, and group participation.

Participation in athletic groups was coded separately, as well as within the group interest category, as were positions of leadership in a class or group. The four measures are described more fully below.

a. Individual interests. This item was based on a count of all notations in each subject's record of special interests or hobbies which did not involve participation in clubs or groups, such as collections, reading, creative writing, current events, painting, music, carpentry, and electronics.

For analysis, subjects were categorized as having either 0 or 1 notations, or 2 or more different notations.

b. Total group participation. This item was based on a count of all notations of membership in a club or group activity in or out of school, such as band or orchestra, debating club, newspaper staff, scouts, nature club, or athletic team. For analysis, subjects were coded as for item a: either as belonging to 0 or 1 groups or 2 or more different groups.

c. Athletic groups. Subjects were coded yes for any notation of participation in an organized athletic team or club.

d. Leadership positions. Subjects were coded yes for any notation in their record that they held one or more positions of leadership in a class or group, such as class officer, club officer, student government representative, team captain, or editor.

All identifying information was removed from the school record data forms and code numbers substituted before any work was done on the records. The systems for categorizing and rating items were set up by a clinical psychologist and an experienced NYC elementary school teacher. The rating was done by the clinical psychologist, and twenty records were also rated by the teacher to test the reliability of the ratings. Reliability was found to be satisfactory, with Kuder-Richardson coefficients .90 or above.

Data Analysis. One of the disadvantages of doing sibling research is that sibships do not always conveniently come same sexed. We did not have enough subjects to use matched comparisons of patients with their own same-sexed sibs, and preliminary analyses indicated the importance of segregating the sexes. Therefore, we have compared all male schizophrenic patients with male sibs of schizophrenic patients and female schizophrenic patients with female sibs of schizophrenic patients (and the same for personality disorders) disregarding family matching.

For comparisons between groups on the category ratings, t tests for independent samples were employed. Chi square or Fisher exact tests were employed for the dichotomous items. One-tailed significance levels are reported for patient-sibling comparisons, since it was predicted that patients would show more problem behaviors. For comparisons between sexes and between diagnostic groups, two-tailed tests were used.

RESULTS

Personality, Elementary School. Table 1 presents the mean ratings for the eight groups in each of the four global personality areas for ele-

Table 1. Means and Statistical Comparisons of Male and Female Patients and Their Sib Comparison Groups on Elementary School Personality Ratings[a]

Ratings	Group Adjustment	Work Habits	Conduct	Personal Adjustment	Mean Elementary
Schizophrenic Group					
Mean personality ratings					
Males					
Patients ($N=15$)	2.2	2.3	1.7	3.0	2.3
Siblings ($N=13$)	1.8	2.0	1.8	2.5	2.0
Females					
Patients ($N=18$)	1.7	1.9	1.2	2.2	1.8
Siblings ($N=14$)	1.1**	1.4	1.1	1.9	1.4*
Significance of sex differences[b]					
Patients: males versus females	N.S.	N.S.	N.S.	N.S.	<.05
Sibs: males versus females	<.05	N.S.	<.05	N.S.	<.02
Personality Disorder Group					
Mean personality ratings					
Males					
Patients ($N=21$)	1.9	2.2	2.3	2.5	2.2
Siblings ($N=12$)	1.7	1.6**	1.3**	2.1	1.7*
Females					
Patients ($N=23$)	1.9	1.9	1.6	2.6	2.0
Siblings ($N=20$)	1.2***	1.3**	1.1**	1.8	1.4***
Significance of sex differences[b]					
Patients: males versus females	N.S.	N.S.	N.S.	N.S.	N.S.
Sibs: males versus females	<.05	N.S.	N.S.	N.S.	N.S.

[a] t tests for independent samples were employed.
[b] Based on two-tailed tests.
* $p<.05$ (one tailed).   ** $p<.025$ (one tailed).
*** $p<.005$ (one tailed).

mentary school. In addition, the mean of the four category ratings for each group is presented to provide an overall problem rating score at each level.

Overall, males had higher ratings than females for virtually every comparison. Sex differences were most pronounced for the schizophrenics: male patients had significantly higher mean elementary ratings than did female patients, and normal brothers were significantly worse than sisters of schizophrenics on group adjustment, conduct, and mean elementary ratings. Male and female personality disorders did not differ significantly on any ratings; brothers of personality disorders were significantly worse than sisters only on group adjustment.

Differences between diagnostic groups were slight, and none approached statistical significance. The trends indicate that male schizophrenics were "worse" than male personality disorders on all ratings except conduct; female personality disorders were "worse" than female schizophrenics on all ratings. Comparisons between the siblings of the two diagnostic groups revealed no significant differences, although brothers of schizophrenics were "worse" than brothers of personality disorders on all ratings.

Male and female personality disorders and female schizophrenics were "worse" than their same-sexed sib comparisons on all of the ratings. For female personality disorders, all of the differences were significant; male personality disorders were significantly worse on work habits, conduct, and mean elementary ratings. For female schizophrenics, group adjustment and the mean elementary school ratings were significantly worse.

A trend for male schizophrenics to be "worse" than male sibs on all ratings except conduct was evident; however, none of these differences was statistically significant. It seems apparent from the data that this does not reflect better adjustment on the part of male schizophrenics compared with the other patient groups; rather, there is a trend toward worse adjustment on the part of the male sibs of schizophrenics compared with the other sibling groups.

Personality, Junior High School. Table 2 presents the junior high school results. The first thing to be noted is that virtually all of the ratings are lower (less abnormal) than they were in elementary school. This is probably due, in part, to the fact that the systematic personality ratings in the NYC junior high school records were less comprehensive than those in the elementary school records. In addition, it is likely that pupils in junior high school (where departmental teaching begins) are less well known to the teacher making the ratings than is the case in elementary school, where pupils are with the same teacher for most of the day. On the basis of these two factors, one can speculate that at least the milder difficulties would be less apt to be noted in the junior high school records.

Overall, boys continued to have higher ratings than girls. Sex differences were most pronounced between male and female schizophrenic patients: three of the four category ratings and the mean junior high ratings were significantly higher for male schizophrenics. In contrast with elementary school, brothers and sisters of schizophrenics did not differ significantly from each other in junior high school. There were no significant differences between male and female personality disorders, nor between their brothers and sisters.

No differences between diagnostic groups, either for patients or sibs, were significant at the junior high level. In terms of directional trends,

Table 2. Means and Statistical Comparisons of Male and Female Patients and Their Sib Comparison Groups on Junior High School Personality Ratings[a]

Ratings	Group Adjustment	Work Habits	Conduct	Personal Adjustment	Mean Junior High
Schizophrenic Group					
Mean personality ratings					
Males					
Patients ($N = 14$)........	1.3	1.9	1.7	2.3	1.8
Siblings ($N = 12$)........	1.2	1.4	1.2*	1.0***	1.2**
Females					
Patients ($N = 17$)........	1.3	1.3	1.1	1.5	1.3
Siblings ($N = 14$)........	1.0	1.3	1.1	1.4	1.2
Significance of sex differences[b]					
Patients: males versus females	N.S.	<.05	<.01	<.05	<.02
Sibs: males versus females...	N.S.	N.S.	N.S.	N.S.	N.S.
Personality Disorder Group					
Mean personality ratings					
Males					
Patients ($N = 20$)........	1.4	1.8	1.9	1.9	1.7
Siblings ($N = 11$)........	1.2	1.6	1.6	1.1*	1.4
Females					
Patients ($N = 24$)........	1.2	1.4	1.4	1.9	1.5
Siblings ($N = 19$)........	1.0	1.2	1.2	1.4*	1.2*
Significance of sex differences[b]					
Patients: males versus females	N.S.	N.S.	N.S.	N.S.	N.S.
Sibs: males versus females...	N.S.	N.S.	N.S.	N.S.	N.S.

[a] *t* tests for independent samples were employed.
[b] Based on two-tailed tests.
* $p<.05$ (one tailed).   ** $p<.01$ (one tailed).
*** $p<.005$ (one tailed).

there was one reversal of the elementary school trends: brothers of schizophrenics were nonsignificantly but consistently "better" than brothers of personality disorders.

In junior high school, patients continued to be "worse" than their sibs on virtually every rating. In contrast with the findings for elementary school, however, male schizophrenics in junior high differed significantly from their sibs on the ratings of conduct and personal adjustment and the mean junior high rating; there were fewer significant patient-sib differences for the other groups in junior high than in elementary school. Only the personal adjustment ratings continued significantly to differentiate male personality disorders from their sibs. Female personality disorders continued to be significantly worse on personal adjustment and the mean junior high rating.

Individual Problem Statements. As would be expected, since the individual problem statements were the basic material for the ratings, the directional trends were found to be very similar, but few items significantly differentiated any groups. The most striking finding was that male schizophrenic patients differed significantly from their male comparison sibs ($p<.005$), from male personality disorders ($p<.01$), and from female schizophrenics ($p<.01$) on having been noted, at least once in their records, as "shy, withdrawn, does not participate" or "has no friends." Some 80 per cent of the male schizophrenics were so noted, compared with 15 per cent of their sib comparisons, 30 per cent of the male personality disorders, and 22 per cent of the female schizophrenics. In addition, male schizophrenics were noted to be hypoactive or lethargic significantly more often than male personality disorders ($p = .05$). (Male personality disorders tended to be called hyperactive, if anything, whereas no male schizophrenics in the sample were noted as hyperactive.)

Although none of the specific (single) nervous habits or symptoms significantly differentiated the groups, male schizophrenics were noted as "nervous child" or as having nervous habits (unspecified) significantly more often than their sib comparisons ($p<.025$) or female schizophrenics ($p<.05$). Female personality disorders were significantly worse than their sibs ($p<.025$) or female schizophrenics ($p = .01$) on "any nervous habits."

Both male and female personality disorders were significantly different from their sibs ($p<.01$) but not from schizophrenics, on the problem statement "parent-child relation seems disturbed." Finally, male personality disorders were more often noted as "undependable, unreliable" than their sibs ($p<.025$) or female personality disorders ($p<.05$), and female personality disorders were more often noted as "frequently unhappy" or "disturbed child" than were their sibs ($p<.05$).

Interests and Extracurricular Activities. There were no significant differences on any comparisons involving the number of individual interests or the number of groups participated in recorded on the school records. The direction indicated that male patients of both diagnostic groups belonged to fewer organized groups than did their male comparison sibs.

Not one male schizophrenic or personality disorder patient was noted to have participated in an athletic group, whereas 30 per cent of the brothers of schizophrenics and 27 per cent of the brothers of personality disorders did participate in some organized athletic team ($p<.05$ for both comparisons).

Significantly fewer male personality disorders (5 per cent) than their sib comparisons (36 per cent) were noted to have held a position of leadership ($p<.05$). No male schizophrenics held leadership positions, but the percentages were very low for their sib comparisons, and for female schizophrenics and sibs.

DISCUSSION

In answer to the first question posed in this research — Do school records differentiate adolescent and young adult psychiatric patients from like-sexed normal sibs? — we have found that the answer is yes, but there are different patterns relating to the school level studied (elementary versus junior high), diagnosis, and sex.

Personality disorder patients of both sexes were significantly differentiated from their sibs at both school levels. Although the differences appear more salient at the elementary level, this may simply reflect the decreased adequacy of the junior high school records. Owing to the absence in the literature of developmental studies of personality disorder patients comparable to ours (i.e., not primarily antisocial or delinquent types), this question awaits further research.

In contrast, the results for our schizophrenic patients reflect sex differences as well as school level differences. At the elementary level, our findings suggest that normal brothers of male schizophrenics had as many behavioral difficulties noted in their records as the patients themselves. This appears contradictory to previous developmental studies of the behavioral characteristics of schizophrenics compared with their normal siblings (Alanen, 1966; Pollack, Woerner, Goodman, & Greenberg, 1966; Prout & White, 1956) or twins (Pollin, Stabenau, Mosher, & Tupin, 1966). These studies all reported significant personality differences between schizophrenics and their sibs in childhood. The most consistent findings were that patients were described as more passive, dependent, unhappy, and less social than their sibs.

Comparison of our findings with these is complicated by the fact that these studies did not analyze their data separately by sex, and that they obtained their information largely from parents' retrospective reports. Characteristics such as passivity, dependency, and unhappiness are less likely to be noted as problems by teachers on school records than they are by parents who are asked to compare one sib with another and are questioned specifically about these traits. Another possibility is that retrospective distortion may have resulted in mothers' underreporting the early difficulties of the normal sibs.

Prout and White's (1956) results do provide some rough corroboration of the school level difference in our findings for male schizophrenics compared with their brothers. They reported that, in childhood, the sibs of pre-schizophrenics were more rebellious and less easy to handle than the pre-schizophrenics were. During adolescence, positive personality changes were reported for the normal sibs and negative changes for the pre-schizophrenics.

The study most comparable with our own in methodology, although the comparison groups consisted of like-sexed classmates rather than siblings, confirms some of our findings. Watt et al. (1970) analyzed teachers' comments on the cumulative school records (elementary through high school) of 17 male and 13 female pre-schizophrenics. The male schizophrenics' records contained significantly fewer positive and more negative teachers' comments than did those of the male controls in two categories: "emotional stability-instability" and "agreeableness-disagreeableness." These are roughly comparable to our categories "personal adjustment" and "conduct," which differentiated male pre-schizophrenics from their brothers at the junior high school level.

An important difference, however, is that our "personal adjustment" category included the problem statements "shy, withdrawn, does not participate" or "has no friends," whereas Watt's study included a separate category called "introversion," which did not discriminate between his groups. In our study, notations on this item were recorded significantly more often for male schizophrenics than for any other group. Thus, in this respect our results are more in line with earlier studies using childhood psychiatric clinic records (Birren, 1944; Frazee, 1953; Gardner, 1967; Ricks & Nameche, 1966; Wittman & Steinberg, 1944); interviews with high school teachers (Bower et al., 1960); and school records (Warnken & Seiss, 1965) which found shy, withdrawn, "shut in" personality traits to be prominent in the premorbid histories of schizophrenics. Some of these studies, like ours, also reported conduct problems or antisocial-aggressive patterns, but these were less salient. An exception is Robins (1966), who found no evidence of a shy withdrawn pattern among 23 male child guidance clinic patients who later became schizophrenic.

Watt's results clearly coincide with ours in finding different patterns on school records for male and female pre-schizophrenics. His female pre-schizophrenics did not differ significantly from their controls on any of his category measures. He concluded from the trends that a pattern of overinhibition, sensitivity, conformity, and introversion was suggested for the girls, in contrast to the pattern of unsocialized aggression for the boys.

This evidence of different patterns in the records of male and female pre-schizophrenics coincides with other findings from our earlier research suggesting that male schizophrenics, more often than female, are characterized by the continuation of an early-recognized deviant socialization pattern (Belmont, Birch, Klein, & Pollack, 1964).

The possibility that sex differences in developmental patterns may in part reflect differing etiologies may be interesting to consider. Rosanoff, Handy, Plesset, and Brush (1934), for example, postulated the involvement of intrauterine defects in the etiology of some early onset male schizophrenics, and a genetic etiology for later onset schizophrenia, which is more characteristic of females.

Turning to the second question posed — Are there specific childhood patterns related to the two diagnostic groups studied? — our comparisons of schizophrenic with personality disorder patients suggest a negative answer. Neither male nor female schizophrenics differed significantly from like-sexed personality disorders on any of the category ratings. Thus, the number and severity of problem statements noted in the records in each category are similar for the personality disorders and the schizophrenics. (The consistency of the trend for pre-schizophrenic girls to show less difficulty than pre–personality disorder girls does suggest the possibility that further work with larger samples will differentiate these groups.)

The individual item analyses did suggest some differentiation in the type of problem within the personal adjustment category: male schizophrenics were more likely to be called shy or withdrawn and hypoactive than were male personality disorders. Although this makes clinical sense, it needs replication before any far-reaching implications can be drawn. There is some corroboration from the retrospective study by Alanen (1966): two thirds of his schizophrenic patients "had been relatively autistic, seclusive persons, even prepsychotically" (p. 367), but none of his neurotic patients had been. In contrast, Fleming and Ricks (1970) found no significant difference between pre-schizophrenics and pre–character disorders (mostly acting out aggressive and antisocial types) on the expression of feelings of isolation and alienation which had been recorded in child guidance clinic therapy session records. Both groups expressed such feelings significantly more often than clinic patients who turned out to be well as adults.

On the whole, it appears that attempts to delineate specific developmental factors for schizophrenia as compared with non-schizophrenic personality disorders have not produced dramatic differential pathognomonic patterns. Roff has reported that blind ratings of peer relationships based on child guidance clinic records predicted later psychoneurosis, severe bad conduct, psychosis, schizoid personality, and homosexuality among males (Roff, 1959, 1961, 1963, 1965, 1966). Costello, Gunn, and Dominian (1968) compared detailed case histories of male inpatient schizophrenics and non-schizophrenics (mostly neurotics and personality disorders) and found them virtually indistinguishable on items relating to family structure, personal history (including school adjustment and childhood neurotic traits), and premorbid social adjustment. Robins (1966) found that male child guidance clinic patients who later became schizophrenic differed significantly from those who became sociopathic only in that they had less often been referred specifically for antisocial behavior, had less often appeared in juvenile court, and had less often associated with bad companions. There were no differences on non-antisocial symptoms, or school problems.

There are several possible explanations for the failure to delineate specific patterns: (a) The data available from records may be inadequate to reflect subtle differences. (b) It may be that schizophrenia is a not too distant cousin of some types of personality disorders, and clear developmental differences should, on theoretical grounds, not be expected. (c) The use of large, heterogeneous diagnostic categories may obscure patterns which might be characteristic of specific diagnostic subgroups. To test this hypothesis one would need inter-rater agreement on diagnostic subgroup classification and a very large population to ensure respectable subgroup sizes. (d) The diagnostic classifications may not reliably distinguish schizophrenia from personality disorder. We would tend to give less weight to this hypothesis for our samples, in view of our careful diagnostic procedure and conservative criteria for the diagnosis of schizophrenia. Furthermore, follow-up studies on Hillside Hospital samples similar to the present one have indicated that patients diagnosed schizophrenic by the research group had a significantly poorer prognosis than did personality disorders (Levenstein, Klein, & Pollack, 1966; Quitkin & Klein, 1967). In addition, independent evaluation of the family members of our present sample revealed a significant overrepresentation of schizophrenia among the relatives of schizophrenic patients, but not among those of personality disorder patients (Pollack, Woerner, Goldberg, & Klein, 1968, 1969).

In conclusion, our results, in the context of the literature discussed, suggest that a significant proportion of adolescent and young adult personality disorders and male schizophrenics give evidence of early behavior or personality difficulty. This is observable on school records, which are not subject to retrospective distortion, and in samples not limited to those who were deviant enough to have been seen in child guidance clinics. The importance of considering the sexes separately and the need for more evidence about female pre-schizophrenics in particular are clearly indicated.

The evidence further suggests that no one premorbid personality pattern characterizes the pre-schizophrenic. Shy, withdrawn, "shut-in" traits, as well as irritable, aggressive conduct problems have been indicated in several studies. The salience of one pattern over another may be a reflection of differing populations, data sources, and definitions of variables.

Finally, although the evidence available is limited, there is little to indicate that the premorbid difficulties manifested by schizophrenics can be clearly differentiated from those of personality disorders. Whether this reflects primarily methodological deficiencies can be determined only by further research.

COMMENTARY

MEDNICK. Did you consider order of birth in terms of the various sibling combinations?

POLLACK. We didn't in this data, but in other analyses with these subjects we found no significance in order of birth. We haven't examined school records with that in mind as yet. I don't think we have a large enough sample to divide by sex, diagnosis, and then by order of birth.

MEDNICK. For your sample, are your male schizophrenic patients equated according to birth?

POLLACK. I don't know if they're equated, but there's no significant difference in order of birth between schizophrenics and their siblings. If you feel strongly about this point, Dr. Erlenmeyer-Kimling might have something more to say on this; she has reviewed all this literature.

ERLENMEYER-KIMLING. All I can say is that the literature in general is negative.

QUESTION. Could you tell how you got your diagnostic labels?

POLLACK. Each of the subjects was interviewed by myself and Dr. Goldberg, one of the research psychiatrists. The charts on the patients were reviewed independently by Don Klein, and we each made an independent diagnosis. Where there was disagreement we reviewed the cases together and argued. Now I realize that this knowledge does not give you an inter-rater reliability number. We used a consensual diagnosis.

For the personality disorders we used the American Psychiatric Association classifications. The framework for the schizophrenics is Kraepelinian and somewhat hard, with the one qualification that we did include the diagnosis of pseudoneurotic schizophrenia. Our framework was that of Donald Klein, as outlined in his book *Diagnosis and Drug Treatment of Psychiatric Disorders* (Klein & Davis, 1969). Our personality disorders might include groups that would be called borderline states by others.

For the normal sibs the criteria were fairly clear — no history of treatment and no rating of abnormality on the psychiatric interview with Dr. Goldberg and me.

QUESTION. Do you have any data on an unselected group of normal kids in the New York City school system and how they are rated by their teachers?

POLLACK. No, we don't. Others are trying to do something like this. Norman Watt is working in a different way in Newton, Massachusetts, using matched controls from the same classes. The one advantage that we have is that we have interviewed the sibs, so we know their psychiatric status, whereas for an unselected control group you don't know the sibs' adult status. For all you know you might be picking quite a large percentage of abnormal cases. This is the point that Merrill Roff has made.

QUESTION. What was the socioeconomic background of the patients? Would you get some differences if, for example, you used patients from another setting that included the schizophrenic kids who are *hyper*active and not *hypo*active?

POLLACK. Well, I can't answer whether this pattern of hypoactivity is culturally or familially related. Perhaps some families suppress hyperactivity or don't allow it. By and large, the families that we have studied are perhaps from a higher level intellectually and culturally than the average New York City family; their parents come mostly from class 3 or 4. But let me point out that we tried at the beginning to work with different cultural groups, and found that the refusal rate for lower-class black and Puerto Rican families was very high. Getting releases for school records and getting the siblings in for interview was very difficult. I'm not saying this can't be done, but it was too difficult for us.

STOTT. I am interested in this improvement in the male sibs as opposed to the female sibs. In several studies involving the use of Bristol Social Adjustment Guide, this is a consistent tendency. It is also found in the improvement of the male subnormals with regard to IQ and in various forms of ill health apart from that. It's certainly something worth following up.

POLLACK. I'm grateful for this information, and I'll be looking for the reference.

QUESTION. What view do you have of the high ratings of the sibs of the schizophrenics in the grade school?

WOERNER. We were surprised because our retrospective studies did not indicate this outcome. It seems that there were a number of male sibs of schizophrenics who had a fair amount of difficulty in the early school years in just about all areas. This needs to be replicated before we speculate about why.

QUESTION. Were these schizophrenic patients ill as children? Is there any indication of any breakdown previously, in school, besides the report of their behavior disorders in the school records?

POLLACK. There were none, if I recall correctly, hospitalized in childhood. Some were referred for testing or treatment of course, but I don't know if that implies breakdown or what.

QUESTION. Were those labeled schizophrenic?

POLLACK. No, I don't think so.

WOERNER. The mean age of the first hospitalization was 19 for the schizophrenics. The mean age of first treatment was 16½, and there were only three who were treated during childhood — in terms of psychiatric treatment. None were called schizophrenic in childhood.

GARMEZY. I'd like to hear some discussion from you and your colleagues about the cooperation of the school system in allowing access to records.

POLLACK. Overall, we got cooperation. We got a letter from the superintendent of schools saying that the principal could give us access to the records. Sometimes our people were left waiting for a day or so because the school clerk was too busy or irascible. Suburban schools and parochial schools seemed to be slightly more cooperative, and perhaps their records were richer. Dr. Rogalski, would you like to comment on that question?

ROGALSKI. In terms of cooperation, I've never learned more about people than when I went to the schools. You go into each school with the same questions — here we have the releases, this is who we are, this is where we come from; there were different reactions from different people.

POLLACK. I don't think that we missed very many, did we?

ROGALSKI. No, we got them all.

POLLACK. That's the point. We got them all. Sometimes it meant going back twice, sometimes it meant a telephone call to somebody else, like the guidance counselor. School records can be obtained. The big problem is that they keep changing them so the same form is not used throughout the child's lifetime, but that's a problem of coding technique. In general, the school people were very friendly.

QUESTION. I'm interested in whether you studied the stability of these variables for these individuals across time.

POLLACK. The only thing we've studied so far is IQ and that's very stable. In fact, it's surprisingly stable considering that they use group tests. The correlations are as good as anything found in the literature for normals.

QUESTION. Was distinction made along the process-reaction dimension in the cases diagnosed schizophrenic?

POLLACK. We're not using any process-reaction dimensions. That's a dirty word around here. We have rated them as to their onset, that is, whether we think there were severe symptoms in childhood or early or late adolescence. For instance, there was no difference in IQ between patients with late adolescent or adult onset and their sibs, but the patients with childhood onset were significantly inferior to their sibs in their adult IQ's; this is true for both the personality disorders and the schizophrenics. So age of onset is a crucial variable. We have not analyzed these data by age of onset; the study has to be replicated before we can make any really good subanalyses. With replication we might get a large enough N.

QUESTION. The transition period between elementary school and junior high school includes within it the advent of puberty, and probably more girls than boys have gone through puberty. Have you made any attempt to consider this or use this in analyzing the data?

POLLACK. We had no good indication of age of menarche in these people or in physical changes in stature of the boy or anything like that. We just don't have any decent indices. It's interesting to speculate why there appears to be a continuity of deviancy from childhood in male schizophrenics whereas in females there appears to be later onset. But our N just isn't large enough to do much with that.

REFERENCES

Alanen, Y. O. The family in the pathenogenesis of schizophrenic and neurotic disorders. *Acta Psychiatrica Scandinavia*, 1966, 42, suppl. 189.

Belmont, I., Birch, H., Klein, D. F., & Pollack, M. Perceptual evidence of CNS dysfunction in schizophrenia. *Archives of General Psychiatry*, 1964, 10, 395–408.

Birren, J. Psychological examinations of children who later became psychotic. *Journal of Abnormal and Social Psychology*, 1944, 39, 84–95.

Bower, E. M., Schellhammer, T. A., Daily, J. M., & Bower, M. High school students who later became schizophrenic. *Bulletin of the California Department of Education*, 1960, 29, 1–157.

Costello, A. J., Gunn, J. C., & Dominian, J. Aetiologic factors in young schizophrenic men. *British Journal of Psychiatry*, 1968, 114, 433–441.

Fleming, P., & Ricks, D. F. Emotions of children before schizophrenia and before character disorder. In M. Roff & D. F. Ricks (Eds.), *Life history research in psychopathology*. Vol. 1. Minneapolis: University of Minnesota Press, 1970. Pp. 240–264.

Frazee, H. Children who later became schizophrenic. *Smith College Studies in School Work*, 1953, 23, 125–249.

Gardner, G. The relationship between childhood neurotic symptomatology and later schizophrenia in males and females. *Journal of Nervous and Mental Disease*, 1967, 144, 97–100.

Klein, D. F., & Davis, J. M. *Diagnosis and drug treatment of psychiatric disorders.* Baltimore: Williams & Wilkins, 1969.

Lane, E. A., & Albee, G. W. Intellectual antecedents of schizophrenia. In M. Roff & D. F. Ricks (Eds.), *Life history research in psychopathology*. Vol. 1. Minneapolis: University of Minnesota Press, 1970. Pp. 189–207.

Levenstein, S., Klein, D. F., & Pollack, M. Follow-up study of formerly hospitalized voluntary psychiatric patients. *American Journal of Psychiatry*, 1966, 122, 1102–1109.

Mednick, S. A., & McNeil, T. F. Current methodology in research on the etiology of schizophrenia. *Psychological Bulletin*, 1968, 70, 681–693.

Offord, D. R., & Cross, L. A. Behavioral antecedents of adult schizophrenia: A review. *Archives of General Psychiatry*, 1969, 21, 267–283.

Pollack, M., Woerner, M. G., Goldberg, P., & Klein, D. F. Psychopathology in the siblings and parents of schizophrenic and nonschizophrenic psychiatric patients. Paper presented at the meeting of the American Orthopsychiatric Association, Chicago, March 1968.

——. Siblings of schizophrenic and nonschizophrenic psychiatric patients: Psychopathology and gender concordance. *Archives of General Psychiatry*, 1969, 20, 652–658.

Pollack, M., Woerner, M. G., Goodman, W., & Greenberg, I. M. Childhood development patterns of hospitalized adult schizophrenic and nonschizophrenic patients and their siblings. *American Journal of Orthopsychiatry*, 1966, 36, 510–517.

Pollack, M., Woerner, M. G., & Klein, D. F. A comparison of the childhood characteristics of schizophrenics, personality disorders, and their siblings. In M. Roff & D. F. Ricks (Eds.), *Life history research in psychopathology.* Vol. 1. Minneapolis: University of Minnesota Press, 1970. Pp. 208–225.

Pollin, W., Stabenau, J. R., Mosher, L., & Tupin, J. Life history differences in identical twins discordant for schizophrenia. *American Journal of Orthopsychiatry*, 1966, 36, 492–509.

Prout, C. T., & White, M. A. The schizophrenic's sibling. *Journal of Nervous and Mental Disease*, 1956, 123, 162–170.

Quitkin, F. M., & Klein, D. F. Follow-up of treatment failure: Psychosis and character disorder. *American Journal of Psychiatry*, 1967, 124, 499–505.

Ricks, D. F., & Nameche, G. Symbiosis, sacrifice and schizophrenia. *Mental Hygiene*, 1966, 50, 541–551.

Robins, L. N. *Deviant children grown up: A psychiatric and sociological study of sociopathic personality.* Baltimore: Williams & Wilkins, 1966.

Roff, M. Preservice personality problems and subsequent adjustment to military service: A replication of "The prediction of psychoneurotic reactions." Rep. No. 58-151, School of Aviation Medicine, USAF, 1959.

——. Childhood social interactions and young adult bad conduct. *Journal of Abnormal and Social Psychology*, 1961, 63, 333–337.

——. Childhood social interaction and young adult psychosis. *Journal of Clinical Psychology*, 1963, 19, 152–157.

——. Some developmental aspects of schizoid personality. Rep. No. 65-4, March 1965, *U.S. Army Medical Research and Development Command*, Contract No. DA-49-007-MD-2015.

——. Some childhood and adolescent characteristics of adult homosexuals. Rep. No. 66-5, May 1966, *U.S. Army Medical Research and Development Command*, Contract No. DA-49-007-MD-2015.

Rosanoff, A. J., Handy, L. M., Plesset, I. R., & Brush, S. The etiology of so-called schizophrenic psychoses. *American Journal of Psychiatry*, 1934, 91, 247–285.

Warnken, R. G., & Seiss, T. F. The use of the cumulative record in the prediction of behavior. *Personnel and Guidance Journal*, 1965, 31, 231–237.

Watt, N. F., Stolorow, R. D., Lubensky, A. W., & McClelland, D. C. School adjustment and behavior of children hospitalized for schizophrenia as adults. *American Journal of Orthopsychiatry*, 1970, 40, 637–657.

Wittman, P., & Steinberg, D. F. Study of prodromal factors in mental illness with special reference to schizophrenia. *American Journal of Psychiatry*, 1944, 100, 811–816.

ROBERT D. WIRT
ANNA C. HAMPTON
PHILIP D. SEAT] *The Psychometric Prediction of Delinquency*

W HENEVER the concept of delinquency is discussed, it becomes immediately necessary to define what is meant by the term in that particular context. The definitional problem is especially difficult because, though *juvenile delinquency* is a legal term, it represents phenomena whose description and explanation are in the realm of the behavioral sciences, especially sociology and psychology. In the field of psychology alone, there are several different classification systems for juvenile delinquency, as well as a number of different theories of etiology. Elsewhere Wirt and Briggs (1965, 1969) have devoted considerable attention to the problem. The various studies claiming to investigate the same problem of prediction of juvenile delinquency have, in fact, dealt with different segments of the general population.

Briggs and Wirt (1965) and Rose (1967) offer comprehensive reviews of the literature in the field of prediction of juvenile delinquency and arrive at essentially similar conclusions. In their opinions none of the predictive procedures available meets the requirements of a well-validated, practical, and useful *predictive* system. This criticism applies to instruments which are still, to a large extent, at an experimental stage, such as the Self-Concept Scale, the delinquency prediction instrument based on the Bristol Social Adjustment Guides, the Mulligan Scale, the Rutter

NOTE: A paper substantially in the form reported here was presented at the 99th Annual Meeting of the Correctional Association of America, August 20, 1969, Minneapolis, Minnesota.

The authors are grateful for the cooperation of the Minneapolis Public Schools, the Hennepin County Juvenile Court, the Minneapolis Police Department, and the Minnesota Highway Department. Financial support for this program of research has been provided, in part, by the Graduate School of the University of Minnesota and the Tozer Foundation.

Scale, the "Guess Who" Inventory, Gough and Peterson's delinquency scale, the Jesness Inventory (all reported in Rose, 1967) and the Nye and Short Delinquency Scale (Nye & Short, 1957). The same statement can be made about the better known instruments which have been studied rather extensively: the Glueck Social Prediction Table (Glueck & Glueck, 1950), the KD Proneness Scale and Check List (Kvaraceus, 1956), and the Minnesota Multiphasic Personality Inventory (MMPI) (Hathaway & Monachesi, 1963).

The Gluecks defined delinquency as referring to "repeated acts of a kind which when committed by persons beyond the statutory juvenile court age of sixteen are punishable as crimes (either felonies or misdemeanors) except for a few instances of persistent stubbornness, truancy, running away, associating with immoral persons and the like" (Glueck & Glueck, 1950, p. 13). This is basically a legal definition; however, their operational definition is quite different. In developing their prediction tables, 500 institutionalized delinquents were compared with 500 nondelinquent boys. Institutionalized delinquents represent less than 5 per cent of the general population as compared with about 25 per cent who met their legal definition of delinquency. The New York City Youth Board Study (Craig & Glick, 1963) was designed to cross-validate the Glueck Social Prediction Table. Although the study repeated the Gluecks' definition of delinquency, cited above, as a criterion for inclusion of a subject in the study, subjects not meeting their criterion were in fact included. Nye (1958) used anonymous, self-reported law violations and antisocial acts as the criterion of juvenile delinquency in developing his delinquency scale. Thus, his group of delinquents represented a larger portion of the population than that of official legal delinquents. Other investigators used nonlegal definitions entirely, concentrating on psychiatric diagnostic categories. Wirt and Briggs (1965) after discussing these examples and some others conclude: "The term *delinquency* is, after all, a legal term. We believe, therefore, that the most sensible, useful, and independent definition of the behavior to which the word refers should maintain a focus upon the legal sense of its meaning, while recognizing the broader social and psychological variables involved. It seems to us that research based on such conception has greater probability of becoming meaningful across disciplines and among different theoretical orientations and various levels of observation" (p. 21). The series of follow-up studies using the MMPI by Hathaway and Monachesi (1963) and by Wirt, Briggs, and their associates (1959, 1960) used the approach recommended above. Since the present study adopted the same approach and in fact used the same classification system of levels of delinquency, a detailed discussion of it will be presented later.

PREDICTION VERSUS IDENTIFICATION OF JUVENILE DELINQUENCY

Although studies of identification of delinquents using behavioral measures can be valuable in a theoretical sense, their practical usefulness is rather limited. A much simpler, as well as more efficient and accurate identification procedure would be the inspection of police and court records — provided, of course, that an essentially legal definition of delinquency is accepted. When the focus is on prevention of delinquency, a procedure which identifies active rather than potential delinquents — in other words, one that identifies rather than predicts — is indeed of little value. The following discussion concentrates on only one aspect of the process of prediction, that of predicting future rather than current behavior.

Only an instrument which was constructed and cross-validated, or at least cross-validated, using the longitudinal or follow-up approach can claim to be predictive of *future* behavior. The only major study in the field using such an approach was the follow-up project of Minneapolis and rural Minnesota ninth-graders by Hathaway, Monachesi, and their associates (summarized in Hathaway & Monachesi, 1963; Wirt & Briggs, 1959). Employing the MMPI as the major personality measurement, Hathaway and Monachesi approached the task of prediction in two different ways. In the first approach, the percentage of children who became delinquents within each MMPI code classification was compared with the general base rates of delinquency. A code type which was found reliably in excess of the delinquency base rate was the 4–9 classification, in which high scale scores were registered on the Psychopathic Deviate (Pd) and the Hypomania (Ma) scales. The delinquency rate within this code type was 38 per cent, representing only 10 per cent above the general base rate. The second approach produced a scale consisting of MMPI items constructed specifically for the prediction of juvenile delinquency. The scale, offered in two forms, was not successful.

The Gluecks compared known delinquents with non-delinquents, constructing their Social Prediction Table from reconstructed retrospective material. The Social Prediction Table is composed of five factors, with the percentage of delinquents in each subcategory of the rating of the factor constituting the weighted failure score on each factor. The prediction of delinquency was based on the total weighted failure score of all five factors (Glueck & Glueck, 1950). The studies evaluating the applicability of their table for the prediction of future delinquent and non-delinquent behavior reported rather disappointing results when compared with predictions based on base rates only. Fairly consistent findings are the over-prediction of delinquency and the large proportion of subjects in the gray area where no reliable prediction can be made (Rose, 1967; Wirt & Briggs, 1960). Craig and Glick (1963) used the follow-up method in their attempt to validate the Glueck Social Prediction Table. However, at the end of the follow-up period they found it necessary to modify the weights of all the factors of the table and eventually to revise the five-factor table into a three-factor table, retaining only two of the original factors. Thus, their study produced essentially a new instrument which has yet to be cross-validated in the predictive sense (Kahn, 1965; Rose, 1967).

Several studies indicate that the KD Proneness Scale and Check List differentiate successfully between delinquents and non-delinquents (Kvaraceus, 1956; see also Briggs & Wirt, 1965; Rose, 1967). The only attempt to assess the predictive validity of Kvaraceus's instruments, made by Bordua (1961), suggests that the scale is unlikely to be a successful predictor of future adjustment. There is not sufficient information available as to the predictive power of the other instruments listed above.

CONSIDERATIONS RELATING TO METHODS OF ASSESSMENT IN PREDICTING DELINQUENCY

Two of the issues relating to behavioral assessment techniques are of particular relevance for practical reasons when the focus is on delinquency prediction. The first has to do with the extent to which a given technique calls for the services of professional personnel, the second with the use of different nonprofessional informants in behavioral studies of children.

The problems involved with the extensive use of mental health professional services for the assessment, scoring, or interpretation of future behavior will be covered first. The Gluecks' prediction tables simply cannot be completed without a long psychiatric interview, and a battery of psychological tests. In the case of the Social Prediction Tables, home visits by a trained social worker are needed. Aside from the legitimate questions often raised about the reliability of such clinical-subjective ratings, one must consider the contamination of the ratings by demographic factors of which the social worker cannot be unaware, and the inapplicability of the factors of "discipline of boy by father," "affection of father for boy," and "cohesiveness of family" to the broken homes which disproportionately contribute to juvenile delinquency (Craig & Glick, 1963; Kahn, 1965). Thus, a serious shortcoming of the Gluecks' table is of a purely practical nature. In view of the severe shortage of professional personnel in the field of mental health, any procedure calling for extensive expenditure of professional time is unlikely to become widely used in any large-scale preventive program. A practical solution to this problem is to use nonprofessional informants.

The second issue is who the best informant would be for a preadolescent subject. Self-reports were used in delinquency studies with the KD Proneness Scale, the various scales derived from the California Personality Inventory (CPI), the MMPI, and Nye and Short's Delinquency Scale. Although self-rating inventories have been used extensively, and often successfully, in personality studies of adults, their applicability in a preadolescent population is questionable. Reading difficulties, short attention span, low motivation level, and in the case of pre-delinquents, lack of cooperation are common problems in young children and are bound to limit the usefulness of self-report methods in delinquency prediction. An alternative approach which has been used successfully by several investigators in the field is the use of ratings by others, in particular by teachers. Studies using the KD Check List, Stott's delinquency prediction instrument, the Mulligan Scale, and several other experimental instruments reported by Rose (1967) found teacher ratings to be easily obtainable and quite useful. Hathaway and Monachesi (1963) also report that, generally, teachers made good informants and produced fairly adequate predictions about the child's future adjustment. However, they found that teachers' judgments were likely to be distorted by the child's level of intelligence and school achievement; teachers also tended to underestimate delinquency in the high socioeconomic levels and made very inaccurate predictions about farm boys.

Surprisingly, none of the assessment procedures in the field of prediction of juvenile delinquency uses the most natural informants about the child, the parents — especially the mother, who is usually more readily available than the father. The objection to mothers as informants often stems from well-established findings relating to distortions in recall, contaminations by personality factors, and defensive styles when the mother is asked to report the presence or absence of past or present behaviors of the child (Dreger, Lewis, Rich, Miller, Reid, Overlade, Taffel & Flemming, 1964; Novick, Rosenfeld, Bloch, & Dawson, 1966; Robbins, 1963; Yarrow, 1963). However, reports "distorted" in the sense of reflecting a given reality inaccurately may still provide *empirically* valid data for prediction. In addition, several recent studies point to the mother as possibly the best nonprofessional informant available in assessing deviant behavior in children. Dreger et al. report a test-retest agreement of 87 per cent, suggesting that mothers are reliable informants. Novick et al. found not only that the mothers were the best single source of "true" information among five possible informants (including teachers) when ascertaining deviant behavior in children, but that they also produced considerably more information on a 247-item inventory than that obtained from *both parents and the child* in the intake interview.

PERSONALITY INVENTORY FOR CHILDREN (PIC)

Using a personality inventory developed by Wirt and Broen (1958), the Personality Inventory for Children (PIC), Hampton (1969) developed a Delinquency Prediction Scale which overcomes some of the objections made to earlier efforts to predict delinquency. The PIC is composed of 600 true-false items covering eleven behavioral domains to be completed by mothers of children between six and sixteen years of age. The result is an MMPI-like instrument. The MMPI has been shown to be a useful diagnostic and research instrument for the study of adults. It was thought that something similar might be useful for the study of children but — as is obvious — an identical approach is not practical because many of the very children one would want to include are unable to read well enough to complete an inventory written in even the simplest language. In a typical child guidance clinic or other agency devoted to work with children, it is usual for an intake worker to interview or otherwise obtain historical, demographic, and psychological data about the child's development and current functioning from informants, chiefly the child's mother. Such data have been found to help the staff greatly in understanding the child and in planning treatment programs and other dispositions for him. It may be reasoned that if such data could be gathered systematically and in quantifiable form, it might be possible to develop scales — something like MMPI scales, perhaps — which would have immediate practical utility and be useful as research tools. Of course, such an approach lacks the flexibility and opportunity for the more extensive, more intensive, and clarifying questioning offered by an interview. No more than any other psychological test is it meant to replace that important function.

The test authors and their associates (chiefly then Norman Bradford and James Greeno) read case records, searched the literature, and depended upon their own clinical experience and that of colleagues. For sampling, eleven general areas of behavior were chosen from factor studies based on observation of children's behavior and from the authors' own biases. The areas were Withdrawal, Excitement, Reality Distortion, Aggression, Somatic Concern, Anxiety, Social Skills, Family Relations, Physical Development, Intellectual Development, and Asocial. Rating scales were developed for these, including a booklet describing in a paragraph a typical child at each of four places along each scale. These have been used by personnel in the many agencies which have cooperated in the total research program. Some 50 items were written for each of the eleven behavioral areas in the form "My child . . . " using language that could be understood by persons having limited reading skill, including items in the negative ("My child does not . . .") and items relating to the parents and others ("The child's father . . ."). Altogether there are 600 items — some are redundant to offer a variety of phrasing from among which the best could be selected for the eventual development of a shorter instrument.

Next, the cooperation of a number of agencies working with children was obtained to collect a large sample of different groups of children (after ten years, cases are still being collected). With the help of the Minneapolis Public Schools a sample of 100 boys and 100 girls at each age level from six through sixteen was gathered from selected schools around the city to provide a representative social class distribution. Race was not recorded, but it is known that the total school population is overwhelmingly white; a study under way involves the collection of a substantial number of protocols from black families. None of these children had ever been referred for psychological, neurological, or social services. Thus, they were at the time perhaps from healthier homes than a truly random sample. Altogether, there are now in this normal sample some 2,400 children.

The development of scales for the PIC is in progress, including scales of General Maladjustment, Delinquency Prediction, Prediction of Learning Disabilities, Delinquent Personality, a scale of Sexual Identification, a scale of Social Introversion, a scale of Depression, a scale to assess Cerebral Dysfunction, an Intelligence Scale, a scale of Somatization, a study comparing mother's personality as reflected in the MMPI with her responses to the PIC, a study comparing mothers' responses to the PIC items with those of fathers, a study comparing mothers' description of their children as reflected in the PIC with those of the adolescent children themselves as reflected in their own MMPI's, and scales of defensiveness and social desirability. The first three of these have been completed, and the findings are encouraging.

THE DELINQUENCY PREDICTION SCALE

Earlier research had shown that if one used a criterion of police records as the definition of delinquency, the rate of delinquency in Minneapolis is about 20 per cent of the adolescent male population (Hathaway & Monachesi, 1963). The PIC study on the prediction of delinquency (Hampton, 1969) followed up the normal sample of boys who were 10 to 12 years of age when gathered in the period 1960–1962. Thus by 1968, it was expected that there would be a reasonable number who had reached the age of 18 and for whom school and police records would be available as the result of continuous residence in the city of Minneapolis. Of 191 boys followed up, 32 were found who had police records (a juvenile delinquency rate of 17 per cent). Of the 32, 2 were classified by clinical judges as non-delinquent because they came to police attention for behavior which was not unlawful. Using a system developed by Hathaway and Monachesi containing four categories of delinquency according to severity, the sample was divided into 30 Delinquents and 161 Non-delinquents.

The Delinquency Prediction Scale was constructed by comparing PIC responses given by the mothers of the delinquent group with those given by mothers of the non-delinquent subjects. The item analysis was based on a method developed by Darlington (1963) and Darlington and Bishop (1966), which, according to the authors and our own earlier experience using it, yields higher scale validities than those obtained using various other methods of item analysis. The two characteristics which distinguish this method are the construction of a scale in stages, several items being added at each stage, and the use made of inter-item correlations. The resulting Delinquency Prediction Scale contains 71 items, of which 38 items are scored in the "true" direction and 33 items in the "false" direction. The items may be divided into the following eight rational content categories: *asocial behavior, maturational level, social skills/peer rela-*

tions, somatic complaints, parent-child relations (discipline, emotional ties), family atmosphere and relations, and others.

To understand further the nature of the test misses, we paired the 17 non-delinquents who were misclassified with test hits, and their personality evaluations recorded by the teacher on the cumulative school records were presented to three judges. Two out of three judges agreed on the classification of 94 per cent of the pairs, of which 65 per cent were correctly classified. Thus, though an incorrect prediction of police contact would have been made for most of these children, they were seen by their teachers as having serious behavior problems in school.

The scale was applied to several samples which had not been used in its construction. The scale identified correctly all but one of 17 delinquent thirteen- and fourteen-year-old boys then at the Minnesota Diagnostic and Reception Center. The score distribution of a normal sample of thirteen- and fourteen-year-old boys from Minneapolis did not differ significantly from the DP Scale score distribution of the construction sample. In another study of a psychiatric population, seven- to twelve-year-old male patients who rated high on the Asocial rating scale received reliably higher scores on the DP Scale than patients who rated low on the Asocial rating scale. The scale construction delinquent group had the highest scores, and the non-delinquent group the lowest; the psychiatric sample with high Asocial ratings ranked in between.

Later, a similar study will be done with children who were younger at the time the normal sample PIC data were obtained, since they will be ending their adolescence soon and will have passed the age at risk of becoming delinquent. The data obtained thus far do suggest that it is possible to identify a sizable percentage of children in elementary school who will or will not have police records before they complete high school.

COMMENTARY

QUESTION. You mentioned identifying thirteen out of fourteen delinquents at another agency. Is there any further cross-validation where there's a good sample size?

WIRT. Not yet. We had to let the younger children become older before we could do that. That second study is now in progress. For further construct validity we are trying to determine if we can identify children who are currently delinquent as well as predicting those who later become delinquent.

GARMEZY. Has account been taken of the type of criticism that Block leveled against the MMPI, that there are many items that disturb people because of their unpleasantness? Has an effort been made to take those out as well?

WIRT. To eliminate objectionable items?

GARMEZY. Yes.

WIRT. No. Remember Butcher and Tellegen's (1966) study of objectionable MMPI items. Their work showed that to try to eliminate such items leaves one without any content. In this item pool we don't have very many items that *you* would think are obviously objectionable. We'd find some people who'd object to some items. Cooperation of the schools and the communication agencies has been encouraging in view of the problem of asking objectionable things and the whole issue of invasion of privacy. We did do a study to try to purge them, but there are doubtless items that some parents would find offensive.

QUESTION. You mentioned that the scale was developed in stages. Could you describe the method a bit more? It sounds like you are zeroing in on something, but I'm not quite clear how.

WIRT. Items were selected in the usual way — that is, by choosing those which correlated highly with a criterion. Then inter-item correlations were used. The method was developed by Darlington. Items are added that contribute to scale validity. If the same item recurs, it is double weighted. If previously utilized items contribute negatively, they are removed. This increases scale validity. The process can be reiterated indefinitely, of course, but after two or three runs you start losing efficiency.

ROFF. How did you get your items to begin with?

WIRT. Mostly out of our heads. We read a good many social case histories in local child guidance clinics in order to cover the areas of concern in the diagnostic process and to get a feeling for the proper language to use. And we took ideas from textbooks and other literature in child psychiatry and developmental psychopathology. And we drew from research reports using behavior observations of disturbed children, such as the factor analytic study by Patterson (1956). To a large extent we depended upon our own clinical experience.

REFERENCES

Bordua, D. J. *Prediction and selection of delinquents.* United States Children's Bureau, Pamphlet No. 17, 1961.

Briggs, P. F., & Wirt, R. D. Prediction. In H. C. Quay (Ed.), *Juvenile delinquency: Research and theory.* Princeton, N.J.: Van Nostrand, 1965.

Butcher, J. N., & Tellegen, A. Objections to MMPI items. *Journal of Consulting Psychology,* 1966, 30, 527–534.

Craig, M. M., & Glick, S. J. Ten years' experience with the Glueck Social Prediction Table. *Crime and Delinquency,* 1963, 9, 249–261.

Darlington, R. B. Increasing test validity through the use of interitem correlations. Ph.D. thesis, University of Minnesota, 1963.

——— & Bishop, C. H. Increasing test validity by considering interitem correlations. *Journal of Applied Psychology,* 1966, 50, 322–330.

Dreger, R. M., Lewis, P. M., Rich, T. A., Miller, K. S., Reid, M. P., Overlade,

D. C., Taffel, D., & Flemming, E. L. Behavioral classification project. *Journal of Consulting Psychology*, 1964, 28, 1–13.

Glueck, S., & Glueck, E. T. *Unraveling juvenile delinquency.* New York: Commonwealth Fund, 1950.

Gough, H. G., & Peterson, D. The identification and measurement of predispositional factors in crime and delinquency. *Journal of Consulting Psychology*, 1952, 16, 207–212.

Hampton, A. C. Longitudinal study of personality of children who become delinquents using the Personality Inventory for Children (PIC). Ph.D. thesis, University of Minnesota, 1969.

Hathaway, S. R., & McKinley, J. D. *The Minnesota Multiphasic Personality Inventory Manual.* (Rev. ed.) New York: Psychological Corporation, 1951.

Hathaway, S. R., & Monachesi, E. D. *Adolescent personality and behavior: MMPI patterns of normal, delinquent, dropout, and other outcomes.* Minneapolis: University of Minnesota Press, 1963.

Kahn, S. J. The case of the premature claims—public policy and delinquency prediction. *Crime and Delinquency*, 1965, 11, 217–228.

Kvaraceus, W. C. Forecasting juvenile delinquency. *Journal of Education*, 1956, 138, 1–43.

Novick, J., Rosenfeld, E., Bloch, D., & Dawson, D. Ascertaining deviant behavior in children. *Journal of Consulting Psychology*, 1966, 30, 230–238.

Nye, F. I. *Family relationships and delinquent behavior.* New York: Wiley, 1958.

——— & Short, J. F., Jr. Scaling delinquent behavior. *American Sociological Review*, 1957, 22, 327–331.

Patterson, G. R. Tentative approach to the classification of children's behavior disorders. Ph.D. thesis, University of Minnesota, 1956.

Robbins, L. C. The accuracy of parental recall of aspects of child development and child rearing practices. *Journal of Abnormal and Social Psychology*, 1963, 66, 261–270.

Rose, G. Early identification of delinquents. *British Journal of Criminology*, 1967, 7, 6–35.

Seat, P. D. The construction of a general maladjustment scale for the Personality Inventory for Children. Ph.D. thesis, University of Minnesota, 1969.

Wirt, R. D., & Briggs, P. F. Personality and environmental factors in the development of delinquency. *Psychological Monographs*, 1959, 73 (15, Whole No. 485).

———. The validity of ten of the Gluecks' predictors. *Journal of Criminology, Criminal Law and Police Science*, 1960, 50, 478–479.

———. The meaning of delinquency. In H. C. Quay (Ed.), *Juvenile delinquency: Research and theory.* Princeton: Van Nostrand, 1965.

———. A definition of delinquency. In R. S. Cavan (Ed.), *Readings in juvenile delinquency.* Philadelphia: Lippincott, 1969, Article I, Section 1, 3–5.

Wirt, R. D., & Broen, W. E., Jr. *Booklet for the Personality Inventory for Children.* Minneapolis: Authors, 1958.

Yarrow, M. R. Problems of methods in parent-child research. *Child Development*, 1963, 34, 215–226.

MERRILL ROFF | *A Two-Factor Approach to Juvenile Delinquency and the Later Histories of Juvenile Delinquents*

THIS PAPER has two quite different parts: first, a two-factor approach to juvenile delinquency and, second, the subsequent histories of juvenile delinquents. The second of these will be presented first.

Increasing experience in the life history area makes it seem more and more important for us to make our terminology increasingly clear and specific. This sharper definition comes, I believe, not from any careful process of word-spinning, but from experience with data which indicate that different things subsumed under the same label may behave differently over time. We need to be able to distinguish between the acute and the chronic, between the benign and the malignant. Although juvenile delinquency may be annoying or even alarming, if we could say that certain types were transient in character, we would normally consider these less serious than misbehavior which seemed likely to be longer lasting.

There is voluminous literature on juvenile delinquency. This is due in part to the fact that delinquency is a matter of record, and in part to the apparent definiteness of the term *adjudicated*, which has made it an attractive criterion. Most studies of delinquency are cross-sectional or retrospective. There are a few life history studies making use of information obtained in the predelinquent period, but these are rare. It is much harder to find studies of what happened to delinquents at later ages than it is to find these cross-sectional studies.

As one part of a long-time research program, I have been following some relatively large samples of delinquents into the young adult period by means of their military service records (Roff, 1961a & b, 1964, 1968, 1969, 1970a). This gives a picture of the later adjustment of individuals with a history of juvenile delinquency which is less pessimistic than studies of, for example, penitentiary inmates, which, when the subjects are followed back, find that most of them had histories of juvenile delinquency. The conclusion is sometimes reached from these studies that the whole probation system is a failure. Although I would not want to argue that the probationary system has reached a state of perfection, I think that it accomplishes more than it is often given credit for doing. At least, most juvenile delinquents straighten out with increasing age.

In prior work with the adult follow-up of child guidance clinic cases, experience in several of the major cities of the country indicated the desirability of working in more than one area. Because of my already existing relationship with S. B. Sells of the Institute of Behavioral Research, Texas Christian University, data collection with delinquents parallel to the work in Minnesota was carried out in Texas. The subjects used in the research reported in this paper were born between January 1, 1928, and December 31, 1935. These dates were selected to include a group who would in general have been too young for World War II, but would have reached an age at which they normally would have completed military service at the time the criterion information was being obtained. In general, they were in service during the Korean War. At that time a larger proportion of the total population entered service than in any later period, so the sampling was better than it was later. Current work is employing the most recent possible samples.

Definition of Delinquency. Although the term *delinquency* sounds definite, its actual definition, and practices in dealing with it, vary from place to place and from time to time. One dictionary definition is "a transgression of law . . . or offense. Or: a tendency to commit such offenses." In practice, there are various degrees of juvenile delinquency, defined not only in terms of offenses but also in terms of the apprehension and treatment of the offender. First is breaking a minor law without being discovered; everyone has done this at one time or another. Another level is being detected by a policeman and verbally corrected, perhaps while remaining anonymous. This may occur with juveniles, as it occurs with adults, for minor traffic offenses; it is impossible to get accurate information on the frequency of these incidents. A degree above this is apprehension and more formal admonition, either by an arresting officer or at a juvenile department. A great many youngsters have no further contact with the law after such an occurrence. Some, however, following further trouble or a more serious offense, are brought into juvenile court where they may be adjudicated delinquent and put under supervision or on probation.

Because it has a certain administrative definiteness, adjudication is the most commonly used single criterion of delinquency in studies in this area. Like many other seemingly clear-cut administrative actions, its definiteness as a criterion is more apparent than real, since the frequency with which youngsters are "adjudicated" varies from place to place, from judge to judge, and from probation office to probation office. In any case, many youngsters never reappear in juvenile court. If there is further trouble, a youngster may be taken out of an unsatisfactory home and neighborhood situation. In both the cities dealt with here, he could be sent to a county training school. It is easily possible to get a count of these individuals. Other work with this Minnesota group (Roff, 1964) indicates that about one out of five boys from the county training school committed subsequent offenses and were sent to the state training school. Later, a higher proportion of those sent to the state training school appear as adult offenders than of those sent only to the county training schools. A small number of these, who represent by this time a *very* small percentage of the total population, are sent to a penitentiary.

Because delinquents are more often dealt with by probation personnel than by psychiatrists, the language of delinquency and its offenses is used here without an attempt at proper application of the various psychiatric labels which might be applicable. Among these are antisocial personality, group delinquent reaction of child or adolescent, and social maladjustment without manifest psychiatric disorder. The first of these is a personality disorder, the second falls under behavior disorders of childhood and adolescence, and the third under conditions without manifest psychiatric disorder. If a youth of sixteen holds up five filling stations, that in itself will attract attention, but the information is not available from these offenses alone to make a proper psychiatric diagnosis.

Samples and Procedure

As expected, it was found that there are differences between both the populations and the administrative procedures in Minnesota and Texas. The Texas delinquent sample was studied first (Sample 1). In addition to the delinquent sample, a control group consisting of a random sample drawn from school files in the same region was employed, to determine base rates for a randomly selected group. Texas is in the highest one third of all states in the proportions of persons rejected for service because of low Armed Forces Qualifying Test scores. This is a simple index, but it should suggest that the results reported for Texas will not necessarily generalize to all other states. Sample 2 was drawn from a metropolitan area in Minnesota, a state which consistently has a relatively small rejection rate for low aptitude.

Apart from population differences between the two states, there was a difference in the method of selection of the delinquent cases. In Sample 1, only those Texas cases were used that had a case file of at least five pages. After adult outcome information had been obtained, appropriate cases were microfilmed for detailed analysis against the criterion data. This meant that a great many minor cases were not included at all, since we were interested only in those cases with enough content to permit analysis of background factors. Thus, Sample 1 was made up of cases more serious than the total set of all youngsters who had had any juvenile court file. On the other hand, for the Minnesota sample (Sample 2) the method of initial case finding was changed to include all cases that had a file at all, so that we could see what happened to the large number of minor cases that had been excluded by taking only the more serious cases in Sample 1. It was considered more important to get information for these additional cases than to replicate exactly the procedures with Sample 1.

Both the population difference between the two states (as reflected in the aptitude scores mentioned above) and the method of case selection would lead to the expectation that Sample 2 would yield a higher proportion of persons who would both enter one of the services and perform satisfactorily there.

Rejection from Service. An analysis of the service outcome of former juvenile delinquents must take into consideration the fact that the in-service sample is a selected one, since there has been some rejection of the candidates who appear lowest on various dimensions. A detailed picture of the service regulations as to who is and who is not acceptable has been given elsewhere (Roff, 1964, 1969).

In these same places, an analysis of rejections has been presented. To summarize briefly, in the Texas delinquent sample a little more than one fourth of the complete delinquent sample were rejected because of histories of bad conduct, juvenile and post-juvenile. For the control sample, randomly selected from the school population in the same area, only about 2 per cent were rejected because of their legal records. For Sample 2, the Minnesota sample which included fewer serious delinquents, about 10 per cent were rejected because of their preservice histories of bad conduct. Thus, there were almost no bad-conduct rejections in the control group, whereas a somewhat larger number were eliminated from the two delinquent groups.

Outcome in Service as Indicated by Service Record. Outcome in service has been classified in four categories, which may be described as follows: (a) The first or "promoted" category consists of all those honorably discharged at the rank of noncommissioned or petty officer or above. (b) The second category includes those honorably discharged without a history of disciplinary problems who did not achieve noncommissioned status. Some of these had rather brief terms of service; the small number who received medical discharges are almost exclusively in this group. (c) The minor disciplinary problems group includes those who had multiple disciplinary offenses that were not serious enough or numerous enough to result in an unsatisfactory discharge. (d) The unsatisfactory group includes all those who received a discharge other than an honorable one, with a disciplinary component in the picture.

Here I shall compare only the category *a* cases with the category *d* cases for the three samples and the four services. A graphic picture of the outcomes is shown in Figure 1. Sample 1 clearly has more unsatisfactory than promoted members in all four branches of service, whereas the control group clearly has many more promoted than unsatisfactory. Sample 2, from Minnesota, is much more like the control group from Texas than it is like Sample 1. There are no consistent and striking differences among the services in their experience with different samples. It is clear that the differences in kinds of persons included in the samples were much more important in determining the results obtained than were the differences among the various services, either in regulations governing initial acceptability or in treatment while on active duty.

Juvenile Confinement as a Predictor of Later Adjustment. There are many factors that may contribute to the prediction of good and poor outcome in service for delinquent samples. An approach could be made by way of type of offense, number of offenses, age at first offense, duration of contact with juvenile authorities, or a combination of these and other factors.

Where the cutting point should be on acceptance or rejection of individuals is a matter of policy that may be influenced by various factors which change from time to time. If it were possible to reject one person who would be unsatisfactory in service at a cost of nine persons who would get along all right, this would almost certainly not be done. If it were possible to reject nine persons who would be unsatisfactory in serv-

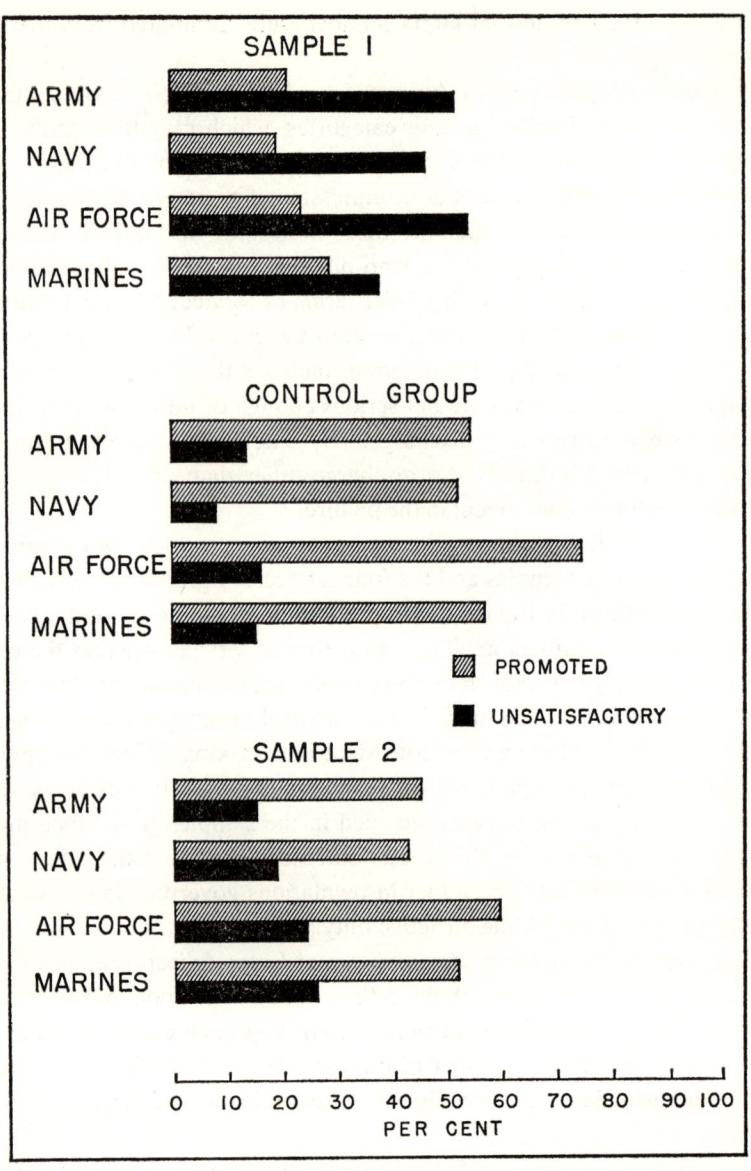

Figure 1. Proportions promoted and unsatisfactory in the three samples, for the four services.

ice at a cost of one person who would get along all right, this would almost certainly be done. For the Minnesota delinquent sample about one out of five of the total group fall in the unsatisfactory category in service. It is desirable to attempt to separate a subgroup of these who would show a larger proportion of unsatisfactory outcomes, if this can be done in a practical way. As a tentative guide in our work we have tried to see whether and how a group could be defined, in terms of preservice information, so that at least one half would prove to be unsatisfactory in service. This is an arbitrary goal but one which seems likely to give results that are of interest. A method of approach which we came to use, because it seemed to work better than anything else, is the disposition made of each case, based on judgments of the individual offender and his life situation made by the responsible correctional authorities in dealing with each case.

As pointed out earlier, delinquency can be considered to have various stages which may be listed as follows: breaking the law without being observed; informal correction by a policeman, perhaps without identification; apprehension and more formal admonition; adjudication and probation; county training school; state training school for boys; adult penal institutions.

As individuals in Minnesota progress through these stages, the number of cases shrinks markedly at each new level. In the Minnesota sample about one in five were sent to the county training school; of these, about one fifth were later sent to the state training school. The state training school group is small in number as compared with the total group treated informally, but it is readily identifiable. A decision to confine a youngster in either the county or the state training school is normally reached on the basis of an appraisal of his history and of the positive and negative factors in his life situation. This is a global kind of judgment, but since the information concerning confinement is readily obtainable, from a predictive point of view it would be useful if it were effective. A search was made in Minnesota at the local and the state training schools to ensure that we would have complete and accurate information on confinement in these institutions.

Outcome in terms of category a (promoted) and category d (unsatisfactory) is shown in Figure 2 for those in Sample 2 with different histories of juvenile confinement. The group sent only to a local training school made the best showing in service. They had a somewhat larger number of promoted than unsatisfactory individuals. The group sent to the state training school following confinement in the local training school made the poorest showing: 60 per cent of these were unsatisfactory, and less than 10 per cent were promoted. The fourth group shown in Figure 2, including those sent to state or federal training schools, is almost as poor as the third group. A cross-validation of this in Texas shows that of those sent to the state or federal training school, about 70 per cent were unsatisfactory and only 7 per cent were promoted. This confinement information is the best predictive data we have found for samples of this kind into the young adult period.

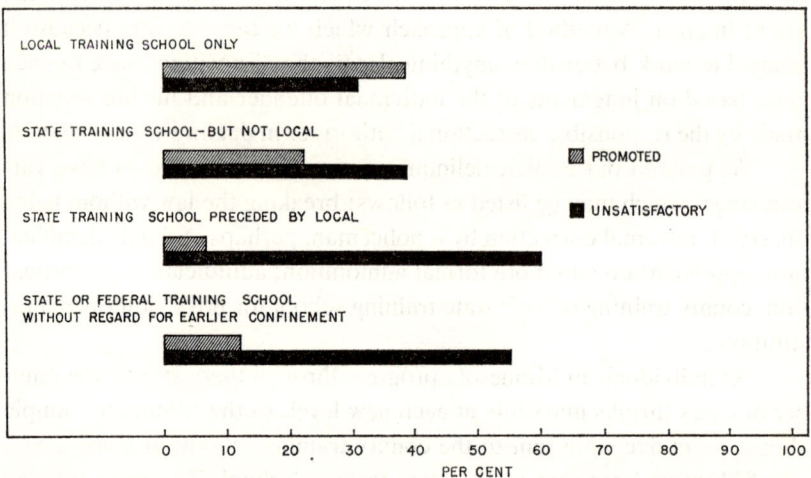

Figure 2. Proportions promoted and unsatisfactory of individuals with different histories of juvenile confinement, Sample 2.

Education and Outcome in Service. Another major variable which we have been studying is amount of education, among the delinquency sample, in relation to later outcome. Amount of education is, of course, related to many other background variables in human lives. It is highly correlated with occupational level and other indexes of socioeconomic status. It has long been regarded by the military services as an effective screening device since it is both easily obtainable and has some predictive validity. A number of studies have shown education to be an effective predictor of outcome in different branches of the service. The general conclusion indicated by this set of studies is that education is related to success or failure in service, but not closely enough to make it unnecessary to try to find better predictors.

The relation between education and outcome in service for the Minnesota delinquent group is shown in Figure 3. The results for the confined

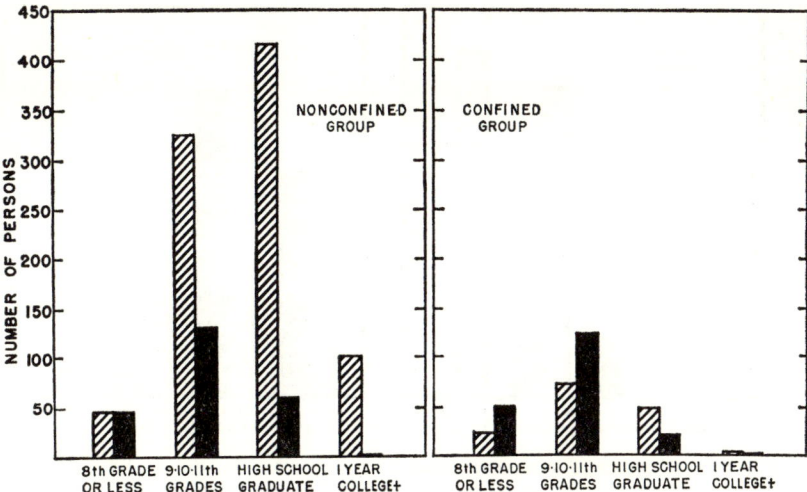

Figure 3. Number promoted (striped bar) and unsatisfactory (solid bar) in relation to amount of preservice education for the nonconfined and confined Minnesota delinquent groups, for the four services.

and nonconfined groups are presented separately; comparisons are made between those promoted and those definitely unsatisfactory, with various levels of education. It is clear that there were many more nonconfined than confined delinquents. For a group of 835 nonconfined, those with an eighth-grade education or less, shown at the extreme left, had about an equal likelihood of being promoted or being unsatisfactory. For the high school dropouts, the ratio of promoted to unsatisfactory was better than two to one, and for the high school graduates, about seven to one. For those who completed at least one year of college, this fact outweighed an earlier history of delinquency to a point where it would be safe to disregard the delinquency. For the confined group, shown in the right half of the figure, those with an eighth-grade education had more than twice as many unsatisfactory as promoted and almost the same ratio held for the high school dropouts. Almost no confined delinquent ever completed a year of college.

For the Texas sample, results are presented (Fig. 4) for the undivided delinquent group, and for a control group from the same region randomly selected from the school population. The picture for the control group is quite similar to that for the non-confined delinquent Minnesota group, except that a much larger proportion attended college. In the Texas delinquent group, we find the same marked shift in proportions suc-

Life History Research in Psychopathology

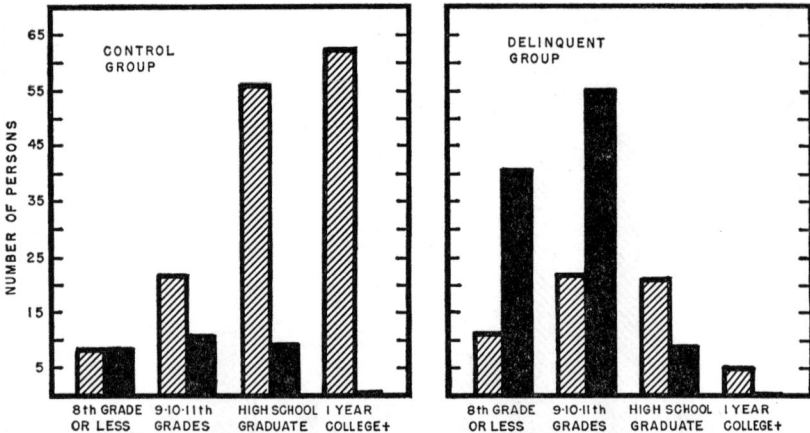

Figure 4. Number promoted (striped bar) and unsatisfactory (solid bar) in relation to amount of preservice education, for Sample 2 and a normal control group, for the four services.

cessful between high school dropouts and high school graduates that we found in the Minnesota confined group.

You may think that the earlier delinquency of those who later attended college would be so minor in character as to be negligible in the first place. That this was not always so can be shown by the case of Rodney, who had some college education and an eventual good outcome. At age 15 he and some other boys were referred for stealing from parked cars. His family was well-to-do, but there was considerable conflict between the parents. The other boys were also from "good" families; only one had been arrested before.

One Month Later. Rodney and three other boys were referred for shooting a rifle into nine homes, causing considerable damage. Rodney was the largest and oldest of the boys and admitted he was the leader. It was found that Rodney had a long record of traffic offenses including, at age 13, driving without a license, two offenses; at age 14, driving without a license; at age 15 speeding (60 mph in a 30 mph zone).

The father often referred to his son as a coward who was afraid to fight for his rights. The principal of Rodney's high school said that the family had given him difficulty previously and was most uncooperative.

Three Months Later (Age 16). Rodney was referred along with five other boys. They were implicated in a theft of approximately 26 automobiles. Rodney wrecked two of the cars, one by intentionally hitting a tree head-on. Although another boy seems to have been the leader in these offenses, Rodney did take about five cars himself. The father seems to be sure his son will be given a suspended commitment to the state training school, and be allowed to enter a military school (he was).

Age 16½: Rodney said he likes the military school and is going back next year. He seems to want to get into difficulty, and the probation officer seems to think he will.

Age 17: Rodney is away at school. Case closed.

Age 17½: Rodney was referred for four traffic violations. He and his mother insisted they did not want the father to know about it because it would create so much disturbance at home. He was placed on unofficial probation.

Age 18: Case closed.

Outcome: Entered service at age 22. He was promoted (personnel specialist) and served overseas for a year. No disciplinary problems. Excellent character and efficiency ratings and honorable discharge. No arrests were recorded after service.

It should be recalled that the Texas delinquents had been selected initially as being somewhat more serious than the Minnesota delinquents, so that inclusion of a total sample of all delinquents from this area of Texas would give a group differing less from the control group than those included here.

The results obtained with the more broadly defined Minnesota delinquent sample indicate clearly that whether or not the result was due to the activities of the probation system, large numbers of youngsters with histories of delinquency made relatively satisfactory later adjustments.

Age. There is a relationship between age of entrance into service and proportion unsatisfactory. In the Army, age is associated with method of entrance (enlisting or being drafted). Many delinquents join the Army as soon as (or even before) their age permits. In general, two thirds of the delinquents who enlisted at an age of 18 or 19 were unsatisfactory. A majority of the third of the delinquents who were drafted were 20 years of age or more; only 20 per cent of these were unsatisfactory. On the other hand, the controls tended to wait until they were drafted or until they reached the age of 20 or more. Those who enlisted had substantially poorer outcomes than those who waited to be drafted.

Various factors may contribute to the large proportion of unsatisfactory cases among the young enlisting men. One significant factor is that those who entered at the age of 20 or later would tend to be those who had refrained from serious offenses in the two or three years before that. The older group can be said to have been roughly screened by their own behavior while they were 18 or 19 years old.

Any attempt to screen out the bad-conduct cases on the basis of age alone would be completely impractical, since it would include so many more successful than unsatisfactory men. The basic research problem here is to develop ways of rejecting the maximum number of those that would be unsatisfactory while rejecting the minimum number of those who got along all right. Thus, age by itself is not usable as a screening procedure, but its part in the total picture should be recognized.

To conclude this part of the paper, I would like to emphasize that the results relating to education stemmed from the actual situation existing at the time. This is a multivariate situation, and attending college is correlated with various other background factors. It is not intended to suggest here that the same results would have been obtained if those who were sent to a training school had been placed in a university instead.

Peer Relations, Socioeconomic Status, and Juvenile Delinquency

The work described up to this point has been concerned with the later history of individuals with records of juvenile delinquency. The period covered is several years into the young adult period after the juvenile delinquency. The second part of the paper has to do with the adjustment of youngsters, in general before the occurrence of juvenile delinquency, and a subsequent follow-up partway through the delinquency period ("early delinquency"). In the course of our earlier work with the adult follow-up of child guidance clinic patients, it was found that poor peer adjustment was frequently a precursor of later severe bad conduct during the young adult period (Roff, 1961a). As has also been reported earlier (Roff, 1970b) poor peer adjustment was found to be an antecedent of various types of adult maladjustment.

These results led to a systematic study of peer relations in a large sample of grade school children, extending through time. It was believed that the children disliked by their peers during grade school constitute a group of major interest to those concerned with the problem of early detection of children who may have subsequent difficulties of various types. In addition to the problem of prediction, it was considered possible that some information concerning the etiology of later problems of various kinds might also be obtained. The grade school situation is an appropriate place for obtaining children's peer choices. It has also been found that teachers can report quite accurately on the reactions of children to their peers. As part of this general program, we are concerned with factors which correlate with acceptance and rejection, both concurrently and over periods of time.

Juvenile Delinquency. Juvenile delinquency is one socially significant later behavior category which we expected to be able to predict from measures of peer acceptance-rejection. The first half of this paper indicated that a record of delinquency is by no means inevitably predictive of adult criminal behavior; in fact, as was seen earlier, the majority of juvenile delinquents eventually get along without serious difficulty. The problem of delinquency during adolescence remains, however, an important one from both a theoretical and a practical point of view.

PROCEDURE

Peer choice nominations were obtained for a total of almost 40,000 schoolchildren in the third through sixth grades in cities in Minnesota and Texas. This project was carried out in partnership with S. B. Sells. Scores were obtained for all pupils in the third through sixth grades of the participating school systems. In the belief that peer group status within the same sex is of primary importance during this age period, choices in each class were made only within and not across sex groups. Each child indicated the four children he or she liked best and the two he or she liked least on IBM Mark-Sense cards.

It was possible to process the Mark-Sense cards through a reproducer and a computer, so that this project was computerized from the beginning. Three scores based on peer group choices were computed for each child, Like-Most, Like-Least, and Like-Most minus Like-Least. The combined scores (LM − LL) are the ones used here. In addition, ratings of each child were obtained from the teachers.

To supplement these scores, a structured interview was conducted with each Minnesota teacher to obtain detailed qualitative information about a partial group selected from the larger sample. Although there is a great deal to be said for the use of precisely derived scores, it is also helpful to have additional qualitative information which will throw light on the meaning of these scores. Interviews were obtained for the lowest boy and the lowest girl in each class, for one high boy or girl in the class, and for a middle boy or girl opposite in sex to the high child. Thus, the interview sample included an equal number of boys and girls, half low in choice status and the other half equally divided between middle and high status. The interviews followed an outline which included questions about appearance, behavior, school personality, and family characteristics. Interviews were completed for just under 2,500 pupils. The present study employs samples of boys only, from Minnesota. Replication of this delinquency study with the Texas part of the sample has not yet been carried out. Follow-up information concerning delinquency was obtained four years after initial testing in St. Paul and three years after initial testing in Minneapolis, so that the older children in the two samples would have completed only the tenth and ninth grades, respectively. We thus refer to the results presented here as relating to "early" delinquency.

The term *delinquency* as used here includes all cases in each city who had contact with the juvenile authorities formal enough to result in the preparation of a case file. Most, but not all, of these were "adjudicated delinquents." Almost all of their offenses occurred before the age of sixteen. One consequence of this is that the difference in total frequency between socioeconomic levels may not be so sharp as it would have been if juvenile delinquents of all ages had been counted. Even if subsequent work with juvenile delinquents of all ages should change the picture presented here, the validity of this study of early delinquents will not be affected. Further follow-up studies might simply lead to the recognition of a difference between early and later delinquency, which has received some, but very little, attention (Neumeyer, 1961).

Subjects. Delinquency information was originally obtained only for St. Paul boys for whom teacher interviews were available. A search of delinquency records was made for "interview" boys in all four grades. Since it was found that those tested in the fifth and sixth grades were more likely to have a delinquency record than those in the third and fourth grades, in Minneapolis a search was made for all fifth and sixth grade boys from the first year of testing, whether or not interviews were available. Since delinquency is much more frequent among boys, the search for a comparable group of girls was postponed. Of the 800 boys in St. Paul for whom a search was made, delinquency files were found for 87, or approximately 11 per cent. A file meant that a boy had been apprehended and had progressed beyond a preliminary consideration; it presented the circumstances of his misbehavior. Since some had moved away from the city, the 87 found cases are more than 11 per cent of those still present in the area. It should be remembered that these boys, who were in the sixth through tenth grades at the time of follow-up, were far from being through the delinquency period.

RESULTS

The St. Paul boys were studied first because (a) the four socioeconomic quartiles for the entire city were represented, (b) the interval since first testing was one year longer than in Minneapolis, and (c) we wanted to have the additional information contained in our interviews for all those with records of delinquency. It was found that the proportion of delinquents in the low peer-status group consistently exceeded the number in the high and middle score groups in the three upper SES quartiles. This was in line with our expectations. In the lowest SES quartile, however, the number of delinquents among the high-choice pupils was about as high as the number in the low-choice group. This was contrary to our expectations and, taken by itself, might seem a chance effect.

A similar study was immediately run in Minneapolis. In earlier work, we had assumed that SES quartiles were a fine enough subdivision for most purposes. We decided however, that it was worthwhile to examine the Minneapolis "interview" sample of fifth and sixth grade boys, which included only the lower two SES quartiles, with each quartile subdivided into upper and lower halves or octiles. Following this division, these octiles were examined for delinquency frequencies in relation to choice scores.

It was found that there were no delinquents at all among the high- or middle-choice boys in SES octiles 5 and 6, and only one in octile 7. There were a substantial number of low-choice boys with delinquency records. In octile 8, however, there were at least as many high-choice boys as low-choice boys with delinquency records, thus replicating the St. Paul results almost exactly. Since there was an observable difference between the seventh and eighth octiles in Minneapolis, we returned to the St. Paul data and separated the third and fourth quartiles into octiles. Again, for octiles 5, 6, and 7, the results were in line with our original expectation that low-choice boys would show substantially more delinquency. For octile 8, on the other hand, delinquency was at least as frequent among the high-choice boys as among the low-choice, in accordance with what was becoming our new, revised expectation.

To fill in the omissions resulting from the use of high-, middle-, and low-choice boys (for whom we had interviews), information concerning delinquency was next obtained in Minneapolis for *all* the 1,729 fifth- and sixth-grade boys for whom first year choice-scores had been obtained. The total number found in the delinquency files was 187, or 11 per cent. Figure 5 shows the percentage delinquent for five standard score class intervals of choice status, for the four octiles of the schools in the lower SES half of the city. Again, our original expectations were approximated closely, except for the high-choice boys in octile 8. Here the proportion delinquent was almost exactly the same as that for the low-choice group, with standard scores of 3.4 and below. The other standard scores for the eighth octile showed the same pattern as the scores in the other octiles.

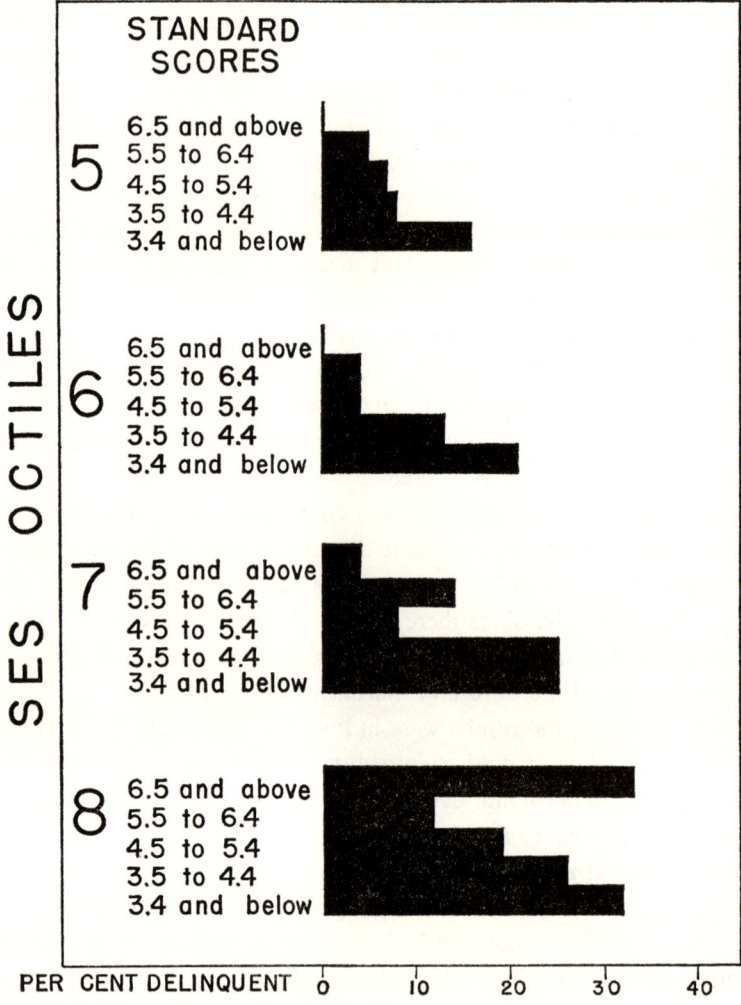

Figure 5. Juvenile delinquency in relation to earlier peer acceptance-rejection at different socioeconomic levels. Reprinted by permission from M. Roff and S. B. Sells, "Juvenile Delinquency in Relation to Peer Acceptance-Rejection and Socioeconomic Status," *Psychology in the Schools*, 1968, 5, 3–18.

ILLUSTRATIVE CASES

The qualitative descriptions of children's behavior and life situations have been useful in many ways. In the present context, they give information not given by the Like-Dislike score about the delinquent as seen by school personnel; they include various factors which may relate to his behavior, both at the time of the interview and later. Space does not permit the presentation of qualitative descriptions for all possible combinations of socioeconomic status and delinquency or non-delinquency. A more comprehensive picture has been presented elsewhere (Roff & Sells, 1968).

SES Octile 8. The SES level of greatest interest here is the eighth octile. In this group, there are as many high-choice as low-choice delinquents. The interviews indicate that, in general, the high-choice boys were in tune not only with the other boys, but also with the teacher and the school. Judging by their peer status and the interview data, they do not seem to have personality problems. On the other hand, the low peer status boys at this SES level are characteristically disliked by the other boys and more likely to be at odds with the teacher and the school. There has been a good deal of talk in the literature about the "delinquent subculture." As a general explanation of all delinquency at this age level, this concept is clearly inadequate. It is closer to the facts to describe these delinquent boys as coming from a bottom economic level, which produces more than its share of delinquents — whether as members of a delinquent subculture or through the operation of other factors, such as family disorganization and "improper" rearing. Edward is a typical high-choice status delinquent from the lowest SES group.

Edward (fifth grade) sometimes looks very neat and clean and other times looks like he climbed out of a ragbag. Occasionally he doesn't even make it to school, apparently because of insufficient clothing. Edward is slender and appears undernourished. He is an attractive boy with a lot of drive. He probably is a good deal more sophisticated in the ways of the world than one would guess from his conversation. He's very nice and polite in school. Edward is a good student, but one handicap is that he rushes to get done.

Edward is a good ballplayer and a good sport and well liked and one of the first to be chosen on any athletic team. In class the youngsters also like him very well and are quick to choose him. He's usually mannerly. He's no bother to anyone, would quickly reach out to help others. He's dependable and is the best-liked boy in class. Good average intelligence. The teacher says that he could not be nicer to her, he's cooperative and courteous, wants to do well. He does things well, is quiet, does not make himself a pest. He does not ask her for help. I think part of this comes from his being forced to be independent of his disadvantaged family.

He comes from a very unfortunate home situation. The mother apparently does try to help work with the youngsters. Neither mother nor father attends conferences.

The father and mother could perhaps be adequate parents if they had one or two children, but with the extremely large family that they have, they are both overwhelmed. As a result the youngsters do not get the proper care and emotional help that they should get. Father is frequently away from home, separated from the mother; mother, in seeking companionship, is apt to reach out to other men and to entertain them in her own home. This probably has some adverse effects on the youngsters. Both parents seem rather immature adults who are apt to satisfy their own needs before satisfying the needs of the youngsters. As a result, the children are many times left without the proper parental attention. Surprisingly enough, they do quite well under these conditions. They are attractive, lovable, and likable boys and girls, who seemingly make the most of what little life has offered them. Currently, there has been talk by the welfare agencies of the possibility of removal of the youngsters from this family. At this point, because of the good adjustment made under these adverse circumstances, they have been reluctant to move the older youngsters; it's the smaller ones that would be most hurt if they should have to leave, yet it's the small ones that perhaps would have the best chance to move on and more fully develop their capacities, with the chance to live somewhere else.

Probation Information. Edward had been arrested for malicious destruction of property and referred to his parents about a year before testing. About a year and a half after testing, he was arrested for shoplifting and put on probation for a year. Six months after this probation, he was arrested for burglary; at that time he admitted nine other burglaries. He was sent to the county training school, where he stayed for six months and remained on probation for another six months after that. This brings him almost to the time of the follow-up.

The family was well known to various social agencies. An older brother was in an adult reformatory, and a second older brother was on probation at the time of the follow-up. The family was described as being unstable without the father. The mother seemed unable to supervise. She had had an illegitimate child about two years before follow-up. The psychological interview report said that there was nothing grossly abnormal or unusual about Edward. Stable mood, emotional reactions generally appropriate, though well guarded; slightly unhappy, has a somewhat poor opinion about himself, is fairly energetic — likes people. A normal person indicated.

Although this family situation seems definitely adverse, apparently this high-choice boy gets along surprisingly well. Of course, there has been some petty thievery, truancy, and so on, but both at the time of the initial teacher interview and at the time of the probation interview, Edward was judged to be a "normal person" who was exhibiting some misbehavior. On the other hand, if we look at a low-choice boy in this bottom SES group, we find not only delinquency but also indications of personality difficulties.

James (sixth grade) is the youngest of three brothers. He is overweight, and self-conscious about it. The children tease him. He is lazy, slow moving, frequently avoids physical effort.

His academic ability is better than his production indicates. It is difficult for him to work; once he starts, he will stay at it. In fact, on occasion he has spent the entire day on arithmetic. He likes questions that require thinking.

James will hit back, kick, or swat anybody who walks past his desk. At times when in difficulty, he looks to the teacher for protection.

On the playground his sportsmanship is better than most of his teammates. His coordination is poor, but he likes to play. His coordination has improved somewhat this year.

In his classroom behavior, he aggressively acts out against the children and against the teacher. Teacher (male) holds him briefly, in his more explosive moments. After he quiets down, he will go to work. Limits have to be set and firmly held for him.

He tries to buy friends through giving candy, gum, and so on. When he does not strike out against the children, some are apt to get him to do so. The children seem to have cast him in a role that will be very difficult for him to change. At the beginning of the school year, he screamed, lashed out at, or walked out on the teacher. Now he still gets angry and will try to fight the teacher, but he recovers from it more quickly and settles down more easily. There has been a slow but fairly consistent growth in self-control.

Children reject him. He almost demands this, despite his wanting to be liked and trying to buy friends. He starts many fights with children over petty things. The children fight back. He is gradually withdrawing from this kind of fighting but if children really start a fight with him he will fight it through.

The teacher has talked with his mother only by telephone. She is interested in James, defends him, and will take his side against any other information that might be offered.

Probation Information. In seventh grade, insubordinate in school; sent to county training school for six months.

Family had eight social agency contacts. Father attempted to murder mother and committed suicide when James was four years old. Mother is unstable, but willing to help. Psychological interview found: Impulsive, aggressive, seeks attention — many somatic complaints — inner self-control lacking. Marked dependency needs — poor peer relations — unresolved emotional conflicts (parents not desirous of seeking help) — not sociable.

Negro Delinquents. Since there is a tendency in some areas for low economic status to be associated with race, it was a matter of concern to see to what extent, if at all, the phenomenon that we are discussing there was attributable to race. We found that delinquent youngsters with both good and poor earlier peer adjustment occurred in the Negro group, as well as among white children. In these cities, less than 4 per cent of the entire grade-school population were Negro at this time, and many of their families were definitely above the lowest socioeconomic level. The pattern found here may not fit other cities such as New York or Chicago, where the proportion of Negro pupils is much larger. It should fit a large number of cities where the ethnic composition does not differ too markedly from that of St. Paul and Minneapolis.

Of the two Negro cases presented here, Willie is not only liked by the other boys, but he is also diligent in his schoolwork, although his ability level is not high.

Willy is a sixth-grade Negro boy, well coordinated and in good physical condition. He is the number two boy in the school in control. The boys respect him and a great many are afraid of him. He seems to be a leader. A consistent good sport on the playground. At times he protects the underdog, but on occasion he may kick him.

Willy is a very dependable monitor. In school he works hard. He is of dull normal ability. Even though he is slow in classwork, he does not want his assignments cut down for him. His effort is great enough to complete his work. He is not always right but he certainly tries.

The teacher (male) gives Willy responsibility in the classroom, and he carries it out consistently. He does not assume responsibility if it is not given to him. Boys respect and like him. There are several boys who would like to take his crown as number two man away from him. He is respectful, cooperative, and responsible. He is recognized by his peers for his leadership qualities. Strangely enough, for the position he holds in the estimation of the boys, he is not an aggressive leader. He always holds his own and gives an excellent account of himself when challenged. He rarely seems to challenge others.

There seems to be a gradual, consistent maturing in Willy this year. Children like his persistent trying, no matter what the job assigned.

His mother is cooperative with the school. She is much interested in her son. She wants him to be a good student and a good boy. Willy respects her and, on occasion, has told the teacher of little things he has bought for his mother. They are a close family.

Probation Information. Two months after testing, charged with immoral conduct and placed on informal probation. One month after that, auto theft and sent to county training school. In spring of seventh grade, truancy and returned to county training school. The following summer, shoplifting. No further trouble until ninth grade when charged with driving without a license and disorderly conduct; informal probation.

Has five older and two younger siblings; two older brothers have histories of delinquency. Father is delivery man, mother is housewife. Probation interview notes "lacks strong male influence — quite close-knit family — good sibling relationship."

On the other hand, Don is actively disliked and consistently nonconforming in the classroom. He has twelve siblings, some of whom also have records of delinquency. He is described as a boy who is not getting along well within his own peer culture.

Don is a dirty, sloppy, well-built, apparently healthy Negro boy (fifth grade). He is a nonconformist with little consideration of others or of the situation. Athletics is Don's only visible asset. His weaknesses are that he presents no apparent reasoning ability, is greatly retarded academically, and is very inconsiderate of others.

On the playground Don tries to run the show, tends to bully, is quick with the fists. He has good athletic ability and skills, but shows poor sportsmanship.

In the classroom he talks constantly. He is consistently nonconforming. Rules are made for everybody but him. With others he is inconsiderate of their feelings; he may even knock heads together. He delights in proving his physical strength, even in adverse ways. He himself is not interested in others except by way of showing his strength.

With the teacher there is no communication either way. He may not answer at all; he often says "I don't know" and there continues to be an impasse, no outright conflict, but no real rapport possible. There has been no change in Don's behavior during the year.

Some children fear him because of his size, some are disgusted with his behavior and lack of cleanliness. He tends to intimidate those who are fearful of him. His tangles with the law tend to appeal to some (but not enough to lead any of them to choose him as Most-Liked). Others may look to his ability in athletic skills. But even with the variety of responses, actual relationship is limited.

Don comes from a very large family. There are thirteen children; he is about in the middle. To observers there may appear to be parental apathy. However, there may be interests which are overlooked because of the overwhelming responsibility heaped upon this family. There is a sweet compliance on the part of of the parents but an inability to follow through with guidance and with real care. The father remains employed, which is a decided family strength, but his livelihood is inconsistent. Actual physical surroundings are bare and sparse. There is sometimes not enough food and insufficient clothing. Some of Don's siblings are retarded, and several are in a great deal of trouble with the law.

Probation Information. First delinquency recorded while in third grade: breaking and entering and petty larceny. In two days during fourth grade charged with four offenses, primarily shoplifting and petty larceny; placed on probation for a year. In fifth grade, insubordinate in school and probation extended. In May of fifth-grade year, bicycle theft, insubordinate in school; committed to county training school for an indefinite period. In fall of sixth grade, assault; probation continued. In spring of sixth grade, insubordinate in school; committed to state training school. Two older brothers and an older sister had repeated records of delinquency.

Discussion

There is a sharp difference between the high- and low-choice boys in the bottom SES octile. The interview material just presented gives a clear picture of the behavior of the low-choice delinquent boys as seen in school; they were obviously not well accepted by their peers, and they seemed to have various adjustment problems. The high-choice boys got along well, not only with their peers, but also with the school. From earlier work, we would expect these high-choice boys of the bottom SES group to make better adult adjustments than the low-choice boys.

This follow-up may be too early to reveal the kind of gang activity which is emphasized in some discussions of delinquency (Cohen, 1955; Short & Strodtbeck, 1965), and a further study of our group may give a somewhat different picture. On the other hand, a careful examination of discussions of gangs and delinquency indicates that they are frequently gang (rather than delinquency) oriented, and do not necessarily apply at all to the large number of cases of individual delinquency. With this reservation, it is of interest to compare the present findings with currently prominent viewpoints on delinquency. The literature on delinquency is extensive, and space does not permit a comprehensive review of it here. To place our findings in the context of one particular part of the literature, reference is made to a conference report from the Children's Bureau, *Sociological Theories and Their Implications for Juvenile Delinquency* (Bordua, 1960). This gives a clear statement of two conflicting points of view, and can be quoted directly to avoid any appearance of caricaturing the position with which our results are in disagreement.

Theories of Delinquency. The two theoretical positions quoted here are frequently advanced to explain the occurrence of juvenile delinquency, including gang activity.

One of these sees the delinquent subculture as arising out of the socially structured gap between the aspirations of lower-class boys and the means realistically available to them to realize these aspirations. According to this view,

lower-class socialization does not equip boys to perform according to the requirements of middle-class dominated institutions such as the school, and consequently the boys suffer "status deprivation" and low self-esteem. . . . The delinquent subculture values precisely what middle-class institutions devalue; e.g., "hanging around" instead of industriousness, aggressiveness instead of self-control.

"Status deprivation," then, provides the motivational core for the lower-class male delinquent subculture. . . . Equally crucial is the fact that "status punishment" in an institution such as the school, tends to be differentially concentrated in lower-class groups who are residentially concentrated in certain parts of any city (Bordua, 1960, p. 3).

The second point of view sees the beliefs and values of the street-corner group as arising, not from any situation of status deprivation, but as simply the adolescent version of "lower-class culture." . . . This position directly opposes the notion that the street gang or group's culture derives from a reaction to the demands of middle-class culture. Instead, it emphasizes the view that "lower-class culture," as a more or less systematized body of beliefs, values, "focal concerns," and even household forms, existed in its own right for generations and need not be considered as a reaction to beliefs, values, and household patterns of the middle class (Bordua, 1960, p. 4).

One question that arose (Bordua, 1960) concerned the evidence that there is a lower-class culture which the adolescents are considered to be reflecting.

Delinquency Theory in Relation to Present Results. Our results give no support to the first point of view, that delinquency arises primarily because of the dissatisfaction of lower-class boys with the middle-class norms of such institutions as the school. They are compatible with the second point of view, that there is a "lower-class culture," but differ from the uniformity implied by the term "lower-class culture" in emphasizing individual difference at all class levels. Our results also show clear-cut indications of differences in the patterns of delinquency at our upper and lowest social levels. At the upper social levels, delinquency appears as primarily a function of personality disturbance as reflected by low peer-group status. *Almost no high-choice boys from the upper levels were delinquent.* At the bottom of our eight social levels, there was still a marked tendency for the low-choice status boys to show delinquency more frequently than the middle boys, but the high peer status boys were delinquent as frequently as the low peer status boys. Qualitative information for high-choice delinquent boys at the fifth- and sixth-grade levels indicates quite clearly that they were not at that time in rebellion against that so-called middle-class institution, the school. They got along well with their associates and exhibited a reasonable amount of ambition scholastically. In some cases a boy had already shown some delinquency at the time of our study, and the teacher sometimes mentioned this as casually as she would mention the color of his hair. Most of these high-choice boys gave a clear picture at this age of being in tune with their associates, with the school, and with the teacher, although they sometimes came from highly pathological family situations.

Our schools were classified into social levels according to the education and income of the adults in each area. It seems clear, and is replicated from one to the other of the two cities, that the lowest of the eight education-income levels produces a substantial number of preadolescent boys who are not in any sense in rebellion, although they may exhibit some delinquency, then and later. On the other hand, there is also a sizable group at the lowest social level which is similar to that found at our higher levels, where the delinquency is accompanied by low peer status, a more general personality disturbance, and a rebelliousness which clearly seems to be personally rather than class oriented.

This difference in pattern at different socioeconomic levels suggests a *two-factor explanation* of juvenile delinquency among boys: the personality factor, as reflected by peer status, operates almost alone at the upper and middle SES levels, whereas sometimes this personality factor and sometimes a social level factor, and not the personality factor, seems to be the primary influence in the lower SES group. The qualitative descriptions illustrate concretely the action of these two factors.

Sociological discussions of delinquency have tended to emphasize gangs and organized group activity in their discussions of delinquency. It is unduly restrictive to limit discussions of delinquency to gang activity. Sociologists have also emphasized the relation between SES and delinquency, but without adequate attention to individual differences. Psychological and psychiatric discussions have focused more on the characteristics of individuals that are associated with delinquency, whether the delinquency is on a group or individual basis. Again, the large literature cannot be reviewed in detail. Mention must be made, however, of Jenkins's distinction between socialized and unsocialized delinquent (1950).

The studies of delinquency employing the MMPI, by Hathaway and Monachesi (1953) and by Wirt and Briggs (1959), contribute important information about differences in personality patterns between delinquents and non-delinquents but do not relate this in detail to SES.

What we have done is to put together the two factors of socioeconomic level and individual differences in personality in relation to delinquency in a way which has not been done before, to the best of our knowledge. We think that it is necessary to deal with these two factors or, if you wish, sets of factors, relating on the one hand to the social milieu and on the other hand to the characteristics of the individual involved if we are to avoid the inadequacies of earlier formulations. We think that the picture given in our data of the relation between choice status, socioeconomic level, and delinquency is new, and we hope that it will help to clarify the situation.

REFERENCES

Bordua, D. J. (Ed.) *Sociological theories and their implications for juvenile delinquency: A report of a Children's Bureau conference.* Washington, D.C.: U.S. Department of Health, Education, and Welfare, Children's Bureau, 1960.

Cohen, A. K. *Delinquent boys: The culture of the gang.* Glencoe, Ill.: Free Press, 1955.

Hathaway, S. R., & Monachesi, E. D. *Analyzing and predicting juvenile delinquency with the MMPI.* Minneapolis: University of Minnesota Press, 1953.

Jenkins, R. L. The psychopathic delinquent. In *Social work in the current scene: Selected papers,* 76th Annual Meeting, National Conference of Social Work, June 12–17, 1949. New York: Columbia University Press, 1950.

Neumeyer, M. H. *Juvenile delinquency in modern society.* (3rd ed.) Princeton, N.J.: Van Nostrand, 1961.

Roff, M. Childhood social interactions and young adult bad conduct. *Journal of Abnormal and Social Psychology,* 1961, 63, 333–337. (a)

———. The service-related experience of a sample of juvenile delinquents. Report No. 61-1, January 1961, U.S. Army Medical Research and Development Command, Contract No. DA-49-007-MD-2015. (b)

———. The service-related experience of a sample of juvenile delinquents. II. A replication on a larger sample in another state. Report No. 63-2, March 1964, U.S. Army Medical Research and Development Command, Contract No. DA-49-007-MD-2015.

———. The service-related experience of a sample of juvenile delinquents. V. The relation between education, number of juvenile apprehensions, and outcome in service. Report No. 68-7, May 1968, U.S. Army Medical Research and Development Command, Contract No. DA-49-007-MD-2015.

———. Juvenile delinquency and military service. In R. W. Little (Ed.), *Selective Service and American society.* New York: Russell Sage Foundation, 1969. Pp. 109–138.

———. The service-related experience of juvenile delinquents. VII. The relation between type of juvenile offense and outcome in service. Report No. 70-9, April 1970, U.S. Army Medical Research and Development Command, Contract No. DA-49-007-MD-2015. (a)

———. Some life history factors in relation to various types of adult maladjustment. In M. Roff & D. F. Ricks (Eds.), *Life history research in psychopathology.* Vol. 1. Minneapolis: University of Minnesota Press, 1970. Pp. 265–287. (b)

———, Mink, W. D., & Hinrichs, G. B. *Developmental abnormal psychology.* New York: Holt, 1966.

Roff, M., & Ricks, D. F. (Eds.) *Life history research in psychopathology.* Vol. 1. Minneapolis: University of Minnesota Press, 1970.

Roff, M., & Sells, S. B. Juvenile delinquency in relation to peer acceptance-rejection and socioeconomic status. *Psychology in the Schools,* 1968, 5, 3–18.

Sells, S. B., & Roff, M. Peer acceptance-rejection and personality development. Final report of Contract No. OE2-10-051, U.S. Office of Education, 1967.

Short, J. F., & Strodtbeck, F. L. *Group process and gang delinquency.* Chicago: University of Chicago Press, 1965.

Wirt, R. D., & Briggs, P. F. Personality and environmental factors in the development of delinquency. *Psychological Monographs,* 1959, 73 (15, Whole No. 485).

FINI SCHULSINGER | *Psychopathy: Heredity and Environment*

NOTHING indicates that the disease or condition we today call "psychopathy" has not been prevalent as far back in the history of mankind as have psychosis, mental retardation, and neurosis. Once psychosis and mental deficiency had been delimited, psychiatrists became interested in describing and classifying those conditions that could not be ascribed to either psychosis, mental deficiency, or gross neurological damage. The real pioneer of today's psychiatry, Philippe Pinel (1801), contributed to the concept of psychopathy, which he described as *manie sans délire* — insanity without symptoms of delirium or delusions. Pinel wrote, "I was much astonished to observe several insane persons who never presented any lesion of their intellect and who were dominated by a sort of instinctual rage, as if the affective abilities alone were damaged."

Esquirol and other French psychiatrists developed Pinel's concept further. The culmination was Morel's 1859 treatise in which he outlined a hierarchy of hereditary degeneration: If the first generation of ill people showed even a simple increase of their parents' nervous temperament, then the following generations would be worse and worse. The fourth generation would include the most defective individuals, idiots and cretins. Psychopathy, as defined today, would probably appear in the second generation.

NOTE: This research was supported by Research Grant R 0016 from the World Health Organization, Geneva, Switzerland. The basic pool of non–family-reared subjects was obtained with financial support from contracts between the U.S. Public Health Service and the Psykologisk Institut (contract number PH93-64-532).

I am greatly indebted to Irving I. Gottesman and L. Erlenmeyer-Kimling, who suggested a number of valuable procedures during the preparation of this paper. Thanks are also due to Miss Agnethe Beck, who did the register searches; Mrs. Lene Kold and Mrs. Karen Nyboe, who did the secretarial work; and Jytte Willadsen, M.D., and Joseph Welner, M.D., who participated in the reliability study.

Pritchard (1835), in his treatise on insanity, described a special form, "moral insanity," a term that has continued to be synonymous with psychopathy far into the twentieth century. Pritchard's concept was rather broad and included a collection of disparate conditions that should be ascribed to a variety of psychoses as borderline or latent forms.

The modern use of the term *psychopathy* was coined by the German psychiatrist Koch (1891) in his book *Die Psychopatische Minderwertigkeiten* (The Psychopathic Inferiorities). Under this heading he included "all, be they inborn or acquired, mental abnormalities that influence the life of a human being but that, even in severe cases, do not provoke psychosis and in the affected persons, even in the best cases, do not let them appear as being in complete possession of mental normality and capacity." Thus, Koch's concept was also rather broad, and many of his cases would today be included among neuroses and organic brain syndrome.

Kraepelin (1915) conceived of the psychopathic conditions as circumscribed infantilism or circumscribed development inhibitions. He described and subclassified the psychopathic conditions into seven groups and presented their sex distribution and prevalence on the basis of a hospital population.

Kahn (1931) and Kretschmer (cited in Schneider, 1934) both tried to correlate psychopathy with other aspects of personality. Kahn described sixteen types of psychopathy, which he then assigned to either a drive, a temperament, or a characterological aspect of the personality. But these aspects of the personality were further elaborated, which again had the sad effect of enabling very few patients to be assigned more easily to one of Kahn's subclasses than to several of the others. Kretschmer's typology was more dynamic; it was based on four psychological stages: the uptake, the retention, the working through, and the release. A person's way of experiencing something could vary from sthenic to asthenic, which made three forms of reaction possible: the primitive reaction, the expansive reaction, and the sensitive reaction. Each of these three forms of reaction were characterized by a different constellation of the above-mentioned four psychological stages.

Obviously, the classification of psychopathy is an intricate problem. Inasmuch as we have been unable to classify psychopathic disorders according to well-known etiologies, the most useful compromise has been to classify them purely on the basis of clinical description. This is what Kraepelin did, and it is what Schneider (1934) called a "system-free typology." Schneider improved Kraepelin's typology to some extent because he added to Kraepelin's mainly transgressive psychopaths some groups of personality deviations that did not necessarily lead to antisocial behavior. Schneider aimed at a concept and classification free of moral values. He conceived of psychopaths as deviants from average norms. The deviations caused the affected individual and/or his environment to suffer. Since the only behavioral norms clearly outlined are those that can be deducted from the penal code, it is difficult to imagine how Schneider could settle on norms without making a choice based on his own moralistic equipment. Apart from this philosophical weakness, Schneider's typology has been relatively easy to apply; and it has, to a large extent, pervaded European and other schools of psychiatry.

Up until 1939, British psychiatry favored a concept of psychopathy mainly as a moral disease. Since then, Henderson (1939), Curran and Mallinson (1944), and Craft (1966) have made classifications of psychopathy on a purely descriptive basis, but much less elaborately than their German colleagues. None of the British authors specified more than three classes. In England the urge for systematic classification has been much less intense than in Continental Europe; and the forensic aspects of psychopathy have been in the foreground, partly because of the existence, until recently, of the death penalty. For this reason, and because of the strong position of social psychiatry, British psychiatrists have focused more on the treatment aspects of this disorder than has been usual in most of Continental Europe.

In the United States, Benjamin Rush (cited in Craft, 1966) wrote: "There are many instances of persons with sound understanding and some of uncommon talent who are affected with this disease in the world. It differs from exculpative, fraudulent and malicious lying in being influenced by none of the motives of any of them. Persons with this disease cannot speak the truth on any subject." Rush thought of psychopaths as having an originally defective organization "in those parts of the body which are occupied by the moral faculties of the mind." He called the condition "moral derangement," and he considered it a valid entity for treatment by physicians.

In the twentieth century, American interest in psychopathy has taken a course that differs in some ways from the European traditions. First, the application of research methods has been more common, perhaps because psychologists and sociologists have had greater academic prestige in the United States than is common in Europe. Second, psychoanalytic theory and practice were integrated into mental health practice much earlier in the United States than in Europe, where integration was delayed partly as a consequence of the opposition of the Nazis to psychoanalysis. The result has been a vast body of more or less sociologically oriented surveys in America on large populations of delinquents and criminals, many of whom were psychopaths. Another result has been several, very different attempts at unifying psychoanalytic and descriptive principles in relation to the concept of psychopathy (Greenacre, 1945; Karpman, 1947; and others). Partridge (1930) proposed the term *sociopathic personality*, which has become the official American term for psychopathy — a term possibly adopted for operational reasons, but with an unavoidable moralistic content, which does not make it easier for modern criminologists to fight the spirit of retaliation in the penal systems.

Alexander (1930) supplied a comprehensive description and explanation of the *neurotic character*, which was the old-time analysts' term for psychopathy. His psychodynamic interpretations of case records are not easy to evaluate from a scientific viewpoint, but his clinical descriptions add much to the otherwise usable, system-free, descriptive classifications of Kraepelin and Schneider. Alexander's description of the neurotic character makes the concept of psychopathy a coherent one. Its focus is on personality traits that are also common, to a large extent, to Kraepelin's and Schneider's subgroups, which then become more meaningful. The essence of Alexander's description is that neurotic characters show a consistent pattern of acting out and that this acting-out is mainly of an alloplastic nature (except, perhaps, for some alcoholics and a few others).

This very sketchy and condensed review of the huge topic of the concept of psychopathy does not pretend to do justice to all facets of the subject and all the authors who have written about it. I find a relatively simple, descriptively based concept of psychopathy the most useful tool in research; however, as will be evident later, Alexander's description has proved most tempting and also operationally useful to me.

ETIOLOGY

Genetics. The very special eugenic ideas of the Third Reich involved some German psychiatric geneticists in the classical type of family studies on relatives of psychopathic probands (Berlit, 1931; Riedel, 1937; Stumpfl, 1936). Their work was carried out in the same neat way as other, respectably intended, genetic work from the famous Munich school. The results of these studies unanimously indicated that heredity plays a role in the etiology of psychopathy.

Life History Research in Psychopathology

The nature-nurture problem has always been particularly pronounced with regard to psychopathy, because therapists of all kinds have always been struck by the terrible environments to which many of their delinquent and/or psychopathic patients have been exposed. Newkirk (1957) stated: "As adopted delinquents permit research on the constitutional separate from the environmental element, thorough statistics on adoption and adopted persons including their ancestry should be devised and collected" (p. 54). Reiter (1930) tried to use this technique in a prospective design; but, for unknown reasons, nothing but a first presentation of the study has been published. Perhaps he feared German eugenics of the 1930's!

Brain Pathology. A number of electroencephalographic (EEG) studies on psychopaths, in different countries, have shown an excess of abnormal EEG's in psychopaths compared with the general population. The more violent or impulsive the psychopaths are, the greater is the number of their EEG abnormalities. The deviations have been shown to be of an unspecific nature, neither focal nor epileptic. Generally, these mild dysrhythmias are viewed as signs of immaturity. Otherwise, it is difficult to interpret certain findings. How much of the abnormality is inherited, and how much comes from insufficient obstetrical care or from series of minor cerebral concussions among the wildest of boys? This physiological correlate of psychopathy cannot yet, in any case, be ruled out as a possible etiological factor.

Cytogenetics. Among tall, violent lawbreakers, the prevalence of the XYY syndrome is greater than among other offenders and the general population (Court Brown, 1968; Nielsen, Sturup, Tsuboi, & Romano, 1969). Such findings are fascinating and encouraging. However, since only about 1 per cent of severe criminal psychopaths in two psychopathic prisons showed this chromosome abnormality, a cytogenetic solution to the etiology of psychopathy is not to be expected in the near future.

Deprivation in Infancy. Broken homes, loss of parents, hospitalization, lack of proper physical and emotional care, and institutionalization are all factors believed by many psychologists and psychiatrists to be of etiological significance in psychopathy, retardation of development, and other mental abnormalities occurring in childhood and later. This belief, or conviction, has been used in many countries to convince politicians and administrators of the value of humane and well-staffed children's institutions. Unfortunately, it is often difficult to provide proper care for children simply because they deserve it.

Writers such as Spitz (1945) and Bowlby (1951) have been influential in a positive way. From a scientific viewpoint, however, most of the classics on early experience and its later effects are more dubious, as has been shown in the more recent works of Clarke (1968), Pinneau (1955), and Heston (1966). A basic methodological error in the classical studies of institutionalization effects was that they were performed without proper genetic control. Heston's study has shown with reasonable certainty that the genetic variable is far more important than institution- versus family-rearing with regard to the later development of psychosis, personality deviations, and other manifest mental disturbances.

PRESENT INVESTIGATIONS IN DENMARK

Inasmuch as any pathological condition is a result of an interaction between genetic and environmental factors, the ideal research should aim at clarification of this interaction. The greater the knowledge about one of the two factors, the greater are the possibilities of planning investigations on the impact of the other factor.

The usual genealogical studies in psychiatry show that the closer the relationship between a family member and a mentally ill proband, the greater is the risk of mental illness for the family member. As already indicated, the relatives in the usual studies share with the probands not only genes but also environment. A realistic way to "isolate" the genetic factor is to conduct studies of probands who have been reared apart from their biological relatives and to analyze the prevalence of mental disorders among their biological and their foster relatives. This idea is not new, but the practical implications of the technique have generally discouraged possible investigators from making serious attempts.

In an investigation initiated by Kety and co-workers (1968) seven years ago, we explored the possibilities in Denmark of conducting such a study on schizophrenia. It turned out that studies of the desired nature were feasible in Denmark, for the following reasons: First, Denmark has a central register of all adoptions, under the supervision of the State Department of Justice. This department, understanding and appreciating our scientific goals, gave us permission to use its registers. (Of course, permission was granted only subject to several discretionary conditions.) Second, Denmark has a central register of psychiatric hospital admissions – meant for research purposes – going back to 1916. And third, Denmark has maintained, since 1924, municipal population registers that make it possible to trace a person if one address from 1924 or later is known. By use of old census lists, it is possible to trace people even further back — in some instances, as far back as the year 1800. In addition, the Danish population is relatively homogeneous, and there are few emigrants.

The schizophrenic probands in the first adoption study were found among 507 adoptees with psychiatric hospital records out of a total pool of 5,483 adoptees, encompassing all the nonfamily adoptions in the city and county of Copenhagen between 1924 and 1947. All the case record material for these 507 adoptees with a record of mental illness was screened and reviewed by two Danish psychiatrists, the writer being one.

During this work I was amazed to find a relatively large number of adoptees who had been in contact with psychiatrists because of personality disturbances. Therefore, I planned to do a family study of psychopathy using this adoptive sample, for which it was possible to separate hereditary from environmental factors. The study began in June 1967, and the collection of data ended in September 1969.

Procedures. The first step was to establish an operational and reliable definition of psychopathy. The following criteria were subjected to reliability testing: (a) A consistent pattern, lasting a reasonable period beyond adolescence, of impulse-ridden or acting-out behavior must be evident. This behavior can be either mainly active, expansive, and manipulating or mainly passive-asthenic (alcohol and/or drug abuse can be an expression of either). (b) The abreactions are inadequate in relation to the precipitating factors (of course, on the basis of very vaguely defined Danish behavioral norms). (c) The abreactions are frequently of an alloplastic nature.

These criteria are all positive. The negative criteria are the following: (d) Character neurosis must be excluded (i.e., a consistent pattern of neurotic restriction of activity and gratification). (e) Borderline psychosis must be excluded. (f) Cases in which acting out is found in an otherwise psychotic person are excluded.

From the 507 mentally ill adoptees whom I had originally given a diagnosis of psychopathy in 1964, before the present study was planned and before the above definition of psychopathy was formulated, 20 cases were picked; 20 other cases with other diagnoses, but with the same amount of case record material and of the same sex and age as the 20 psychopaths, were selected from the same pool. All the available sets of records for the two groups were then mixed into a common group and evaluated, again blindly, by two other experienced psychiatrists and me, following a discussion of the criteria. Each of the criteria was rated on a four-point rating scale. I now found 21 persons of the 40 who could be classified as psychopaths. The other psychiatrists considered 17 and 16 of these 21 cases, respectively, to be psychopathic. In 14 cases all three of us agreed upon the diagnosis of psychopathy; and as the raters had classified, respectively, 21, 22, and 20 persons as psychopaths, the overall agreement among the three raters was 67 per cent. However, one of the criteria, that the acting-out behavior should have lasted a reasonable time beyond adolescence, was applied differently by the three raters. An exclusion of the cases below 20 years of age from the screening raised the overall agreement to 74 per cent among the three raters. If agreement about absence of psychopathy were included, the overall agreement would increase to 82 per cent.

It turned out that the scoring system discriminated very well between psychopaths and character neurotics. One or two raters characterized 8 of the 40 persons as possible borderline psychotics. The total scores of these 8 were rather varied with regard to psychopathy, but none of them was high. As a result of the reliability testing procedure, the original definition was changed on one point: it was now required that the psychopathic symptoms should have lasted beyond the age of 19.

On the basis of the definition thus established, it was possible to select 57 psychopathic probands from the 507 adoptees with known mental disorders. Then from the pool of nearly 5,000 adoptees who were not mentally ill, a control was selected for each of the 57 index probands. For every adoptee in this pool there was a form in the central register showing sex, age, and age at first transfer to the adoptive family; names and birthdates of the adoptive parents; occupation of the adoptive father, his stated annual income and financial status, and his address at the time of the adoption; and the names, birthdates, occupations, and addresses of the biological parents. Starting with the form on the index proband, an alternating forward and backward search was made until four possible controls had been found. A control had to be of the same sex and born during the same period, to avoid the different influences of a changing society. They were also matched for age at transfer to the adoptive home and for the social class of the adoptive parents, on the basis of a Danish classification by Svalastoga (1959).

A pretransfer history was prepared for every index proband and the four possible controls — that is, a report of how long, with whom, and where each stayed until the transfer to the adoptive parents. In almost every one of the 57 cases it was possible to find a perfect control, with exactly the same age, social background, length of institutionalization, length of stay with biological relatives, and number of environmental shifts before the transfer. It was easy to match for social class, and in many cases to match even for the same section of the city of Copenhagen. The comparability of the two groups is evident in the accompanying summary.

	Index Ss	Controls
Number of females	17	17
Average age of females	35.8 yrs.	35.8 yrs.
Number of males	40	40
Average age of males	36.7 yrs.	35.8 yrs.
Number of environmental shifts	1.18	1.21
Months of institutionalization	5.63	5.62

The total number of biological and adoptive relatives age 20 or above was 854. Their distribution in terms of relationship was fairly similar for the two groups, as the accompanying tabulation indicates. Three biological fathers of index probands and one biological father of a control could not be identified. Three adoptive mothers of probands were unmarried at the time of adoption. Adoptive full sibs are offspring of both adoptive parents; adoptive half sibs are offspring of only one of the adoptive parents.

	Index Biological	Index Adoptive	Control Biological	Control Adoptive
Half sibs	169	12	156	8
Full sibs	25	8	16	11
Fathers	54	54	56	57
Mothers	57	57	57	57
Total	305	131	285	133

Findings. Mental illness among the relatives was found through a search for the names of all 854 relatives in the archives of all the psychiatric institutions in Denmark. A research assistant traveled throughout the country and spent several days at each institution searching the files (with greatly appreciated assistance from the local secretaries). I reviewed and summarized all the available case record material and did a diagnostic classification blindly, without knowing whether the person was related biologically or by adoption to an index proband or to a control. The findings on mental illness in the various categories of relatives are summarized in Table 1.

The prevalence of mental illnesses of all types among the relatives is shown in Table 2 (total number of ill relatives, 129). It may be noted that the rates of illness are approximately the same in both groups of adoptive relatives and in the biological relatives of the controls. The overall rate of illness for the biological relatives of the index probands, however, is considerably higher than the rates for the other three subgroups of relatives.

Table 1. Distribution of Mental Illnesses in Relatives of the Index Probands and Controls

Relative	Total N	Mentally Ill	Spectrum Disorders	Core Psychopathy
Biological				
Father				
Index	54	15	14	5
Control	56	5	5	1
Mother				
Index	57	16	7	
Control	57	12	2	
Sister				
Index	13	2	2	
Control	11	1		
Brother				
Index	12	3	3	1
Control	35	2		
Half sister (maternal)				
Index	35	4	3	1
Control	33	5	2	
Half brother (maternal)				
Index	35	6	5	2
Control	33	4	3	1
Half sister (paternal)				
Index	46	7	6	1
Control	51	4	3	1
Half brother (paternal)				
Index	53	5	4	2
Control	39	4	4	1
Total index	305	58	44	12
Total control	285	37	19	4
Adoptive				
Father				
Index	54	7	5	1
Control	57	3	1	
Mother				
Index	57	9	4	
Control	57	7	3	
Sister				
Index	3			
Control	6			
Brother				
Index	5	1	1	
Control	5	3		

Table 1. Continued

Relative	Total N	Mentally Ill	Spectrum Disorders	Core Psychopathy
Half sister (maternal)				
Index..............	4			
Control............	2	1	1	1
Half brother (maternal)				
Index..............	3			
Control............	1	1	1	1
Half sister (paternal)				
Index..............	5	1		
Control............	3			
Half brother (paternal), control............	2	1	1	
Total index........	131	18	10	1
Total control.......	133	16	7	2

The quality of the case record material, of course, varied according to the institution, the tradition of the time, and, especially, the length of institutionalization. It therefore seemed most useful to operate with a *spectrum* of personality disorders, in which psychopathy was the nuclear disease. In some cases a diagnosis of psychopathy was rather likely, but the case record material did not permit application of all the criteria from the definition of psychopathy. These cases were classified as "observation for psychopathy" (probable psychopathy). Some cases were too mild or too inconsistent to be classified psychopathic according to the definition, and they were just classified as "character deviations." If the case record material was relatively sparse in such cases, they were classified as "observation for character deviation." A number of cases had to be classified as evidencing either criminality, alcoholism, or drug abuse, with no other clarifying diagnosis. (In my view, they probably belong to the spectrum of personality disorders more or less related to psychopathy.) A few cases had to be diagnosed as hysterical character deviation (but not conversion hysteria). These cases were counted within the psychopathy spectrum. A single case of an obsessive-compulsive character was not included in the psychopathy spectrum, nor were cases of completed suicide for whom there was no psychiatric information.

The prevalence of psychopathic spectrum disorders among the relatives is shown in Table 2. It is immediately evident that there is a great surplus of such disorders among the biological relatives of the index probands, more than 14 per cent of whom have a psychopathic spectrum disorder compared with 5–8 per cent among the other three relative groups.

Table 2. Prevalence of Mental Illnesses among Probands' Relatives

Illness and Relative	Biological	Adoptive
Mental illnesses among all relatives		
Index	58/305 = 19.0 ± 2.3%	18/131 = 13.7 ± 3.0%
Control	37/285 = 13.0 ± 2.0%	16/133 = 12.0 ± 2.8%
Psychopathic spectrum disorders among all relatives		
Index	44/305 = 14.4 ± 2.0%	10/131 = 7.6 ± 2.3%
Control	19/285 = 6.7 ± 1.5%	7/133 = 5.3 ± 1.9%
Psychopathy among all relatives		
Index	12/305 = 3.9 ± 1.1%	1/131 = 0.8 ± 0.8%
Control	4/285 = 1.4 ± 0.7%	2/133 = 1.5 ± 1.0%
Psychopathy among parents		
Index	5/111 = 4.5 ± 2.0%	1/111 = 0.9 ± 0.9%
Control	1/113 = 0.9 ± 0.9%	0/114 = 0
Psychopathy among fathers		
Index	5/54 = 9.3 ± 4.0%	1/54 = 1.9 ± 1.9%
Control	1/56 = 1.8 ± 1.8%	0/57 = 0

Among the biological relatives of the index probands, 76 per cent of "mental illnesses of all types" belong to the psychopathy spectrum, compared with 44–56 per cent in the other relative groups. The differences between the biological relatives of the index probands and the other relative groups would have been even greater if the diagnosis of hysterical character deviation had been omitted from the psychopathy spectrum.

Base rate figures for the expectancy of psychopathic spectrum disorders as classified here are not available for the Danish population. It may be seen, however, that the rates of disorder are again about the same in all of the relative groups except the biological relatives of the index probands.

The prevalence of the core disease, psychopathy, among the relatives is also shown in Table 2. Psychopathy is certainly overrepresented among the biological relatives of the index probands. This difference is even more marked when the distribution of psychopathy is compared in the four parent groups only. In fact, since none of the mothers in any group received the diagnosis of core psychopathy, the comparisons may be confined to the fathers only. Psychopathy occurs more than five times as frequently among the index probands' biological fathers as among their adoptive fathers or the biological fathers of the controls (Table 2).

Referring back to Table 1, it will be noted that there is an overall tendency for the psychopathic spectrum disorders, and for core psychopathy in particular, to appear more frequently among the male than among the female relatives. The sex differences, however, are not so marked and consistent in the sibling and half-sibling subgroups as in the parent subgroups. Table 1 also shows that the differences between the biological relatives of the index probands and the controls do not increase consistently as one moves from the comparisons of rates of mental illness in total to rates of psychopathic spectrum disorders to core psychopathy. The differences between the index and control relatives increase substantially, for example, as one goes from the psychopathic spectrum disorders to core psychopathy in the biological fathers, whereas in the biological mothers the increase occurs between the all-mental-disorders category and the spectrum-disorders category. It is not entirely clear from these preliminary analyses, therefore, whether the psychopathic spectrum as classified here is meaningfully related to the definition of core psychopathy. The difference in the patterns of the mothers and fathers may reflect the generally agreed upon fact that males are more likely than females to be classified as core psychopaths in Denmark. The symptomatology involved in the author's definition of psychopathy is more easily recognized in males who have to go to a hospital.

Assuming, however, that the psychopathy spectrum *is* appropriately classified, it is of further interest to examine the distribution of spectrum disorders in the family. The accompanying tabulation indicates the number of the psychopathic spectrum disorders in the affected families, the presence of such a disorder in a biological or adoptive family being indicated by + and its absence by −.

	Index	Control	Total
Biological +, adoptive −	27	11	38
Biological −, adoptive −	22	39	61
Biological +, adoptive +	5	4	9
Biological −, adoptive +	3	3	6
Total	57	57	114

A chi-square test for this distribution (with the second and third groups combined) resulted in $p<.005$.

DISCUSSION

The conclusion to be drawn from these findings is that genetic factors play an important role in the etiology of psychopathy. The definition of psychopathy that we used is purely descriptive, and, applied to case record material, it requires only a minimum of interpretation of the data. The definition has proved reliable, and it probably has face validity as well.

The selection of controls was made with due respect to possible etiological factors. Social background in the adoptive homes was matched, as was the period of birth. Even the possibility of deprivation during infancy was partially taken into consideration, as the controls and the index probands had been subject to the same number of environmental shifts, had spent the same amount of time in institutions, and had been with their biological relatives the same length of time before placement in their adoptive homes.

The assistant who visited all the psychiatric institutions to find the mentally ill relatives processed all the relatives as one group, without knowing whether they were index or control cases or adoptive or biological relatives. I selected the index probands and the controls during 1967 and did not, at that time, make any notes about them. When I reviewed the case record material of the mentally ill relatives about two years later, I was not able to tell whether the relative belonged to an adoptive or biological family or to an index proband or a control, with few exceptions. In three cases I felt, because of very peculiar last names, that I could identify a relative as belonging to the biological family of an index proband. In a few cases I could identify relatives as adoptive relatives of probands, but did not know if these probands were controls or index cases. In each such instance, a note to this effect was made in the case summary. It turned out that these few cases of recognition had no influence on the results of the study.

Although the design of this study aims especially at demonstrating possible genetic factors in the etiology of psychopathy, this does not at all mean that the findings exclude environmental factors. However, the tabulation on page 114 indicates that the frequency of psychopathy and related disorders in the adoptive families can be excluded as an important etiological factor in this sample. Only three of the index probands had a unilateral prevalence on the adoptive side, and three of the controls also had this environmental load. Only five index probands and four controls had a bilateral load of psychopathic spectrum disorders.

Another possible environmental factor is deprivation during early infancy, as expressed in number of environmental shifts and length of institutionalization in early childhood. If this factor were to be tested in the study, it would have to be a test of, for example, the hypothesis that psychopathic spectrum disorders would be less frequent among the biological relatives of the index probands who were transferred late to their adoptive homes than among those transferred at an early age.

In order to make a statistical analysis of these data, it is necessary to take into account the great difference in the number of relatives between the biological families and the adoptive families. It is also necessary to take into account that fathers, mothers, and full siblings are first-degree relatives whereas the half siblings are second-degree relatives. The following scoring system was used for our provisional analysis: no disorder, 0; disorders other than psychopathy spectrum, 1; criminality, alcoholism, drug abuse, 2; character deviations and observations for psychopathy, 3; and psychopathy, 4. Each disease score was multiplied by one if the disorder appeared in a half sib and by two if it appeared in a first-degree relative. Then the disease scores were totaled separately for each of the proband's two families (biological and adoptive), and the total score for each was divided by the number of relatives in the family group. In order to avoid 0 in the numerator, a score of 1 was added to the total disease score of each family before dividing. That is, family score = [Σ(disease score $\times$ relationship score) + 1]/number of relatives.

Of the index probands, 15 were one month old or less at the time of transfer to their adoptive home; 42 were older than this at the time of transfer. No significant difference in the frequency of psychopathic spectrum disorders among biological family members of the two subgroups was found when the biological family scores were compared by a t test ($p > .15$). Therefore, early deprivation could not be held responsible for psychopathy in the index probands. Further, a repetition of this analysis, but with one year of age as the time of transfer as the separation factor, also revealed no significant difference ($p > .15$).

One of the possible etiological factors in psychopathy is brain damage. The case record material available for the relatives does not permit an evaluation of this factor, which would require an examination of all the relatives. However, a relevant factor could be pregnancy and birth complications. A search for the official midwife reports about the births of the 114 probands and controls yielded 107 reports. Information on the births of 50 matched pairs of probands and controls was thus available.

The content of older midwife reports is difficult to evaluate. There is some agreement in Denmark that not every complication is registered in these reports. On the other hand, if something is registered, one can feel sure that it really happened. In other words, the midwife reports yield minimum information. Every midwife report was rated according to a five-point rating scale devised in collaboration with Professor F. Fuchs, Chairman of Gynecology and Obstetrics at Cornell Medical School, New York. This scale, based on the relatively primitive type of information in the midwife reports, ranged from 0 (no complications) to 4 points (for severe complications); the total score could be 5 or more points.

The accompanying tabulation compares the pregnancy birth complications of the index and the control probands:

	Index Ss	*Controls*
Number with birth records	53	54
Total scores	94	105
Average score	1.8	1.9
Number with birth records for both groups	50	50
Total scores	80	97
Average score	1.6	1.9
Number with score of 0	24	19
Number with 1–4 points	21	19
Number with 5+ points	5	9
Number with single scores of 3 and/or 4	8	5
Number with single scores of 4	6	3

This analysis does not establish a brain damage etiology of psychopathy, at least insofar as brain damage from birth complications is concerned. If there were such brain damage etiology, we could expect the index probands without obstetrical complications to have a more severe genetic load of psychopathic spectrum abnormalities than the index probands with complications. Twenty four index probands had not suffered any pregnancy/birth complications (score 0), and 14 had a total score of 3 or above. To obtain a score of 3+, they had to have experienced one or more serious complications, or a combination of minor complications. Comparing the biological family scores for psychopathic spectrum disorders for the two groups, using the t test, we found no significant difference in the genetic load in the two groups ($p > .20$). Therefore, this analysis, too, failed to yield support for an etiological role of pregnancy/birth complications in psychopathy per se.

In summary, this study of the 854 biological and adoptive relatives of 57 psychopathic adoptees and their 57 matched controls shows the frequency of mental disorders to be substantially higher in the biological relatives of the psychopathic probands than among their adoptive relatives or than among either group of relatives of the controls. The difference is even greater when only psychopathic spectrum disorders are considered. The study supports a hypothesis of heredity as an etiological factor in psychopathic spectrum disorders. Deprivation during infancy and brain damage caused by pregnancy/birth complications were not found to be etiologically significant, at least as measured by the somewhat crude indices of this investigation.

REFERENCES

Alexander, F. The neurotic character. *International Journal of Psychoanalysis*, 1930, 11, 292.

Berlit, B. Erblichkeitsuntersuchungen bei Psychopathen. *Zeitschrift für die Gesamte Neurologie und Psychiatrie*, 1931, 134, 382.

Bowlby, J. *Maternal care and mental health*. WHO Monograph Series No. 2. Geneva: WHO, 1951.

Clarke, A. D. B. Problems in assessing the later effects of early experience. In E. Miller (Ed.), *Foundations of child psychiatry*. Oxford: Pergamon, 1968.

Court Brown, W. M. Males with an XYY sex chromosome complement. *Journal of Medical Genetics*, 1968, 5, 341.

Craft, M. *Psychopathic disorders*. Oxford: Pergamon, 1968.

Curran, D., & Mallinson, P. Psychopathic personality. *Journal of Mental Science*, 1944, 90, 266.

Greenacre, P. Conscience in the psychopath. *American Journal of Orthopsychiatry*, 1945, 15, 295.

Henderson, D. K. *Psychopathic states*. New York: Norton, 1939.

Heston, L. L. Psychiatric disorders in foster-home–reared children of schizophrenic mothers. *British Journal of Psychiatry*, 1966, 112, 819.

Kahn, E. *Psychopathic personalities*. New Haven: Yale University Press, 1931.

Karpman, B. The myth of the psychopathic personality. *American Journal of Psychiatry*, 1947, 104, 523.

Kety, S. S., Rosenthal, D., Wender, P. H., Schulsinger, F. The types and prevalence of mental illness in the biological and adoptive families of adopted schizophrenics. In D. Rosenthal & S. S. Kety (Eds.), *The transmission of schizophrenia*. Oxford: Pergamon, 1968.

Koch, J. L. A. *Die psychopathische Minderwertigkeiten*. Ravensburg: Maier, 1891.

Kraepelin, E. *Psychiatrie*. (8th ed.) Vol. 4. Leipzig: Barth, 1915.

Newkirk, P. R. Psychopathic traits are inheritable. *Diseases of the Nervous System*, 1957, 18, 82.

Nielsen, J., Stürup, G., Tsuboi, T., & Romano, D. Prevalence of the XYY syndrome in an institution of psychologically abnormal criminals. *Acta Psychiatrica Scandinavica*, 1969, 4, 383.

Partridge, G. E. Current conceptions of psychopathic personality. *American Journal of Psychiatry*, 1930, 10, 53.

Pinel, P. *Abhandlung über Geistesverirrungen oder Manie*. Wien, 1801.

Pinneau, S. R. The infantile disorders of hospitalism and anaclitic depression. *Psychological Bulletin*, 1955, 52, 429.

Pritchard, J. D. *Treatise on insanity*. London: Sherwood, Gilbert, & Piper, 1935.

Reiter, H. Auswirkung von Anlage und Milieu, Untersucht an Adoptierten Unohelicho Geborenen. *Klinische Wochenschrift*, 1930, 9, 2358.
Riedel, H. Zur empirischen Erbprognose der Psychopathie. *Zeitschrift für die Gesamte Neurologie und Psychiatrie*, 1937, 159, 648.
Schneider, K. *Die psychopathischen Personlichkeiten*. Leipzig: Thieme, 1934.
Spitz, R. A. Hospitalism. *Psychoanalytic Study of the Child*, 1945, 1, 53.
Stumpfl, F. *Die Ursprünge des Verbrechens*. Leipzig: Thieme, 1936.
Svalastoga, K. *Prestige, class and mobility*. Copenhagen: Gyldendal, 1959.

MARC SCHUCKIT
DONALD W. GOODWIN
GEORGE WINOKUR] *The Half-Sibling Approach in a Genetic Study of Alcoholism*

FAMILY history studies have proved useful in suggesting genetic factors in human illness. In psychiatry this method has been of particular use in schizophrenia (Kallman, 1938), manic-depressive illness (Winokur et al., 1969), and alcoholism (Schuckit et al., 1969). The family history method has its limitations. Though it allows one to study people of similar genetic make-up functioning in grossly similar environments, it tells him little of the interaction of similar genetic make-ups with dissimilar environments or different genotypes within similar environments.

This paper presents a method of family investigation that may be used to study people of varying genetic closeness raised in similar as well as dissimilar environments. This is the half-sibling approach, a derivative of a method suggested by Kallman (1953) and by Rüdin (1923), but subsequently neglected. Through this approach, it is possible to study various genotypes in various environments.

Methods. The authors are presently applying the half-sibling method to alcoholism. The population studied represents an eleven-month period of admissions to the alcoholic unit of Malcolm Bliss Mental Health Center, a public hospital, as well as alcoholic admissions for two months to Renard Hospital, a private psychiatric hospital. All but four of the patients reported here were from the public hospital.

Patients admitted to the hospital were screened for the diagnosis of primary alcoholism, that is, alcoholism in the absence of any pre-existing psychiatric disorder. Thus excluded were persons with serious antisocial behavior, hysteria, or drug addiction predating alcohol abuse or those with a clear depressive or schizophrenic illness antedating alcoholism. Alco-

NOTE: This study was supported, in part, by U.S.P.H.S. Grants MH-09247, MH-05804, and MH-05938.

holism was defined as drinking which seriously interfered with health or social adjustment using specific criteria outlined elsewhere (Schuckit et al., 1969).

The study included only those primary alcoholics who had a half-sibling, related to the proband through only one of his biologic parents. All primary alcoholics with half-siblings were then administered a systematic interview recording the history of psychiatric illness in biologic parents, parent surrogates, full siblings, and half-siblings as well as in the biologic parents and parent surrogates of the half-siblings.

One to five selected relatives were given the same interview as the proband to establish validity of the history. The number of people interviewed depended on how reliable the histories thus far obtained were judged to be, as well as upon relatives' availability and willingness to serve as informants.

Results. There were 41 probands, representing about 12 per cent of the public hospital alcoholic unit admissions during the eleven-month period; 36 were male, 5 female. Their average age was 36 years with a range of 22 to 54 years old. Of the 41 probands, 25 were Negroes.

Interviews were completed with 59 relatives. One proband, who gave a clear family history, knew of no living relatives. The relative interviewed was a mother in 24 cases, a father in 5, a brother in 2, a sister in 11, a half-brother in 4, a half-sister in 5, and more distant family members in 8 instances. When informants disagreed upon the presence of illness for any person, the consensus of reports was used.

The incidence of alcoholism reported in family members is shown in Table 1. A high incidence of alcoholism occurred in male biologic relatives, whereas in female biologic relatives this finding was less striking.

The present study focuses on the relative influence of genetic load for alcoholism versus the effect of being reared in an environment with an alcoholic parent figure. First examined was the effect of having an alcoholic biologic parent as a predictor of alcoholism in the half-sibling. This is shown in Table 2. It may be seen that, to a highly significant degree, more alcoholic half-siblings than nonalcoholic half-siblings had alcoholic biologic parents.

The biologic parent shared by proband and half-sibling was usually the mother, seen in 29 probands. The father was the shared biologic parent for 8 probands, and 4 had half-siblings through both biologic mothers and fathers.

Next examined was a gross environmental factor — that is, had the

Table 1. Alcoholism in Families of Probands and Half Siblings

Member of Family	N	Alcoholic
Proband[a]		
Biologic father	41	39%
Biologic mother	41	5
Biologic parental pairs	41	41
Surrogate father	19	0
Surrogate mother	12	8
Full brothers	40	38
Full sisters	37	8
Half-brothers	53	34
Half-sisters	45	11
Half Siblings[b]		
Biologic father	49	16
Biologic father shared with S	12	17
Biologic father different from S	37	16
Biologic mother	45	7
Biologic mother shared with S	33	6
Biologic mother different from S	12	8
Biologic parental pair[c]	49	20
Surrogate father	21	29
Surrogate mother	9	0

[a] $N = 41$.   [b] $N = 98$.

[c] In only one parental pair for half-siblings were both biologic parents alcoholic.

Table 2. Factors in Half-Siblings of Alcoholic Probands

Factor	Alcoholic Half Sibs ($N=23$)	Non-Alcoholic Half Sibs ($N=75$)
Incidence of at least one alcoholic biologic parent for half-sibs	61%	19%[a,b]
Incidence in half-sibs of living with *any* alcoholic parent figure for 6 or more childhood years	30	30
Incidence in half-sibs of living with an alcoholic surrogate parent figure for 6 or more childhood years	0	12[c]
Incidence of broken homes among half-sibs	91	81

[a] Difference significant: $\chi^2 = 16.1410$, $df = 1$, $p < .0005$, using Yates correction for continuity.

[b] Only one of these 14 half-sibs never lived with his biologic alcoholic parent. He, however, was raised by an alcoholic surrogate parent.

[c] The alcoholic parent figure was a surrogate mother for 1 and a surrogate father for 8.

half-sibling lived with an alcoholic parent figure for six years or more? Parent figure here refers to the adult with whom he resided as a child, whether his biologic parent or a parent surrogate. Alcoholic half-siblings lived with an alcoholic parent figure no more frequently than did nonalcoholic half-siblings. This finding was unchanged when we considered those living with an alcoholic parent figure during adolescence (age 13 and over). Alcoholic and nonalcoholic half-siblings experienced broken homes to an equal extent.

To be certain that these findings could not be attributed to differences in years at risk for alcoholism, those half-siblings over age 35 were examined separately, since they would have lived through most of the age of risk for alcoholism. A biologic parent of alcoholic versus nonalcoholic half-siblings over 35 years old was alcoholic in 70 per cent versus 16 per cent of the cases, respectively. Again there was no difference in incidence of broken homes or development of alcoholism in half-siblings associated with living with an alcoholic parent figure. These results were almost identical with those given in Table 2.

Thus, having an alcoholic biologic parent predicted a high incidence of alcoholism, irrespective of whether the half-sibling was reared by an alcoholic parent figure. In support of this conclusion is the accompanying tabulation, where half-siblings who did have an alcoholic biologic parent were examined. It is apparent that once a half-sibling had an alcoholic biologic parent, living with the parent at any time did not increase his chances of becoming an alcoholic. The differences shown were not significant, and the conclusion that living with a biologic alcoholic parent decreased the risk of being an alcoholic was not proved by the present data. The tabulation also shows that living with an alcoholic parent figure did not increase the rate of alcoholism for those half-siblings without an alcoholic biologic parent.

To determine if there was any critical time of exposure to an alcoholic parent figure in the home, the authors looked at the ages at which the half-siblings lived with an alcoholic parent figure. No predictive pattern appeared, but as yet the numbers are quite small.

	Alcoholic
Half-sibs with alcoholic biologic parent ($N = 29$)	
Alcoholic parent figure ($N = 15$)	40%
No alcoholic parent figure ($N = 14$)	57
Half-sibs with *no* alcoholic biologic parent ($N = 69$)	
Alcoholic parent figure ($N = 14$)	14
No alcoholic parent figure ($N = 55$)	13

Further data analysis was conducted to determine whether the families in which alcoholic probands were reared were especially alcohologenic. Half-siblings and siblings who grew up in the same household as the alcoholic proband were examined. Table 3 reveals that sharing the family household with alcoholic probands was not associated with increased rates of alcoholism. Rates were high only when the half-sibling himself had an alcoholic biologic parent. Although the number of full siblings not raised with the proband was too small for valid comparison, like the half-siblings, those raised apart from the proband had even higher rates of alcoholism than those raised with him. Thus different genotypes — that is full versus half-siblings — sharing the same gross environment revealed alcoholism largely along the lines of their genetic load rather than of their shared environment.

Table 3. Alcoholism in Half- and Full Siblings Brought Up with Proband

Characteristic	Brought Up with S		Not Brought Up with S	
	N	Alcoholic	N	Alcoholic
Half Siblings				
Those with alcoholic biologic parent	7	29%	22	55%
Those with *no* alcoholic biologic parent ..	45	9	24	21
Full Siblings				
Those with alcoholic biologic parent	38	26	2	[0][a]
Those with *no* alcoholic biologic parent ..	31	13	6	[4][a]

[a] These are frequencies rather than percentages because of the small number of full siblings not reared with the proband.

In every evaluation performed which compared environmental experience against having an alcoholic biologic parent, the genetic load for alcoholism appeared the dominant factor. Yet, there remains an apparent discrepancy in the support of a genetic theory of alcoholism which requires explanation. One expects that, given an alcoholic proband, relatives with whom he shares more genetic material (i.e., 50 per cent of genes being shared with full siblings) should have more alcoholism than those with whom he shares less genetic material (i.e., 25 per cent of genes being shared with half-siblings). Yet, as shown in Table 1, half- and full siblings both had about the same incidence of alcoholism (21 versus 23 per cent). The basis for these findings seems to be a relatively low incidence of alcoholism in the full siblings with alcoholic biologic parents. Whereas 14 of the 29 half-siblings with an alcoholic biologic parent (48 per cent) were alcoholic, only 10 of the 40 full siblings with alcoholic biologic parents (25 per cent) were alcoholic.

There is an interesting possible explanation. One might expect that children reared by alcoholic parent figures and thus exposed at close quarters to the destruction caused by alcohol abuse would tend to avoid excessive alcohol intake themselves. The tabulation on page 123 reveals that those half-siblings with alcoholic biologic parents reared by an alcoholic parent figure had less alcoholism than those reared by nonalcoholic parent figures. The same pattern was found for full siblings. Of the 27 full siblings with an alcoholic biologic parent who were reared by an alcoholic parent figure, only 19 per cent themselves became alcoholic, whereas there was a 38 per cent incidence of alcoholism in those 13 full siblings with alcoholic biologic parents who were reared by nonalcoholic parent figures. The presence of an alcoholic parent figure, therefore, was associated with lower risks for alcoholism in both full and half-siblings. And full siblings were a little more often reared by alcoholic parent figures than were half-siblings (38 versus 29 per cent). The higher rate of alcoholism expected on a genetic basis for full siblings as opposed to half-siblings of alcoholics may then have been counterbalanced by the fact that more full siblings were reared with alcoholic parent figures. Perhaps observing the consequences of alcoholism in a parent figure while growing up influenced some of these potential alcoholics to avoid intemperate drinking.

The lower incidence of alcoholism associated with living with an alcoholic parent in those with a genetic load for alcoholism is not statistically significant. However, the finding is so contrary to expectations about the effect of parental models on behavior as to warrant further research in this area.

Another possible explanation for the findings is that the 33 mothers shared by probands and half-siblings may have subtly encouraged alcoholism in their children. Each of these women had produced at least one alcoholic offspring. The mothers were also remarkable in that 58 per cent had children with one alcoholic man, and 3 (9 per cent) had children with 2 different alcoholics. Thus, even when not alcoholic, these mothers evidenced an unusual proclivity for selecting alcoholic mates and may somehow have created an alchologenic environment for their children. One means of resolving the question is to study half-siblings raised by *neither* the biologic father nor mother. The numbers of such individuals in our study are as yet too small to provide an adequate answer.

Discussion. This study involves applying the half-sibling approach to an American alcoholic population. The design circumvents the limitations inherent in a family history study where it is impossible to distinguish the relative importance of heredity and environment. This half-sibling study measures the relative importance of having an alcoholic biologic parent versus living with an alcoholic. Studying the half-siblings of alcoholic probands provides a largely untreated sample with a high risk for alcoholism, thus avoiding the biases found in a treated population.

The investigation started with a population relatively likely to have come from broken homes — that is, the inpatient alcoholic population of a public hospital. The probands were then interviewed to select those who were primary alcoholics and had half-siblings. The probands were questioned in detail regarding their family history, with emphasis on the environment and genetic linkage to first-degree relatives and half-siblings. Relatives also were interviewed, and histories compared. In general, the histories given by the probands were consistent with ancillary reports from interviewed relatives.

In analyzing the data, the most valuable information related to the half-siblings themselves. The population chosen had a high incidence of broken homes, making it possible to study (a) the children of alcoholic biologic parents reared with alcoholic parent figures throughout their childhood; (b) those living with an alcoholic parent figure for only part of their childhood; and (c) those who were never reared with an alcoholic parent figure. In a similar manner, the childhood relationship to alcoholic parent figures of half-siblings born of nonalcoholic biologic parents also could be measured. We could observe the outcome in half-siblings reared with the alcoholic probands and thus sharing an environment that had already been shown to produce an alcoholic. The latter environment was found to have little if any "alcohologenic" effect on children of nonalcoholic parents. Having a biologic alcoholic parent was the strongest predictor of alcoholism in the half-siblings. The presence of a rearing alcoholic parent figure resulted in no increased alcoholism for full or half-siblings but, on the contrary, was associated with lower levels of alcoholism for them.

COMMENTARY

KNUPFER. I think it's encouraging that the elegant methods which have been suggested in the literature for some time are now actually being used.

WIRT. I agree. This is the kind of approach that could be used to study criminality, psychosis, and all kinds of other things rather more cheaply than some of the approaches we are now using.

MYERS. Have you analyzed your data in terms of family size? When you report on half-siblings, for example, do you include all half-sibs, regardless of family size? Thus, if one has five half-siblings and another only one, is your N six half-sibs or two family units?

WINOKUR. I think that it's throwing away data to count family units in which alcoholism is present rather than the number of people alcoholic. If you get enough families at high risk to avoid sampling bias, counting the number of people alcoholic gives you a better estimate of any illness in the family.

KNUPFER. You brought up the fact that in many cases the alcoholic parent of the half-sib was a non-shared parent.

SCHUCKIT. Out of the 29 alcoholic parents, 20 were non-shared parents for the half-siblings. Now we're getting into something that's very hard to follow. The typical family had a nonalcoholic mother who had children with an alcoholic father.

KNUPFER. Can you get at anything like assortive mating?

SCHUCKIT. With such small numbers of Ss, it is difficult to give a definitive answer. We are presently looking at the groups of half-siblings that were reared with neither biologic parent. So far, those half-sibs reared by neither biologic parent but with an alcoholic biologic parent are alcoholic 100 per cent of the time. The N, however, is only three. As we increase the N that's one of the answers we'll be looking for.

WINOKUR. The question of assortive mating is a matter of some interest to us. We have studied assortive mating in 259 alcoholic Ss. There was assortive mating in those Ss, with the alcoholic Ss marrying spouses who were depressed or alcoholic. Further, we did a family history study of the families of the ill spouses and the families of the well spouses of the alcoholic Ss. There was a highly significant increase in the history of illness in the ill spouses' families.

REFERENCES

Kallman, F. J. *The genetics of schizophrenia.* New York: J. J. Augustin, 1938.
———. *Heredity in health and mental disorder.* New York: Norton, 1953.
Rüdin, E. Über Vererbung geistiger Storungen. *Zeitschrift für die Gesamte Neurologie und Psychiatrie*, 1923, 81, 459.
Schuckit, M., Pitts, F. N., Jr., Reich, T., King, L. J., & Winokur, G. Alcoholism I. Two types of alcoholism in women. *Archives of General Psychiatry*, 1969, 20, 301–306.
Winokur, G., Clayton, P., & Reich, T. *Manic depressive illness.* St. Louis: C. V. Mosby, 1969.

REMI J. CADORET | *Family Differences in Illness and Personality in Affective Disorder*

AFFECTIVE disorder is broadly defined as psychiatric illness in which the predominant change is one of mood and where other symptoms (such as delusions) can be understood as arising out of the altered mood state. Manic-depressive illness, psychotic depression, and depressive reaction are some of the diagnostic names associated with affective disorders. Recent work with longitudinal and family studies has indicated that affective disorder can be subdivided into two types: bipolar affective illness, in which individuals have both manic and depressive mood states, and unipolar affective illness, wherein only the depressive mood state occurs. This dichotomy of affective disorders has proven to be a fruitful one for finding clinical differences between the two types of patients (in addition to the obvious qualitative difference of presence or absence of mania). For example, the age of onset of bipolar illness is generally earlier than for unipolar (Dorzab, Baker, Winokur, & Cadoret, 1970; Kinkelin, 1954; Perris, 1966; Weinberg & Lobstein, 1936). Bipolar illness occurs in more frequent episodes, but the length of these episodes is generally shorter than those of the unipolars (Angst, 1966; Kinkelin, 1954; Leonhard, 1966; Perris, 1968). More recently, Reich and Winokur (1970) reported that bipolar females had higher postpartum rates for illness, in contrast to Baker et al. (1970), who found no evidence for increased rate of illness during the postpartum period. Dunner et al. (1970) recently found that bipolar families had a higher incidence of suicide than unipolar. In all fairness, however, it must be added that some series have not reported a difference in suicide in relatives (Angst, 1966; Perris, 1966; Weinberg & Lobstein, 1936), whereas others have (Leonhard et al., 1962; von Trostorff, 1968).

NOTE: This work was supported, in part, by U.S.P.H.S. Grants MH-05804, MH-13002, and MH-09247.

A number of studies have demonstrated that the incidence of psychoses is higher in relatives of bipolar than of unipolar patients (Asano, 1967; Dorzab, Baker, Cadoret, & Winokur, 1970a; Kinkelin, 1954; Leonhard, 1966; Neele, 1949). The commonest psychiatric illness in relatives of affectively ill probands is affective disorder (Angst, 1966; Perris, 1966; Winokur & Pitts, 1965). A higher rate of disorder in relatives of bipolar patients suggests either that mania is more easily detectable than depression or that bipolar and unipolar affective disorders may be two distinct illnesses with different patterns of inheritance. This paper will be concerned with differences in the sex patterning of affective disease in families of affective disorder patients when a bipolar member is or is not identified. It will also report on personality and temperament differences in these family members. If the patterning by sex and the personality and temperament types are associated with the bipolar-unipolar distinction, this will serve as additional evidence that the bipolar-unipolar dichotomy is a meaningful one. I shall investigate not only overall rates of affective disorder in relatives but also whether the sex distributions among first-degree relatives (parents, siblings, and children) are consistent with the hypothesis that there are two separate illnesses with distinct types of heritability. The data to be analyzed come from a number of series in which individual cases and families were reported in sufficient detail to permit classification of families as unipolar or bipolar. Details of selection of the series and their analysis can be found in Cadoret et al. (1970). The identification of families as bipolar or unipolar differed slightly among the studies included (Hoffmann, 1929; Majer, 1941; Stenstedt, 1952, 1959; Winokur & Clayton, 1967), but the differences in definition are trivial.

Division of the data according to the sex of the patient and the sex of the first-degree relatives showed marked contrasts in the patterns of occurrence of affective disorder between unipolar and bipolar families. The most marked difference was found in the patients' children (Table 1). Morbid risk for affective disorder (the probability of a relative's becoming ill) is computed by the abridged Weinberg method as described in Cadoret et al. (1970). Sons of unipolar mothers have a significantly lower risk than daughters in contrast with children of bipolar mothers, whose sons and daughters share equal risks. Sons and daughters of male probands share equal risks, whether the father is unipolar or bipolar.

Among siblings (Table 1), sisters of female probands have a greater risk than brothers in both unipolar and bipolar families, whereas sisters of male probands have risks equal to brothers in both unipolar and bi-

Life History Research in Psychopathology

Table 1. Morbid Risks for Affective Disorders in Relatives of *S*s in Unipolar and Bipolar Families[a]

	Male *S*s		Female *S*s	
Relative	Unipolar Family	Bipolar Family	Unipolar Family	Bipolar Family
Son				
Ill	2	3	8	11
Number at risk	40	20	91	48
Morbid risk	5.9	15.0	8.8	22.9
Daughter				
Ill	3	2	24	9
Number at risk	46	14	94	38
Morbid risk	6.6	14.8	25.5	23.7
Brother				
Ill	36	12	44	4
Number at risk	228	42	595	60
Morbid risk	15.8	28.6	7.4	6.7
Sister				
Ill	27	8	82	16
Number at risk	231	45	624	69
Morbid risk	11.7	18.0	13.1	23.4
Father				
Ill	23	2	39	9
Number at risk	185	30	407	53
Morbid risk	12.4	6.8	9.6	17.1
Mother				
Ill	22	9	51	12
Number at risk	197	34	434	52
Morbid risk	11.2	26.5	11.8	23.3

[a] Data from Hoffmann (1921), Majer (1941), Stenstedt (1952, 1959), and Winokur & Clayton (1967).

polar families. Thus, among siblings, increased risks in sisters are associated with the sex of the proband but no contrasting pattern is found between unipolar and bipolar families.

In morbid risks for parents (Table 1), another significant unipolar-bipolar difference emerges: mothers of bipolar males have a higher risk of illness than fathers. No significant differences are found by sex of parent of unipolar male or female probands or bipolar females, although mothers of ill daughters are slightly more frequently ill than fathers. Thus, the parents and children, but not the siblings, of affectively ill patients show different patterns of illness in unipolar and in bipolar families.

One possible explanation of the differences found in the sex patterning of illness of the relatives of bipolar and unipolar probands is that there are two kinds of transmission of illness. If one uses a genetic model of inheritance, then the bipolar pattern is more consistent with an X- or sex-chromosome linked dominant inheritance than is the unipolar pattern. (A dominant type is argued by the approximately equal rates for probands' parents and children.) If an X-linked, dominant gene were involved, then the following consequences should hold: (a) An ill mother should have an equal number of ill sons and daughters. This is the case for the bipolar families, but *not* for the unipolar. (b) An ill father will have ill daughters but should not have ill sons. This is not supported, since male patients have as many ill sons as daughters. However, the bipolar male probands have many more ill mothers than fathers, consistent with the sex-linked hypothesis. This difference is not found in the unipolar group. The inconsistent findings of two cases of father-son bipolar illness transmission in the bottom of Table 1 and three cases in the top should disprove an X-linked dominant hypothesis except for the possibility that the mother's (the proband's wife) side of the family (despite her own apparent health) might contain a genetic factor for the illness. This interpretation is strengthened by the fact that in one of these families where father-son transmission occurred (the Majer series) one of the "well" mother's sibs was said to be "schizophrenic." (c) Ill males should have equal numbers of ill brothers and sisters (since their inheritance would be through the mother, who can produce ill siblings of both sexes); ill females should have more ill sisters than ill brothers (since the female can inherit from either father or mother, but her brothers only from the mother). The middle of Table 1 shows that the bipolar results are consistent with this. However, the pattern for siblings of unipolar probands is also consistent with this hypothesis.

Thus, the overall findings show that the *pattern* of inheritance for bipolar families is compatible — with the exception noted in (b) above — with an X-linked dominant inheritance. The inheritance for unipolar families does not fit the pattern, since only siblings show a pattern consistent with this hypothesis. The probability of an X-linked dominant inheritance for bipolar families is further supported by the finding of significant association of red-green color blindness, a proved X-linked condition, with bipolar illness in two families (Reich et al., 1969), and the significant association reported by Tanna and Winokur (1968) between the X_g serum protein, also controlled by a gene on the X-chromosome, in several bipolar families. Alongside this evidence for association of bipolar illness with the X-chromosome must be placed evidence from at least two series of bipolar cases (Dunner et al., 1970; Perris, 1968) reporting many more cases of father-son transmission of illness. However, in these cases it is possible that a diathesis for illness could have been present on the mother's side as well.

Aside from the linkage studies of the color blindness and the X_g protein in bipolar illness, there is no conclusive evidence of a genetic factor. The data about transmission of unipolar illness shows that it is decidedly different from bipolar. To what extent genetic and environmental factors contribute to this different pattern remains for future studies to clarify. There are a few points, however, regarding genetic and environmental effects to be made from these data. The overall tendency for more females to be ill in unipolar disorder, an effect most marked in children of female probands suggests that some process of learning or identification with a same-sexed individual might be operating. But if this were the case, then why do not ill bipolar mothers show a similar excess of ill daughters? Clearly, other factors are at work. For example, the learning situation might be different because of personality differences between the bipolar and the unipolar mothers, so that study of the personality types found in affective disorder families would be very relevant. That personality types differ in these two kinds of families has been reported by Leonhard et al. (1962), who investigated first-degree relatives of unipolar and bipolar probands.

Since Leonhard's data are not readily available in the psychiatric literature in English, I have summarized them in Table 2. More relatives with a hypomanic personality are found in bipolar families than unipolar; in contrast, more subdepressives are found in unipolar families. No significant difference is found for the cyclothymic temperament, although the trend is for more bipolar relatives to have this characteristic. One of the difficulties with the Leonhard study is the probable absence of a double-blind method for diagnosing family members (no such precaution is mentioned). However, it has been possible to find data on personality types in children of manic-depressive patients by Hoffmann (1921) — data collected years before the unipolar-bipolar distinction was developed. In these data, a division of families into bipolar and unipolar was possible on the basis of information given about probands and ill relatives. The results of this new division of the data are shown in the bottom of Table 2. As in the Leonhard data, bipolar probands appear to have a higher number of children with a hypomanic personality. The depressive temperament also tends to be associated with unipolar illness in the parent, but this comparison fails to reach statistical significance. On the other hand, the cyclothymic personality shows a significant association with unipolar illness. This

Table 2. Temperament in Relatives of Unipolar and Bipolar Ss[a]

Relative	N	Hypomanic		Subdepressive		Cyclothymic		Total	
		N	%	N	%	N	%	N	%
Bipolar illness in S									
Siblings	94	16	17	5	5.3	14	15	35	37
Parents	80	21	26	6	7.5	12	15	39	49
Total	174	37	21	11	6.3	26	15	74	43
Children	97	15	15	2	2.1	3	3.1	20	21
Unipolar illness in S									
Siblings	143	13	9.1	19	13	11	7.7	43	30
Parents	120	17	14	27	23	13	10	57	48
Total	263	30	11	46	17	24	9.2	100	38
Children	73	2	2.7	6	8.2	10	14	18	25
χ^2 difference (unipolar vs. bipolar)									
Total siblings and parents		7.10**		10.55***		2.95		0.71	
Children		6.15*		2.28		5.22*		0.19	

[a] Data on parents and siblings from Leonhard et al. (1962); data on children from Hoffmann (1921).
* $p<.025$.   ** $p<.01$.   *** $p<.005$.

is a different pattern than shown by the Leonhard data. An adequate explanation of this discrepancy is not immediately evident.

The data from the Hoffmann series partly support the Leonhard findings, and together both studies strongly suggest that unipolar and bipolar families differ in the incidence of personality or temperament types. This has important implications for epidemiologic studies. It is possible that the background of "well" relatives with certain types of behavior (such as hypomanic temperament) could furnish a child with a model to pattern himself or herself after, so that the type of illness could represent learned behavior. The present data do not permit us to distinguish what the importance of this possible environmental factor as compared with a genetic factor, to say nothing of the interaction of the two. The relevant direction of further studies would seem to be to determine the relative contribution of genetic and environmental influences to personality and illness. In such studies, the use of homogeneous groups of patients may lead sooner to the solution of these complex epidemiologic questions.

COMMENTARY

KLEIN. The argued X-linked heredity of bipolars implies that if you have a male proband, he shouldn't have any male children with the illness.

CADORET. Yes, that's correct.

KLEIN. I believe that the top of Table 1 showed that the incidence of male and female children was the same.

CADORET. This number (three ill male children) came from the Hoffmann series. The other series contained in that table was consistent with an X-linked hypothesis in that no sons were ill. The particular family which is inconsistent with an X-linked hypothesis occurred in the Majer series. The family has a mother who is described as schizoid and who had, I believe, a sister who was hospitalized with chronic schizophrenia. Thus, it's possible that some diathesis for illness came from the maternal side, which could explain this inconsistency.

KLEIN. One other point. We were also doing some work with depressive patients. One thing that we had some difficulty in doing was separating patients with bipolarity from periodic unipolar depressives — because frequently if you ask patients about hypomanic episodes they deny them. But we've seen, after treatment with antidepressants, that some go out of their depression into a frankly hypomanic state; if you ask them if they've ever behaved like this before, they say, "Oh, is that what you meant?" People don't consider hypomania pathological; they consider this normal for them.

CADORET. This would mean that a unipolar group could be "contaminated" with bipolars, but with luck, contamination would not occur frequently. As an example, in the present unipolar depression study we have carried out in St. Louis involving 100 probands, only one patient developed hypomania following treatment and was accordingly dropped from the study. This would argue for a low rate of contamination.

SCHULSINGER. I would like to ask about your patients with depressions but without manic episodes. There are so many of them. My partner and colleague, Dr. Welner, has analyzed the concept of neurotic depressions without real depressive delusions. They can appear several times in the same person, but if we go back and do a retrospective analysis of the hospital records, they most often turn out to be character disorder patients with depressive spells.

CADORET. Well, separation of unipolars from bipolars is difficult. Perris solves it by accepting as unipolar only those patients who have three or more discrete episodes of depression. He claims that in this way he has excluded most of the bipolar patients. He feels that only about 10 per cent of bipolar patients would slip through this screening. I don't know how carefully he screens for moderate hypomanic episodes, however, and this is a problem because, as Dr. Klein mentioned, people often don't recognize hypomanic episodes, especially the patient himself. The unipolar sample in our present study includes people who have only a history of depression and for whom we can get no history of hypomania from either the patient or a relative.

SCHULSINGER. Does that mean that you include any depression without manic episode?

CADORET. Yes. In the study that we're doing now there are 11 characteristics of depression. If an *S* has 7 out of 11 of these characteristics of depression, he would be accepted for this study. The characteristics include such things as slow thinking, motor retardation, change of affect to depressed mood, the vegetative symptoms such as appetite changes, sleep disturbance, and decrease in libido.

ROBINS. I think you may have left out something that Dr. Schulsinger was talking about . . . that these have to be primary affective disorders. If they have any other psychiatric disorders they're eliminated.

REFERENCES

Angst, J. Zur Ätiologie und Nosologie endogener depressiver Psychosen. *Monographien aus dem Gesamtgebiete der Neurologie und Psychiatrie*, No. 112. Berlin: Springer Verlag, 1966.

Asano, N. Study of manic-depressive psychosis. In H. Mitsuda (Ed.), *Clinical genetics in psychiatry*. Kyoto: Bunko-sha, 1967.

Baker, M., Dorzab, J., Winokur, G., & Cadoret, R. J. Depressive disease: The effect of the postpartum state. Unpublished MS., 1970.

Cadoret, R. J., Winokur, G., & Clayton, P. Family history studies: VI. Manic-depressive disease versus depressive disease. *British Journal of Psychiatry*, 1970, 116, 625–635.

Dorzab, J., Baker, M., Cadoret, R. J., & Winokur, G. Depressive disease: Familial psychiatric illness. Paper presented at the meeting of the American Psychiatric Association, San Francisco, May 1970. *American Journal of Psychiatry*, 1971, 127, 1128–1133.

Dorzab, J., Baker, M., Winokur, G., & Cadoret, R. J. Depressive disease: Clinical course. Unpublished MS., 1970.

Dunner, D., Gershon, E., & Goodwin, F. Heritable factors in the severity of affective illness. Paper presented at the meeting of the American Psychiatric Association, San Francisco, May 1970.

Hoffmann, H. Die Nachkommenschaft bei endogenen Psychosen. In E. Rudin (Ed.), *Studien über Vererbung und Entstehung Geistiger Störungen*. Berlin, 1921.

Kinkelin, M. Verlauf und Prognose des Manisch-depressiven Irreseins. *Schweizer Archiv für Neurologie, Neurochirurgie und Psychiatrie*, 1954, 73, 100–146.

Leonhard, K. *Aufteilung der endogenen Psychosen*. Berlin: Akademie Verlag, 1966.

———, Korff, I., & Schulz, H. Die Temperamente in der Familian der monopolaren und bipolaren phasischen Psychosen. *Psychiatria et Neurologia*, 1962, 143, 416–434.

Majer, O. Beitrag zur Erbbiologie involutwer, klimakterischer und reaktwer Depressionen. *Zeitschrift für die Gesamte Neurologie und Psychiatrie*, 1941, 172, 737–790.

Neele, E. *Die phasischen Psychosen nach ihrem Erscheinungs und Erbbild*. Leipzig: Johann Ambrosius Barth Verlag, 1949.

Perris, C. A study of bipolar (manic-depressive) and unipolar recurrent depressive psychoses. *Acta Psychiatrica Scandinavica*, 1966, Suppl. 194, 1–188.

———. Genetic transmission of depressive psychosis. *Acta Psychiatrica Scandinavica*, 1968, Suppl. 203, 45–52.

Reich, T., Clayton, P., & Winokur, G. Family history studies: V. The genetics of mania. *American Journal of Psychiatry*, 1969, 125, 1358–1369.

Reich, T., & Winokur, G. Post partum psychoses in patients with manic depressive disease. *Journal of Nervous and Mental Disease*, 1970, 151, 60–68.

Stenstedt, A. A study in manic-depressive psychosis. *Acta Psychiatrica et Neurologica Scandinavica*, 1952, Suppl. 79.

——. Involutional melancholia. *Acta Psychiatrica et Neurologica Scandinavica*, 1959, Suppl. 127.

Tanna, V. L., & Winokur, G. A study of association and linkage of ABO blood types and primary affective disorder. *British Journal of Psychiatry*, 1968, 114, 1175–1181.

von Trostorff, S. Über die hereditäre Belastung bie den bipolaren und monopolaren phasischen Psychosen. *Schweizer Archiv für Neurologie, Neurochirurgie und Psychiatrie*, 1968, 102, 235–243.

Weinberg, I., & Lobstein, J. Beitrag zur Vererbung des Manisch-depressiven Irreseins. *Psychiatrische en Neurologische Bladen*, 1936, 1, 339–370.

Winokur, G., & Clayton, P. Family history studies: I. Two types of affective disorders separated according to genetic and clinical factors. In J. Wortis (Ed.), *Recent advances in biological psychiatry*. Vol. 9. New York: Plenum, 1967.

Winokur, G., & Pitts, F. N., Jr. Affective disorder: VI. A family history study of prevalences, sex differences and possible genetic factors. *Journal of Psychiatric Research*, 1965, 3, 113–123.

LEE N. ROBINS] *An Actuarial Evaluation of the Causes and Consequences of Deviant Behavior in Young Black Men*

THE ATTRIBUTION of cause is one of the most important and most perplexing problems facing the researcher in life histories. Using either a longitudinal design, in which life events are sampled at two or more points in time, or a retrospective design, in which subjects review their life histories up to the time of interview, the researcher is faced with the problem of interpreting the sequence of events presented. He wants to know why one event regularly follows another. Are both events consequences of some earlier experiences, in which case their regularly falling in a particular order may be due only to a higher age requirement for the second event than for the first (as being court-martialed must necessarily occur later than being held back in first grade)? Or does the occurrence of the earlier event to some degree increase the probability that the subject will experience the second — that is, is it a "cause" of the second? In some instances the causal connection between two events is clear: being convicted of a crime is a necessary but not a sufficient condition for experiencing parole supervision. But in many instances an event which is neither necessary nor sufficient may contribute to a later event, since there may be more than one path to the second event. Thus, having been convicted of a crime may lead to unemployment (as well as to parole), since some employers refuse to hire ex-convicts, but certainly unemployment may occur without a prior conviction.

When employers state that they are reluctant to hire ex-convicts, it is not difficult to decide that unemployment regularly following conviction implies a causal connection between the first event and the second, but

NOTE: This paper was prepared with the assistance of Susan M. Le Vine and Marsha Richardson. The research reported here was partly financed by research grants MH-09247, MH-18864, and MH-36598.

often there is no such statement to guide our interpretation. It is known, for example, that the less educated have more drinking problems than the better educated (Cahalan, 1970), but we do not know whether this should be interpreted to mean that low education is a direct cause of drinking problems, perhaps via the frustrations attendant on restricted job opportunities, or whether persons with low frustration tolerance both drop out of school and drink excessively. Whereas the first interpretation implicates dropping out of school as a cause of alcoholism, the second interpretation does not. According to the second interpretation, the order of events would depend only on the fact that schooling occurs early in life and drinking problems appear only after some years of exposure to heavy alcohol intake. Both interpretations can be simultaneously correct, of course: even if low education did cause alcohol problems, the relationship might be further intensified by the effect of personality factors that increase risks of both school termination and excessive drinking.

Our problem, therefore, is not to choose between these alternative interpretations, but rather to find out whether the causal interpretation is reasonable by seeing whether earlier experiences can *fully* explain both events without invoking a causal relationship.

The ability to draw causal inferences has obvious utility in planning intervention. If the alcoholism of the school dropout were entirely a matter of pre-existing personality factors, remediation would lie in modifying his character, not in making schools attractive or education mandatory. Conversely, if dropping out itself were an important contributing factor to alcoholism, one would recommend in-school counseling, work-study programs, and other ways of encouraging school attendance.

The need for causal analysis is one of the chief motivations behind the choice of long-term follow-up designs over cross-sectional study designs. Through follow-up studies, it is possible to select a sample more homogeneous with respect to early life history factors than would be obtained in a cross-sectional study, so that some of the factors that might simultaneously account for both events in a sequence are ruled out. In addition, the sample can be chosen so that factors that do vary within the sample at initial evaluation are simultaneously controlled and thus do not confound one another as causes of later events. Follow-up studies also allow ascertaining the temporal order between some events. Events experienced before the initial evaluation clearly predate events first reportable at time of follow-up. Furthermore, follow-up studies allow making uniform the length of exposure to risk of an outcome. If the whole sample is selected as of the same date and if, no matter how long the follow-up interval, the re-examination is carried out over a brief period, all subjects will have had an approximately equal period at risk of experiencing events they had not yet experienced at initial evaluation. (The period at risk becomes synonymous with the follow-up interval, which is thus kept constant for all subjects.) It is this set of features that makes the follow-up study a particularly attractive method for doing research into the causal meaning of sequences of life events.

In planning our own research into childhood variables explaining the adult success of young black men, we attempted to exploit these assets of the follow-up design. From elementary school records, we chose a sample homogeneous with respect to a number of variables: sex (all male), race (all black), place of birth (all born in St. Louis), schools attended (all attended St. Louis public schools for six years or more), and adult residence (all lived in St. Louis at some time between 1959 and 1964, and were thus exposed to the same job market and police practices). The range of ages and IQ's was restricted by choosing subjects born between 1930 and 1934 with IQ scores of 85 or higher. The childhood factors we wanted to explore as predictors of adult success were simultaneously controlled with respect to one another (more fully described in Robins, Murphy, & Breckenridge, 1968) by selecting the sample so that father's presence in the home (as indicated by the name of the guardian on the elementary school record), school performance (as indicated by attendance records and repetition of grades), and socioeconomic status (as indicated by the guardian's occupation) were all uncorrelated. Further, the sample was selected so that these variables were uncorrelated with age and IQ. The factors allowed to vary were all known to precede the events they might predict since they were ascertained from school records made before any of the outcomes in which we were interested had occurred. Finally, the period at risk of the outcomes was held constant for the whole sample by obtaining all records through the same date (December 31, 1964) and confining interviewing to a 15-month period. Interviews with 223 men (95 per cent of the target sample) were obtained between June 1965 and September 1966.

This sample design is useful when we wish to argue that events occurring before leaving elementary school may cause later events. But the design is not very helpful in answering whether events occurring after leaving elementary school cause still later events. Events such as high school dropout, conviction, and alcohol problems all occurred during the follow-up interval (i.e., between ages 14 and 33). These events may in part be caused by early childhood experience, but they may also themselves form a causal chain. None of the controls instituted at initial sample selection helps us to decide whether they do so. With respect to causal relations among post–elementary school events, we are in exactly the same position as the researcher using a cross-sectional design and obtaining all his information retrospectively. Like him, we find that many of the life events during the follow-up interval are statistically associated, but the interpretation of these associations is ambiguous.

INFERRING CAUSAL DIRECTION AMONG FIVE LIFE EVENTS

The present paper discusses five such associated events occurring during the follow-up interval in our sample of young black men: dropout, alcohol problems, jail, heroin use, and divorce. *Dropout* refers to leaving school before high school graduation for one quarter or more (with or without subsequent return and graduation). The age of first dropout was obtained by interview. An *alcohol problem* refers to any complaint about excessive drinking by a family member, a health problem owing to alcohol, an arrest because of drunkenness, or job problems attributable to drinking. Neither intake of large amounts of alcohol nor a personal concern about drinking too much qualified as a problem. This information was obtained by interview. *Jail* refers to incarceration in any reformatory, city jail, workhouse, or penitentiary. Information was obtained by reviewing juvenile court, police, prison, and parole records. Incarceration in military stockades was not included. *Heroin use* refers to the use of opiates (unless prescribed by a physician) one or more times. Again information was obtained by interview. *Divorce* refers both to formal divorce and to permanent separation not yet legalized. Separation from a woman with whom a subject was living but to whom he was not legally married was not counted. Associations reported between divorce and other variables are based on the ever-married portion of the sample only (i.e., excluding bachelors). Information about divorce came from the interview.

Statistical Association. The first requirement for causal inference is statistical association. Associations among these five variables are presented in Table 1. Each variable was statistically significantly associated with each of the others. Seven of the ten associations were very strong, and only one was weak — dropout versus divorce. (The contingency coefficient for fourfold contingency tables has an upper limit of .70. The minimum value statistically significant for a sample of 223 is .13.) Clear-

Table 1. Contingency Coefficients among Five Deviant Outcomes

Outcome	Dropout	Alcohol Problems	Jail	Heroin Use	Divorce
Dropout	...	.35*	.22*	.22	.15
Alcohol problems		...	.24*	.23*	.18
Jail			...	.45*	.30*
Heroin use				...	.25*

* $p<.001$.

ly, these five outcomes tend to occur together in the life histories of young black urban males. Such findings confirm previous observations by criminologists that low educational achievement and alcohol problems typify convicts (Guze, Goodwin, & Crane, 1969; Reckless, 1955). Studies of heroin addicts have similarly noted that their histories frequently include both heavy drinking and criminality (O'Donnell, 1969). But these statistical associations do not necessarily imply causation, nor do they tell us in what direction causality flows, if it exists.

Age at Onset. Both cross-sectional and follow-up studies can arrive at some intimation about the *direction* of causality, assuming causality exists, by ascertaining age at first occurrence of each event. The earlier in the life history an event typically occurs, the more likely it is to have preceded another event, and thus the greater the chance that it is the cause rather than the effect of other events with which it is correlated. A rough estimate of the direction of influence can be achieved simply by calculating median age of first occurrence, as we have in the accompanying tabulation. Age of first occurrence was obtained by asking, "How old were

	f	%	Median Age of Onset
Dropout	109	49	16
Heroin	30	14	19
Jail	48	22	22
Alcohol problem	105	47	23
Divorce	97	43	25

you the first time you . . .," for events reported in interview and by noting the age at first incarceration in prison and police records. In this sample, dropout was typically the earliest of the five outcomes, divorce the latest. The ranking by median age at onset suggests that when dropout is one of a pair of associated variables it is likely to precede the second, and therefore to be a potential cause, whereas divorce is likely to follow and thus to be a potential effect. But the direction of causality inferred from age of onset in the total sample may be incorrect, since events may occur in a different order within the subset who actually experience both events.

Order of Occurrence. In Table 2, the order of events is examined for all persons who experienced both of a pair of events. Persons who first experienced both events at the same age are omitted, since for them we do not know the order of onset. For this reason, the columns "A first" and "B first" do not add up to 100 per cent.

As we had been led to expect from the tabulation above, dropout tends to occur before each of the other four events, when both occur. However, divorce does not always follow each of the other events. In fact, alcohol problems, divorce, and jail seem to occur in virtually random order. Knowing the median age of onset for these events in the total sample was no help in predicting which of these events was more likely to be cause and which was more likely to be the effect in the subsample in which both occur. Nor does knowing that two events occur in virtually random order answer the question about the direction of causality between them. The finding of random order among alcohol problems, divorce, and jail would be compatible with three interpretations concerning their mutual causality: (a) the relationships may be spurious, both events being the consequence of some third event that precedes them both; (b) there may be a reciprocal causal relationship, in which the occurrence of either event makes the other more probable; or (c) there may be a causal relationship in one direction and a spurious relationship in the other.

AN ACTUARIAL APPROACH TO CAUSALITY

The remainder of this paper will present a way of using our knowledge about the age of onset of various outcomes which seems to solve

Table 2. Order of Occurrence between Two Outcomes: From Clear Temporal Precedence to Random Order

Both Outcomes Occurred	N	A First	B First	Difference
A, dropout; B, divorce..........	52	98%	2%	96%
A, dropout; B, heroin use........	23	96	0	96
A, dropout; B, alcohol problems...	67	91	4	87
A, dropout; B, jail...............	34	79	15	64
A, heroin use; B, divorce........	19	79	16	63
A, heroin use; B, jail............	22	77	14	63
A, heroin use; B, alcohol problems	22	64	14	50
A, alcohol problems; B, divorce....	48	60	29	31
A, divorce; B, jail...............	30	50	40	10
A, alcohol problems; B, jail.......	32	53	44	9

some of the ambiguities concerning causal direction and possible spuriousness of relationships among life history events. Like the use of median age of onset in the tabulation on page 141 and the use of order of occurrence between events affecting the same persons in Table 2, it is a method equally appropriate to follow-up and cross-sectional data. Its advantages over the method used in Table 2 are two: First, it not only considers zero-order correlation and sequence of occurrence as we have already done, it also takes into account the fact that persons who experience a first event are at risk of the second event for less time and during a different age span than persons who do not experience the first event. Second, it investigates possible spuriousness of the association by holding constant other variables that predict both the life events between which we posit a causal relationship.

The method is based on the actuarial technique for calculating risks from a truncated combined-risk life table. The procedure involves three steps: First, the actuarial technique is used to show that when Event A occurs, Event B subsequently occurs significantly more frequently than among persons who have not experienced Event A, once the reduced period at risk of experiencing Event B among persons experiencing Event A is compensated for. Second, the actuarial technique is used to identify other variables preceding both Events A and B which might make spurious the association between them discovered in the first step. Third, each person who experienced Event A while still at risk of Event B is matched on all significant precursors with a person who did *not* experience Event A during this period, and their outcomes compared. If the rate of Event B outcomes among the members of the matched pairs who experienced Event A is still significantly higher than the rate among those without Event A, the investigation of Event A as a cause of Event B has passed the tests for temporal precedence, for age adjustment of the risk period, and for spuriousness. When these three tests have been passed, we can plausibly consider that Event A *may* be a cause of Event B, and then plan experiments to test the causal relationship by manipulating rates of the Event A and observing whether the expected change in rates of Event B then occurs.

Computing Actuarial Rates. Before the report of findings with respect to the five life events our sample experienced, a brief description of the calculations involved in the actuarial method may be useful. The actuarial method assigns each member of the sample to one of three possible states during each year of his life. State 1 is the state of being at risk of

Table 3. Actuarial Method for Calculating Age-Adjusted Outcome Rates

Age	A No Cause, Still at Risk	B Outcomes Among A	C Age-Adjusted Outcome Rate for A[a]	D With Cause, Still at Risk	E Outcomes Among D	F Ever at Risk, for D
1........	223	0	$0.0 = 0\ (0/223)$	0	0	0
15.......	223	3	$0.0 = 0\ (3/223)$	0	0	0
16.......	$220 = 223 - 3$	5	$0.0 = 0\ (5/220)$	0	0	0
17.......	$203 = 220 - 5 - 12$	3	$0.0 = 0\ (3/203)$	0	0	0
18.......	$196 = 203 - 3 - 4$	8	$0.4898 = 12\ (8/196)$	12	6	12
19.......	$185 = 196 - 8 - 3$	20	$1.0811 = 10\ (20/185)$	$10 = 4 + 12 - 6$	3	4
Total ...			$\overline{1.5709}$[b]		$\overline{9}$[c]	$\overline{16}$

[a] $D(B/A)$.   [b] $1.5709/16 = 9.81$ per cent.   [c] $9/16 = 56$ per cent.

both the hypothetical cause (Event A) and the hypothetical effect (Event B). State 2 is the state of being at risk only of Event B, having already experienced Event A. State 3 is the state of being at no risk of Event B, either because Event B has already occurred, because some other event precluding the experience of Event B has occurred (as graduation from high school precludes dropping out), or because observation has ended (i.e., the last interview or record check has occurred or the subject has died).

Table 3 provides an abbreviated illustration of how the computer program assigns individuals to States 1, 2, and 3 and adjusts the age span at risk of Event B for persons without the experience of Event A to the age span at risk of Event B for persons who do experience Event A. Column A lists the number of persons in State 1 at the beginning of each year of age. Note that all 223 interviewed subjects begin in State 1. All remain in State 1 until age 15, when 3 persons experience Event B (see Column B) and are removed to State 3 (i.e., removed from Column A the following year). At age 17 the first 12 persons in State 1 experience Event A and therefore leave State 1 at age 17 to enter State 2 (Column D) at age 18. At age 18, 6 persons in State 2 experienced Event B (Column E) and therefore exited from State 2 (Column D) to State 3 the following year. Because Table 3 is abridged, it shows no exits from States 1 and 2 into State 3 the year following interview or death. Such exits begin in our sample at age 31. (The oldest exits at age 37.)

Column C shows how the period at risk of Event B is adjusted for the group not experiencing Event A to the risk period for the group experiencing Event A. The proportion in State 1 (at risk of B, without having experienced A) who experience Event B at a given age is multiplied by the proportion of those ever in State 2 (ever at risk of B after having experienced A) at risk of Event B at the same age. This adjustment compensates for the fact that persons enter State 1 at birth, but enter State 2 only after some of the period of risk of Event B has passed. For example, suppose we wanted to learn whether divorce (Event A) increases the chances of incarceration (Event B). We noted in the tabulation on page 141 that by the time the average divorce occurs, most of the risk period for first incarceration has passed. Therefore, we must compare risks of incarceration subsequent to divorce with risks of incarceration during the same age period for men who have not been divorced. The adjustment in Column C assures that the same age periods are investigated for the divorced and the still married.

Significance of difference is calculated using a fourfold contingency table (see accompanying tabulation, where $\chi^2 = 24.1$, $p<.001$). Contingency tables require both marginal totals, to allow calculation of expected frequencies and observed frequencies with and without the outcome of interest. For the "with cause" group (those ever in State 2), the marginal total and the observed frequencies with which Event B did or did not oc-

	With Cause	Without Cause	Total
With outcome	9	.0981 (207)	9 + .0981 (207)
Without outcome ..	7	207 − .0981 (207)	223 − 9 − .0981 (207)
Total	16	223 − 16 = 207	223

cur are available. For the "without cause" group, those who never entered State 2, marginal and observed frequencies must be adjusted to the risk period of the "with cause" group. By subtracting the "with cause" group from the total, we obtain the marginal total for the without cause group and we can calculate pseudo-"observed" frequencies, by multiplying the marginal total by the age-adjusted rate for Event B to provide appropriately adjusted figures for the statistical test.

RESULTS OF THE ACTUARIAL ANALYSIS

Step 1, Showing That Event B Tends to Occur Once Event A Has Occurred. Actuarial computations as described in Table 3 were applied to all possible pairs among the five life events, using each event as both a potential cause and a potential effect of each other event. This yielded twenty possible relationships (i.e., the ten correlations in Table 1, each considered in both directions). Thirteen of these twenty relationships were found to be statistically significant (Table 4). There were three pairs of events for which causation might be reciprocal: jail and divorce, jail and alcohol problems, jail and high school dropout, since significant differences were found in both directions. Dropout predicted each of the four other events at statistically significant levels, and heroin use predicted each event except dropout. Although dropout was the universal predictor, heroin use was the strongest predictor, with $p<.001$ in each case. Divorce was the weakest predictor, predicting only incarceration, and that at a low level of statistical significance.

Step 2, Identifying Common Precursors of Events A and B. The second step was to use this actuarial method to find other variables which might account for the significant relationships among the five events ana-

Table 4. Actuarial Analysis of Mutual Effects among Five Behaviors

Behaviors in Order of Occurrence	N	Percentage of Those with First Behavior Showing Second	N	Percentage of Those without First Behavior Showing Second
Reciprocal Predictors				
Jail, alcohol problems......	29	48	186	25*
Alcohol problems, jail......	82	21	133	6**
Dropout, jail.............	102	26	120	10**
Jail, dropout	6	83	216	31**
Jail, divorce	18	67	169	30**
Divorce, jail	82	18	108	3**
One-Way Predictors				
Dropout, alcohol problems..	98	62	116	20***
Dropout, heroin use.......	107	21	114	5***
Dropout, divorce	87	59	103	37**
Heroin use, alcohol problems	22	64	192	28***
Heroin use, jail...........	25	68	197	5***
Heroin use, divorce........	18	83	171	28***
Alcohol problems, divorce..	60	48	118	24**

* $p<.02$. ** $p<.01$. *** $p<.001$.

lyzed in Step 1, and thus explain these relationships as spurious rather than causal.

In addition to the five events studied in Step 1, there were ten other life events which occurred reasonably frequently and for which we knew the age at first occurrence. These included nine behaviors by the subjects themselves (drinking, arrest, use of three drugs other than heroin, sexual intercourse, departure from home, marriage, and entry into the armed services) plus the parents' breakup through separation or divorce. Events such as sexual intercourse, marriage, drinking, and leaving home occur universally and can be considered as possibly predictive of deviant behavior only when they begin at an unusually early age. Therefore, we considered these as potential causes of our five deviant behaviors only when they occurred before age 16 for sex and drinking or before age 18 for marriage and leaving home. Similarly, we assumed that parental separation and divorce would be important in shaping later behavior only if it occurred early in the child's life. Thus, parental breakup was counted only when it occurred before subjects were 16. (These assumptions were tested by comparing results with and without age cutoffs for some of these events. As expected, correlations with the five deviant outcomes were stronger when an age cutoff was used. It would be possible to use the actuarial method to select the particular cutoff age providing maximum predictability, but we have not yet attempted to do this.)

Each of these ten variables was treated as a potential cause (Event A) with respect to each of the five deviant behaviors explored above (Event B's). Results are presented in Table 5. Arrest and marihuana use predicted each of our five life events; use of amphetamines and barbiturates, early sex, and early drinking each predicted four of the five outcomes. Leaving home for good before age 18 predicted three; early marriage and parental divorce predicted two; and entering service only one — alcohol problems.

Table 5. Predictors of Deviant Outcomes for Young Black Males

Predictors	Alcohol Problems	Jail	Dropout	Divorce	Heroin Use
Arrest	x	x	x	x	x
Marihuana	x	x	x	x	x
Amphetamines	x	x	x	x	
Barbiturates	x	x		x	x
Early sex	x	x	x		x
Early drinking	x	x	x		x
Left home early	x		x	x	
Early marriage		x		x	
Parental divorce	x		x		
Military service	x				

Looking at these relationships from the point of view of the five life events to be predicted, we note that nine of the ten variables predicted alcohol problems, but only five predicted heroin use. The relative scarcity of predictors of heroin use was also notable in Table 4. Of the four relationships between pairs of life events in which heroin use was treated as the effect (Event B), only one was statistically significant — when dropout was Event A. When alcohol problems were treated as Event B, three of the four relationships were statistically significant. Thus, alcohol problems were predicted by twelve of the fourteen variables we examined as possible predictors; heroin use by only six. These findings probably reflect the fact that alcohol problems were much more common in this sample than heroin use, thus providing larger samples on which to base statistical tests. But it is also possible that alcohol problems were more an expression of a general predisposition to deviance than was heroin use.

Step 3, Showing That Event B Follows Event A When Precursors Are Held Constant. Our final step was to test the power of the relationships in Table 4 when all the variables which predicted both the hypothetical cause (Event A) and the hypothetical effect (Event B) were held constant. We included any of the five life events that predicted both events, as well as any of the ten variables in Table 5 significantly related to both events. For example, in evaluating the possible causal effect of alcohol problems on serving a jail term, we held constant dropout and heroin use as well as the first six variables in Table 5, since each of these eight variables significantly predicted both alcohol problems and jail.

To hold these predictors of both events constant, we attempted to match each person ever in State 2 (i.e., having experienced the Event A in which we were interested while at risk of Event B) with a person without Event A who shared the same set of predictors of A and B at the age the person for whom he was to serve as a match first experienced Event A. To be sure our matching procedure was unbiased, we first put the whole sample in random order. A computer program then located the first person with Event A, observed which precursors he had already experienced at the age he first experienced Event A, and then selected as a match the next person in the random series who either had never experienced Event A or at least had not by the age he first experienced Event B and who had experienced the same precursors by the age at which the person to be matched experienced Event A. No match was attempted for persons experiencing Event A if information was missing either about age of first experiencing the precursors or about age of first experiencing Event B. Cases for whom no perfect match was found were dropped from consideration. Members of each successfully matched pair were compared with respect to their later experiencing Event B. They could be concordant (00 or ++) or discordant (0+ or +0) for outcome. Significance of differences was tested by McNemar's test for individually matched samples. This test evaluates the probability, among the discordant pairs only, that the true proportion in which Event B occurred to the pair member with Event A is greater than 50 per cent.* Results are shown in Table 6.

$$*\chi^2 = \{ [\Sigma(+0) - \Sigma(0+) - 1]^2 \} / \{ \Sigma(+0) + \Sigma(0+) \}$$

Only four of the thirteen significant relationships were still striking when persons with and without the cause were matched on all precursors. Heroin use remained a striking predictor of all three forms of later deviance, and school dropout continued to forecast alcohol problems. Although not statistically significant, school dropout continued to show some relationship to divorce, heroin use, and jail.

Comparing percentages in the last column of Table 6 with percent-

Table 6. Predictors of Later Events When Matched for Precursors and Age at Risk

Behaviors in Order of Occurrence	No. Precursors Matched	No. Matched Pairs	No. Discordant Pairs	Percentages with Positive Outcomes	
				With Cause	Without Cause
Plausible Causes					
Heroin use, divorce........	4	13	9	85	15****
Heroin use, jail...........	6	17	10	53	18**
Heroin use, alcohol problems	6	15	10	67	27**
Dropout, alcohol problems..	8	52	28	52	33***
*Possibly Significantly Related**					
Dropout, jail	5	66	18	23	17
Dropout, heroin use.......	4	68	15	16	9
Dropout, divorce	5	64	35	59	48
Alcohol problems, divorce..	8	39	15	54	41
Not Significant					
Alcohol problems, jail	8	47	11	19	17
Divorce, jail	8	42	6	12	7
Jail, divorce	8	15	7	67	60
Jail, alcohol problems......	8	16	7	50	44
Jail, dropout	5	4	2	75	75

* $p<.25$. ** $p<.10$. *** $p<.05$. **** $p<.005$.

ages in the last column of Table 4, we note that for most of the "without cause" cases, rates of later deviant behaviors in Table 6 exceed rates in Table 4. This, of course, follows from the fact that the precursors on which they were matched with the "with cause" cases predicted both the cause and the outcome studied. The high-risk "without cause" cases have been selected as matches for the "with cause" cases.

There is a less striking tendency for rates of outcomes in the "with cause" group to be lower in Table 6 than in Table 4. This occurs because the cases which had experienced more precursors were less often matchable than those that experienced fewer. For instance, cases that could *not* be matched among dropouts at risk of heroin use constituted 63 per cent of those with three or four predictors of both dropout and heroin use, but only 3 per cent of those with none or one of the predictors. As one would expect, then, later heroin use was less frequent among the dropouts who *could* be matched (16 per cent) than among those who could not be (34 per cent). Had we achieved the same proportion of precursors in the matched as in the original sample, we might well have found a significant influence of dropout on later heroin use.

Because we cannot match every case from our rather small pool of "without cause" members of the sample, the matching procedure is a very tough test of the impact of these events on each other. The total number of cases is reduced (yielding only a small number of discordant pairs for the McNemar test), and the reduction is disproportionate among high-risk cases. It should be noted that even when these life events no longer show a statistically significant prediction of later events, the rate of later events was always higher when the potential cause had occurred than when it had not (except for the jail-followed-by-dropout relationship, for which there were only four matched pairs, since assignment to a correctional institution rarely occurred to boys still enrolled in school). Finding that "with cause" rates are always higher than "without cause" rates does not necessarily mean that our criteria for statistical significance are unduly rigid, however, since each person with the causal event has experienced one more precursor of the outcome than the person with whom he is matched (i.e., he had an equal number of precursors other than the causal variable, plus the causal variable). If it is the *number* of precursors that matters, rather than the particular event such as dropout or jail, we would expect a slightly greater rate of positive outcomes for the case with the cause, whatever the cause may be, than without it.

What we can conclude is that the use of heroin has a remarkably powerful effect on chances of marital breakup and incarceration and that both heroin use and dropping out of school are sharply associated with the later development of alcohol problems, even when all the factors that may lead to the use of heroin or dropping out are considered. We cannot conclude that the other relationships found significant in Table 4 are clearly *not* causal until we explore them again in a larger sample and using a matching method that allows one less precursor for the "without cause" group than for the "with cause" group, to equalize the number of indicators of deviance.

CONCLUSIONS

This study of the relationships among five life events in a sample of young urban-born and urban-reared black men shows that all five events are intercorrelated: school dropout, heroin use, divorce, jail, and alcohol problems. All five events are also predicted by earlier experiences, particularly by arrest and marihuana use, precocious sexual activity, and drinking. Finding such nesting of problem behavior is the rule, rather than the exception, in research in life histories. The problem then arises of how to interpret such intercorrelations. Are they simply expressions of a general tendency toward deviant behavior? Or do they constitute a set of causal chains, in which one deviant behavior makes the next more probable?

This question has been explored by an actuarial technique that takes into account the order of events, the age span of exposure to risk, and the precursors common to the possible cause and the possible outcome. Our findings indicate that heroin use clearly predicts later deviant behavior, independently of the past behaviors that led to the use of the heroin. Dropping out of school also seems to increase the risks of later problems — clearly so for alcohol problems, and possibly so for the other three behaviors as well. Alcohol problems also may increase the risk of marital breakup, independently of whatever caused the alcohol problems.

The most elaborate causal chain suggested by the data is that dropping out of school predicts heroin use which in turn predicts alcohol problems which then predict divorce. There are also a number of shorter chains: dropout followed by heroin use which is then followed by both jail and divorce (without alcohol problems intervening), and dropout followed by alcohol problems which are then followed by divorce (without heroin use intervening). Jail and divorce appear only as consequences of the other three variables, never as their predictors. None of the possible reciprocal relationships we had identified survived the test of matching cases on all shared precursors.

If our findings are correct, we have three points of attack that might be expected to reduce the social problems of young urban blacks: facilitating high school completion, discouraging heroin use, and discouraging excessive drinking. The most certain benefits would be achievable by reducing exposure to heroin. Heroin users form a much smaller proportion of the population than high school dropouts or excessive drinkers. This fact means that it would be less costly to work on heroin abuse than on other problems — but at the same time, success in reducing heroin use would create gains in the social welfare of only a small proportion of those with problems.

COMMENTARY

MYERS. What did you match your subjects on?

ROBINS. We matched them on all the variables that predicted both outcome variables. For instance, when testing to see whether dropout leads to alcohol problems, we matched on each variable significantly related to both (i.e., where there was an x in both the alcohol problem and the dropout column in Table 5).

MYERS. Could you have had only marihuana and amphetamines, or could you have had any of the variables preceding dropout?

ROBINS. Well, if the dropout had them, then the match had to have them. If the dropout did not have them, then the match could not have them. The match had to be exactly like the dropout with respect to each of those precursors, at the age of first dropout. We also required that he still be free of alcohol problems at the dropout age, as the dropout was.

GUZE. If you are going to use this method to get clues about etiology, it's very important that you compare factors of commensurate weight. For example, it may be that the use of heroin even once is more important than having a single alcohol problem, that going to jail is more important than any single alcohol problem. In other words, the general psychiatric and social implications seemed to be comparable for each of the variables you are comparing.

ROBINS. Well, as long as we can find a match who has had exactly the same history, there's no problem. Even if one variable is a more potent predictor than another, since we've matched on both, the match is appropriate. However, it is true that we may be failing to find a match because of one small difference between a case and its only potential match. So far we have insisted on perfect matches, perhaps unnecessarily.

GUZE. My point is that one could conclude, for example, that alcoholism isn't very important as a cause, if only one alcohol related problem was enough for this diagnosis. The pressure of three or four alcohol problems may have significance similar to the use of heroin even once.

ROBINS. Certainly, other definitions of "alcohol problems" or any other outcome might be more useful than the ones we used. If we had defined alcohol problems more stringently, it would have made the matching a lot easier. Since fewer people would have qualified as having problems, we would have had a much bigger pool remaining to match from. It also might have been more sensible. There's nothing holy about the particular definitions we chose. However, if one defined alcohol problems as a number of problems, which could occur at differing ages, it would be hard to decide what the proper age of first occurrence is.

THOMAS. Isn't Lee's method of research answering the question that concerns you? In other words, if she can find out by this method whether the use of heroin once is equivalent to the use of alcohol as a problem once, or not, or whether one is a greater problem, then this method will help to identify which variable seems to be more significant. If we find that one use of heroin is much more significant than one alcohol problem, we could then go on to see whether two alcohol problems are equivalent to one heroin problem or three alcohol to one heroin.

ROBINS. The question I have posed here is, Does having even one alcohol problem predict divorce and jail? I agree with Dr. Guze that that may not be the best question to ask, but that's the only question I've asked here.

WINOKUR. It seems to me that one can use Table 5 somewhat imaginatively. Parental divorce seems to predict alcohol problems and dropouts. But if one looks again, early drinking, which must to some extent be predicted by parental divorce, predicts alcohol problems, jail, dropout, and heroin use. Now, the question is, Can you use this method to describe a chain of events? You may well be able to set it up so that one thing will lead to another, then another, and so on in a reasonable sense.

ROBINS. Well, we only looked for chains in those five variables but there was no reason why all the rest of the variables for which we have age data could not have been included. We just would have had considerably more computer output.

THOMAS. The question then arises, What causes parental divorce?

ROBINS. Most arguments for causal variables have been based on face validity. That is, what would logically come before what else? We assume that the mother's personality predates dropout and jail or what have you. There is no reason why you couldn't add into this system variables which you know by face validity must come first, even when we have no specific age of onset. We could arbitrarily assign such variables an age of occurrence of zero, so that they predate all behavior on the part of the individual. In this way events present at birth — such as parental characteristics, sex, race, ethnicity — could all be handled by the computer along with events occurring later in the individual's life. In this paper, we looked only at variables that do occur for the first time during the life-span of the child because we wanted to explore the method. There's no reason why things present at birth could not also be included.

REFERENCES

Cahalan, D. *Problem drinkers.* San Francisco: Jossey-Bass, 1970.

Guze, S. B., Goodwin, D. W., & Crane, J. B. Criminality and psychiatric disorders. *Archives of General Psychiatry,* 1969, 20, 583–591.

O'Donnell, J. A. *Narcotic addicts in Kentucky.* Washington, D.C.: Public Health Service Publication No. 1881, 1969.

Reckless, W. C. *The crime problem.* New York: Appleton, 1955.

Robins, L. N., Murphy, G. E., & Breckenridge, M. B. Drinking behavior of young urban Negro men. *Quarterly Journal of Studies on Alcohol,* 1968, 29, 657–684.

HAROUTUN M. BABIGIAN | *The Role of Psychiatric Case Registers in the Longitudinal Study of Psychopathology*

PSYCHIATRIC case registers have been increasingly used as epidemiologic research tools over the past few years. Baldwin (1968) describes registers by stating, "Their essential characteristic is the development of individual- rather than event-oriented cumulative files on all patients entering psychiatric treatment in a defined geographic area, thus improving the validity and reliability of measures of treated morbidity and enabling the tracing and linkage of all an individual's treatment experiences over the course of both the initial and subsequent illnesses and recurrences." He concludes, "The register is thus a powerful tool which it will take time to learn to use to the full, but it is already encouraging research which probably would not otherwise have been attempted and, whether or not the research itself proves significant, the exercise is a worth-while training experience."

The Monroe County (New York) Psychiatric Case Register entered its second decade of operation in 1970. Those compiling the register have struggled with technical problems of assuring accurate reporting, proper maintenance, and rapid retrieval of data. But the unique contributions of this research instrument have been demonstrated and found to justify the operational costs involved. The initial goals of the project, delineated by Gardner et al. (1963), were clinical, epidemiological, and service evaluative (administrative). As investigators become more familiar with the register, its potential uses in various research designs are being realized.

Initial efforts were devoted to the development of the instrument and the provision of more precise data on diagnosed incidence and prevalence of mental disorders. Since a register is a longitudinal record of every individual receiving psychiatric care over a period of time, studies of utilization of services, of admissions and readmissions to hospitals, of diagnostic change over time, and of the influence of social class on type of care provided were undertaken. It takes time to learn to use the register to the full, especially in longitudinal studies of psychopathology. On the other hand completed research from registers has proved to be significant and valuable.

One of the most important factors in the limited use of register data has been the lack of familiarity with potential contributions of the instrument in basic research designs, particularly in the selection of experimental and control populations from a community for longitudinal and cross-sectional studies. Bahn (1968), in discussing the register as a tool for planning and evaluation, outlines four major uses for registers: "as a continuous monitoring or surveillance of the psychiatric services being provided the community; as an index of cases which can be used as a sampling frame for the conduct of intensive field investigations; as a data resource against which records of other agencies or programs can be matched to evaluate their differential or combined impact on the community's mental health; and as a basis for comparison with data on random or selected segments of the population." She illustrates each of these areas with studies from the registers of the states of Maryland and Hawaii, the Monroe County Psychiatric Case Register, and the North Carolina Tricounty Area Case Register.

In this paper, after a description of the operation and maintenance of the Monroe County Psychiatric Case Register and the presentation of summary data for eight years (1960–1967), I shall discuss some completed and current studies illustrating the role of the register in longitudinal research under three separate headings: (a) the register itself as a longitudinal study, (b) the register as an aid to other longitudinal studies in the community, and (c) the register as a sampling base for longitudinal and cross-sectional studies of high-risk populations and follow-up studies of selected groups.

THE MONROE COUNTY CUMULATIVE PSYCHIATRIC CASE REGISTER

The Monroe County register is maintained and operated by the Department of Psychiatry of the University of Rochester School of Medicine and Dentistry. It is the major research undertaking of the Division of Preventive and Social Psychiatry. Compiling of the register began on January 1, 1960, following a six-month pilot study in 1959 supported by the Ford

Foundation. Initial support came from grants from the National Institute of Mental Health and the Millbank Memorial Fund. The National Institute of Mental Health supported the register for ten years. As of October 1969, the support for the maintenance of the register was assumed by the New York State Department of Mental Hygiene, the Monroe County Board of Mental Health, and the University of Rochester. In addition to maintenance support, the National Institute of Mental Health, the New York State Department of Mental Hygiene, and Monroe County provided grants and contracts for many studies utilizing data from the register.

Monroe County had a population of approximately 700,000 in 1970. It is an urban industrial community, with approximately 40 per cent of the population living in the city of Rochester and the remainder residing in suburban and rural areas. On January 1, 1960, all patients under psychiatric care were registered. Since that day patients contacting public and private inpatient and outpatient psychiatric facilities of Monroe County have been reported regularly, including those who consulted private psychiatrists. The reporting facilities comprise a university hospital with inpatient, outpatient, and emergency services; the Rochester State Hospital with its inpatient, outpatient, alcoholism, and home care facilities; an acute inpatient observation unit; a Veterans Administration hospital; a children's treatment center with inpatient, outpatient, and day care facilities; two child guidance clinics; a court clinic; and 56 of the 60 practicing private psychiatrists in Monroe County. Since January 1967, a new mental health center with inpatient, outpatient, day care, emergency, and consultation services for both adults and children has reported to the register. The alcoholism clinic and one child guidance clinic were incorporated into this center. As of July 1968, another community mental health center with five essential services for children and adults began operating and reporting. The children's treatment center with all its services became a part of this new mental health center.

The register reporting form consists of seventeen items with two carbon copies. The information gathered regularly consists of patient's name, address, birth date, age, sex, race, marital status, psychiatric service received in the past, psychiatric diagnostic impression with four impressions allowed for each patient contact, type of service given (diagnostic, treatment, or consultative), date of initial encounter, date of termination of service, type of treatment given, current frequency of therapy, reasons for termination, condition on termination, and name of the reporting facility and doctor. Obviously, many additional items could have been incorporated in reporting. The major reason for restricting the number of items to a practical minimum was to ensure the cooperation of reporting persons and facilities over a long period of time. Complicated and cumbersome reporting forms are not favorably received by busy clinicians and overburdened facilities.

Each facility reports all patient contacts. A contact may be a single visit to a psychiatric emergency department or a period of hospitalization or outpatient care. A patient may have several contacts for one episode of illness.

To assure complete reporting, register staff are assigned to different psychiatric facilities in the community where they check the facility's records and determine whether a specific patient was reported to the register. Register personnel also help some of the private psychiatrists to complete their reporting forms. With regard to those physicians who do not want register personnel helping them, we are unable to know exactly how many reports are missing. Some psychiatrists have agreed to check the names of patients reported to the register against their own records to determine whether they have missed reporting any patients.

Once a report is received, the patient's name is checked against an alphabetic listing of previously registered individuals. If the patient is already in the register he retains the same serial number, and if he is a new patient a new serial number is designated. The data are then coded, keypunched, and verified. At three-month intervals the data are edited for intra- and inter-record errors, the errors are corrected, and the master tapes are updated. Data are kept on two separate master tapes: one with name, residence, date of birth, sex, race, and social security number, when reported; the other with serial number and all information gathered except name. All analysis is done on the latter data file to assure the maintenance of confidentiality.

Reports from acute inpatient facilities are filed on discharge. Longer term facilities send an initial form a few days after admission with a tentative diagnosis which is updated periodically and on discharge. Reports on outpatients are received following the first few interviews, and followup information is requested every three months if the patient continues under treatment. In addition to these patient data, the register receives death certificate data for every deceased resident of Monroe County from the New York State Department of Health. Each death record is matched against the register, and death data for each registered individual are added. In 1960–1966 approximately 10 per cent of the register population (3,809 individuals of 39,475) had died.

As of January 1, 1969, the Monroe County Department of Social Services began reporting all individuals in families receiving public welfare assistance. Reporting is by name of parents and children, birth date, age, sex, race, type of assistance, and length of time that they received assistance. This welfare register has opened up new areas of research. Every individual reported is matched against the psychiatric case register. Of approximately 30,000 individuals who received public assistance in 1969, 2,500 were already in the psychiatric register by the end of 1968. Name-matching continues, and the psychiatric and public assistance data are combined on those individuals who are in both registers. This additional register brings us closer to the more comprehensive reporting systems recommended by Srole (1967) and others.

In 1960–1967, some 45,200 individuals were reported to the psychiatric register. Table 1 represents the total register population for this period by age, sex, race, and average yearly rates (eight-year prevalence rate divided by eight). Approximately 1 per cent of county residents are reported to the register each year. The rates of contact are higher for nonwhites than for whites. The 15–24-year-old group has the highest representation, followed by the 25–44-year-old group. Rates for males are slightly higher than for females.

Table 2 presents the number of individuals served by psychiatric facilities in Monroe County in 1967 by major diagnostic categories and type of contact. Approximately 2 per cent of the population of Monroe County (13,436 individuals) received some type of psychiatric care in

Table 1. Average Yearly Rates and Total Number of Patients in the Register from 1960 to 1967 by Age and Sex[a]

Patient and Rate	0–14 Years	15–24 Years	25–44 Years	45–64 Years	65+ Years	Total
Male white	3,488	4,327	7,002	4,344	1,981	21,142
Rate	5.22	17.76	12.23	9.30	9.21	9.76
Female white	1,470	4,461	7,746	4,090	2,719	20,486
Rate	2.30	16.24	12.52	8.07	9.58	8.81
Male nonwhite	270	370	940	348	48	1,976
Rate	6.70	28.24	31.43	28.21	17.80	20.10
Female nonwhite	172	452	719	199	54	1,596
Rate	4.19	29.34	23.40	17.30	16.67	15.66
Total	5,400	9,610	16,407	8,981	4,802	45,200
Rate	3.89	17.57	13.11	9.01	9.51	9.64

[a] All rates are age-adjusted per 1,000 Monroe County (1960) population.

Table 2. Number of Patients Served in 1967 by Diagnosis and Type of Contact

Diagnosis	First Lifetime Contact		First Register Contact[a]		Previous Register Contact		Care Continued from 1966		Total
	No.	%	No.	%	No.	%	No.	%	No.
Chronic brain syndrome..	341	26.5	68	5.3	111	8.6	767	59.6	1,287
Affective disorder	130	16.7	66	8.5	157	20.3	422	54.5	775
Schizophrenia	327	11.0	242	8.1	691	23.1	1,726	57.8	2,986
Neurosis	885	34.9	261	10.3	475	18.8	912	36.0	2,533
Personality disorder	947	39.3	252	10.5	566	23.5	645	26.7	2,410
No diagnosis	125	68.3	22	12.0	27	14.8	9	4.9	183
Other[b]	1,619	49.6	319	9.8	851	26.1	473	14.5	3,262
Total..............	4,374	32.6	1,230	9.2	2,878	21.4	4,954	36.8	13,436

[a] But previous contacts with psychiatric facilities (before 1960).
[b] Other diagnoses include acute brain syndromes, psychophysiologic reactions, adjustment reactions, and suicide attempt.

1967: 4,374 (32.6 per cent) experienced their first lifetime contact with psychiatric facilities, 1,230 (9.2 per cent) were reported to the register for the first time but claimed to have received psychiatric care before the register was initiated seven years previously, 2,878 (21.4 per cent) re-entered care following termination of care in the previous seven years, and 4,954 (36.8 per cent) continued in care from the previous year. Of the total eight-year population, 30 per cent (13,436 out of 45,200) received care in a single year (1967).

THE REGISTER AS A LONGITUDINAL STUDY

As noted previously, the register is a longitudinal data file of all individuals with diagnosed mental illness in Monroe County. Most longitudinal studies have been a result of specific interest of an investigator directly involved in the operation of the register. Since a primary national interest focuses on the planning and development of community mental health centers, Miles (1966), Gardner (1967), and Gardner, Bahn, and Miles (1969) studied the movement of patients between different facilities in the community over a period of time. They noted that private and public community services, including private practice, assumed the responsibility of triage, and the state hospital system was burdened with the care of the chronic schizophrenics and elderly patients, mainly on an inpatient basis. They emphasized the fact that "the community services provided most of the treatment for patients diagnosed neurotic or personality disorder. This substantiates the belief that these services spend considerable time with minor mental illness." Gardner and Babigian (1966) compared low and high socioeconomic areas with respect to the overall mental illness rates and patterns of psychiatric services, re-emphasizing the need for more adequate outpatient services for lower socioeconomic groups.

A study of diagnostic consistency (Babigian et al., 1965) and patterns of change over time showed that chronic brain syndrome is the diagnosis given with the highest consistency (90 per cent), followed by schizophrenia (70 per cent). Lowest consistency (40 per cent) was found with the affective psychoses. This study also showed that difficult-to-manage patients with repeated contacts were ultimately diagnosed schizophrenic and admitted to the state hospital.

A study of the mortality of individuals who had received psychiatric care showed that the relative risk of death of the register population was 2.5 to 3 times that for the comparable general population (Babigian &

Odoroff, 1969). The relative risk of death for the register population was greater than 2 times the general population for both sexes for all causes of death with the exception of neoplasms. After removal of groups that are known to contribute to the high mortality rate, such as the aged, the alcoholic, and the chronically ill, the relative risk of death remained 1.5 to 2 times that of the general population. Even patients with no hospital experience whatsoever, those treated by private psychiatrists and clinics, showed twice the mortality rate of the general population. With this general study there was difficulty identifying areas of preventable mortality. It was obvious that other methods of investigation are required in order to uncover causes of the excessive mortality in the psychiatric population.

An eight-year study of schizophrenia in Monroe County (Babigian, 1970) showed that approximately one of every thousand individuals receives the diagnosis of schizophrenia every year, and four out of a thousand are hospitalized with this diagnosis yearly, spending a total of half a million days in hospitals. Adolescents and young adults (ages 15–24) have the highest incidence rates of schizophrenia. Investigation of incidence and prevalence rates by socioeconomic levels and age showed that in the 15- to 24-year-old group the incidence rates of schizophrenia are almost equal for all socioeconomic levels and do not appear to be related to social class. All other age groups show higher incidence and prevalence rates in the lower classes. This makes us wonder whether schizophrenia with onset in adolescence and young adulthood may not be more genetically determined and less dependent on social stress than is schizophrenia with later onset. A study of rates of readmission to hospitals found that a schizophrenic patient is more likely to be readmitted to a hospital than is a non-schizophrenic patient. Within 100 months after discharge approximately 50 per cent of schizophrenics are readmitted as compared with 38 per cent of non-schizophrenics. We were unable to show any relation between rehospitalization of schizophrenics and age, sex, marital status, length of first hospitalization, or socioeconomic class.

One major use of the register is the provision of a sampling base for follow-up studies of representative cohorts. A follow-up of 214 schizophrenic and 23 nonpsychotic males was undertaken by Gardner et al. (1966). We are currently following up a cohort of 569 psychotically depressed individuals seven years after their entry into the register. This cohort includes all new patients with the diagnosis of psychotic depression in the years 1961–1962. A longitudinal follow-up in the register indicated that 6 per cent were seen only once in an outpatient area, diagnosed as psychotic depression, and never received treatment; 50 per cent had one clear depressive episode, were treated, and have not returned for care in seven years; 24 per cent had multiple depressive episodes; 20 per cent had one depressive episode followed by other episodes not diagnosed as depression. A representative sample of each group was interviewed in 1969 to determine their current level of functioning and degree of pathology.

THE REGISTER AS AN AID TO OTHER LONGITUDINAL STUDIES

The register is able to add meaningful longitudinal follow-up over a period of many years to studies of early case detection and prevention. Two such studies are those of Cowen et al. (1963, 1966). These investigators screened all primary grade children in a school and identified those children who were already manifesting moderate to severe adaptation problems or in whom the likelihood of such problems was judged to be incipient. Of all grade school children, 30 per cent were "red-tagged" and followed up with control groups over a period of ten years; most of the children in the first group are now in their late teens or early twenties. All records included name, address, birth date, sex, race, and names of parents. We are currently matching all children and parents in both the experimental and control groups with the register to learn whether they have already entered psychiatric care or will enter care in the future. This information plus information on psychiatric care of parents will give an added perspective to an already completed longitudinal study.

THE REGISTER AS A SAMPLING BASE FOR
HIGH-RISK POPULATIONS

With an increasing interest in studies of the etiology of schizophrenia, investigators have begun to study children who are considered to have a high potential for developing psychopathology in adolescence or early adulthood. *Vulnerability research* is the current term for the general area of studies of high-risk populations. Garmezy (1971), in his paper "Vulnerability Research and the Issues of Primary Prevention," states, "Vulnerability research involves the selection of those children in a community who are at high risk for the later onset (typically in late adolescence and adulthood) of severe psychopathology. Selection criteria may be based on genetic loading within the family (as revealed by the psychiatric status of parents or relatives), evidence of excessive family disorganization or the undesirable effects generated by a disordered environment. In essence, the status of a child as 'vulnerable' or at 'high-risk' . . . typically is derived from the three basic models that characterize our speculations about the etiology of mental disorder: (1) genetic transmission of the predisposition or the diathesis, (2) pathological disorganization within the near environment (the family) or (3) within the molar (sociocultural) environment of the child. We can also identify a fourth model that is coming to prominence, although its applicability to adult psychopathology is not yet clear — one stressing deprivation within the prenatal and neonatal period in which faulty maternal care and inadequate nutrition can serve to render the infant vulnerable to subsequent stressors."

Interest in vulnerability research within our department during the past two years has led to the development of a family-oriented record file. For ten years the register remained individual-oriented, but to meet the need for identification of high-risk children and for the selection of control groups, we have developed a family linkage system whereby each individual reported to the register is checked to find out if he is related to others in the register. The initial group we were looking for is the most vulnerable: the families with both parents having the diagnosis of schizophrenia (dual-mated schizophrenic parents).

The family register file allows easy access to cohorts with different combinations of vulnerability factors, starting with dual-mated schizophrenic parents, to schizophrenic mothers with a father who has received psychiatric care but was not diagnosed schizophrenic, to a schizophrenic father with the mother having a non-schizophrenic diagnosis, to schizophrenic mothers with "normal" fathers and vice versa, and to siblings, one of whom has a diagnosis of schizophrenia, but with neither parent in the register. Subgroups of the above combinations can be obtained using socioeconomic variables.

The accompanying tabulation lists families containing more than one patient in the register within nine years (1960–1968); 14 per cent of the total register population (7,267 individuals of a total of 51,392) have a primary relative also in the register.

There are multiple diagnostic combinations within the families identified in the register. Having a primary interest in the schizophrenic disorders, we found the following patterns: Of the total 3,380 families with more than one registered patient, 1,366 had both husband and wife in the register. Of these 1,366, 125 couples were dual-mated schizophrenics, 413 couples had one member schizophrenic and the other with a different diagnosis, and 828 couples did not have a diagnosis of schizophrenia.

	No.
Father, mother, and two or more children in the register	37
Father, mother, and one child	165
Husband and wife	1,167
Father and two or more children	50
Mother and two or more children	99
Father and one child	434
Mother and one child	758
Siblings	656
Other	14
Total number of families	3,380
Total number of related individuals	7,267
Total number of unrelated individuals	44,125

From these families, investigators can select cohorts for studies of the offspring. In addition to providing a sampling base, the register becomes the monitoring instrument for those children under study over a period of years to identify them as having contacted a psychiatric facility for minor or major psychopathology.

One major vulnerability study that is being facilitated by the availability of the register is the current research into neonatal factors in serious mental disorder by Sameroff and Zax. Pregnant women with the diagnosis of schizophrenia are being identified through the register, and their newborn infants are being compared with newborns of a control group and with newborns of women with the diagnosis of depression. The children are then followed up during the first year of life. We are planning a follow-up study of both children and their mothers over a longer period of time.

Several other epidemiologic and vulnerability studies are being designed to study the pregnancy and birth experience of children of schizophrenic and non-schizophrenic mothers, and the children of schizophrenic fathers. The pregnancy and birth experiences of children already in the register will be compared with those of their siblings who have not demonstrated any psychopathology.

CONCLUSIONS

During the decade of the sixties we witnessed national commitment to the prevention of mental illness and the provision of adequate mental health services to all citizens in need. Current knowledge about the etiology of major psychiatric disorders is minimal and thus does not allow us to design effective primary prevention programs. We are much better equipped to practice secondary and tertiary prevention while continuing the investigations that would give us clues about etiology.

The role of psychiatric case registers is crucial in epidemiologic studies, in providing a sampling base for the study of vulnerable groups, and in the longitudinal monitoring of high-risk individuals under study. Beyond these contributions, registers are invaluable in the planning of mental health services in a community and particularly in providing longitudinal data on existing and new mental health services. Registers facilitate the evaluation of the impact of new mental health services on a community. For community mental health centers to be able to focus primarily on prevention, we need more definitive data on etiology which can be easily translated into action programs.

COMMENTARY

ERLENMEYER-KIMLING. Dr. Babigian, I suspect that you have more than half of this audience green with envy over this instrument. For myself, having spent a long time trying to collect dual mating cases and sibling pairs, I can only say "wow"!

WIRT. My first comment would be applause for Monroe County. I think we'd be interested in having you tell us how you sold those agencies and private practitioners on the register.

BABIGIAN. This is a question that comes up frequently. I think that the register was made possible by the nature of the organization of service in Monroe County and the people involved. The Department of Psychiatry of the University of Rochester Medical Center was founded in 1946. Its chairman since then and a founder of the register is Dr. John Romano, and the majority of the practicing private and other psychiatrists in responsible positions were trained under him. The other founders of the register were Dr. Elmer Gardner, who at that time was in private practice, and Dr. Harold Miles, the Director of Monroe County Mental Health Services. They were able to convince all the agencies and the practicing psychiatrists that confidentiality would be maintained and that they would dispose of the records before making them available to any third party.

After the establishment of the register, all physicians and agencies were provided with follow-up information on their patients which they found extremely valuable. All agencies and the majority of the practicing psychiatrists continue reporting to us. I do not want to minimize the problems involved in private reporting; we still have to keep in continuous contact with some physicians and provide help for reporting. We know that we are losing about 15 per cent of private practice patients because some doctors do not report, and others report by code, without names. Some of the ones who report by code provide the names to me, trusting me as a consultant. So we have all kinds of arrangements with physicians by which we try to accommodate their needs. In ten years we have encountered no problems with leakage of any type of identifying information.

QUESTION. Do you include psychologists?

BABIGIAN. We include psychologists, social workers, everybody who sees patients in psychiatric facilities. We had reporting from Family Service for a two-year period, and we're analyzing the data now.

ROBINS. One of the things that I was particularly impressed by was your recognition of the fact that you can't take those diagnoses at face value and your insistence that if you're going to treat the diagnosis seriously you have to go out and look at the record and the patient. This raises the question, What about confidentiality? Do you have any problem about using these names to go out and re-interview people?

BABIGIAN. We've interviewed schizophrenics and depressed patients of private practitioners. If the patient's last contact was with the University Hospital, there is no problem. We're representing the University Hospital so we go there as such. The State Hospital has given us permission to do the same thing — to represent the State Hospital — so the facilities are no problem. If the patient is with a private practitioner, we call the psychiatrist, tell him what we're doing, and ask him for permission to see his patient. If he says no, it's no. We don't try to sell it to him. We go to the next person. If he wants to talk to the patient, even though the patient has terminated, before we see that patient, we allow him to do that. Some of them say go ahead, and there's no problem.

MYERS. Is there any pressure in New York State for a confidentiality law? Such a law was enacted in Connecticut and at the present time, it is exceedingly difficult to do follow-up or other studies based on the identification of persons through psychiatric or other records.

BABIGIAN. I know that at least the New York State Department of Mental Hygiene would not like this law because the Department is getting reports from all mental health facilities today and it is trying to get these reports by name so that a register can be established for the State of New York. I agree that if we do not have names, then we don't have to have registers. The law we are functioning under in New York State is one that allows physicians to report their patients to a research study for research purposes, if it is strictly research and connected with the Department of Mental Hygiene — and we are connected with the Department of Mental Hygiene. As for new laws that restrict reporting, we just hope that there will not be any.

MYERS. Has there been some pressure?

BABIGAN. There has been some pressure but not major, to my knowledge, up to now.

THOMAS. The State of New York Department of Mental Hygiene did enact a regulation about a year ago requiring voluntary and private psychiatric facilities to report the cases on a register form to the State, as is also being required of the city, county, and state facilities. At least in New York City, there was a tremendous uproar about this, especially from the private facilities, over the issue of confidentiality. The state has given the assurance that the names in the register are kept entirely separate and that only code numbers are being used in the actual registers to which people have access. This has calmed the issue down for the time being. I'm not sure that it will do so permanently. I think some device such as you have to ensure absolute confidentiality is essential if there is to be any chance of such registers developing, especially with more and more issues being raised by groups such as the Civil Liberties Union about the invasion of privacy, the constitutional rights of hospitalized mental patients, and so on. The register of Monroe County is a model of the kind that should be done. I just want to say, as a word of caution for the future, that the register employed by the New York State Department of Mental Hygiene for its reporting system throughout the state is a model of what should not be done. First of all, it involves a sheet which, instead of having seventeen simple items, has forty or fifty items including symptomotology, some of which are in such fine print that one must puzzle over the items. Secondly, the register forms are usually filled out by overburdened physicians, clerks, and residents in busy hospitals, and from our own experience we know that the reliability or validity of information on forms when filled out this way probably approaches chance level. I'm willing to assume that it's as good as chance level, but sometimes it may not be, in terms of negativistic reactions of staff. In all seriousness, I assume that some time in the future, five or ten years from now, there will be a number of volumes issued reporting findings from the New York State Register and unless one is aware of how the data are gathered one might conclude that this information is worth paying attention to. I think that it is very important continuously to distinguish the Monroe County register and the way it works from the register of the state as a whole.

BABIGIAN. To amplify this, Monroe County facilities report to our register at the Department of Psychiatry by name without too much problem, but some report to the Department of Mental Health by code, not name.

REFERENCES

Babigian, H. M. Schizophrenia in Monroe County. Paper read at "Schizophrenia — The Implications of Research Findings for Treatment and Teaching," a conference sponsored by the National Institute of Mental Health and John E. Fogarty International Center, National Institutes of Health, May 31, June 1 and 2, 1970.

———, Gardner, E. A., Miles, H. C., & Romano, J. Diagnostic consistency and change in a follow-up study of 1,215 patients. *American Journal of Psychiatry*, 1965, 121, 895–901.

Babigian, H. M., & Odoroff, C. L. The mortality experience of a population with psychiatric illness. *American Journal of Psychiatry*, 1969, 126, 470–479.

Bahn, A. Research tools for planning and evaluation. In R. H. Williams & L. Ozarin (Eds.), *Community mental health*. San Francisco: Jossey-Bass, 1968. Pp. 292–301.

Baldwin, J. A. Evaluative function of a case register. In R. H. Williams & L. Ozarin (Eds.), *Community mental health*. San Francisco: Jossey-Bass, 1968. Pp. 305–322.

Cowen, E. L., Izzo, L. D., Miles, H. C., Telschow, E. F., Trost, M. A., & Zax, M. A preventive mental health program in the school setting: Description and evaluation. *Journal of General Psychology*, 1963, 56, 307–356.

Cowen, E. L., Zax, M., Izzo, L. D., & Trost, M. A. The prevention of emotional disorders in the school setting: A further investigation. *Journal of Consulting Psychology*, 1966, 30, 381–387.

Gardner, E. A. The use of a psychiatric case register in the planning and evaluation of a mental health program. *Psychiatric Research Reports of the American Psychiatric Association*, 1967, 22, 259–281.

───── & Babigian, H. M. A longitudinal comparison of psychiatric service. *American Journal of Orthopsychiatry*, 1966, 36, 818–828.

Gardner, E. A., Bahn, A. K., & Miles, H. C. Patient experience in psychiatric units of general and state mental hospitals. *Public Health Reports*, 1964, 79, 755–767.

Gardner, E. A., Miles, H. C., Iker, H. P., & Romano, J. A cumulative register of psychiatric services in a community. *American Journal of Public Health*, 1963, 53, 1269–1277.

Garmezy, N. Vulnerability research and the issues of primary prevention. *American Journal of Orthopsychiatry*, 1971, 41, 101–116.

Hetznecker, W., Gardner, E. A., Odoroff, C. L., & Turner, R. J. Field survey methods in psychiatry. *Archives of General Psychiatry*, 1966, 15, 427–438.

Miles, H. C., & Gardner, E. A. A psychiatric case register. *Archives of General Psychiatry*, 1966, 14, 571–580.

Srole, L., Discussion. *Psychiatric Research Reports of the American Psychiatric Association*, 1967, 22, 282–290.

BARBARA SNELL DOHRENWEND
BRUCE P. DOHRENWEND ⦎ *Social Class and the Relation of Remote to Recent Stressors*

WE ARE concerned with the impact on individuals of events that, for better or for worse, disrupt the usual activities of most people who experience them — events such as death of a loved one, change in job, or, even, a trip to participate in a conference on life history research. The reason for our interest in these disrupting events is that we suspect they play a significant part in explaining why such large portions of general populations and, most strikingly, of the lowest socioeconomic class have been found in recent epidemiological studies to be suffering from what appear to be symptoms of psychiatric disorder (Dohrenwend & Dohrenwend, 1969, p. 17).

As our work in relations between social factors and psychopathology has progressed we have become more and more impressed with Tyhurst's comments in 1957. On the basis of his clinical observation of "transition states," such as marriage, childbearing, promotion, retirement, migration, and physical disaster, Tyhurst wrote: "Our tendency to regard the appearance of symptoms as invariable signs of illness, and therefore a need for psychiatric treatment, requires some revision. It would be probably more appropriate if we regarded the transition state and its accompanying disturbance as an opportunity for growth. When an impasse develops in the resolution of the 'hitch' we may speak of illness. Signs of psychological distress — somatic, emotional or intellectual — are thus not necessarily equivalent with that person's being a case of mental illness . . . Thus, for example, prevalence surveys of such symptoms . . . can have little meaning for the incidence of mental illness unless the *contextual relevance*

NOTE: The research reported here has been supported by Grants MH-10328 and MH-13356 from the National Institute of Mental Health, U.S. Public Health Service.

and timing of the symptoms is determined at the same time. If symptom incidence [sic] is not close to 100 per cent in such surveys, this is probably because the survey has been incomplete in some way or the memories of informants were faulty" (1957, p. 161).

PROBLEM

We are far from alone in our interest in the nature and rates of stressful events in different groups. In studies of the role of stress in both physical illness and psychiatric disorder, investigators have asked people about a variety of stressful events (or *stressors* as, borrowing across disciplines from Selye [1956], we prefer to call them) (e.g., Brown & Birley, 1968; Murphy, Robins, Kuhn, & Christensen, 1962; Paykel, Myers, Dienelt, Klerman, Lindenthal, & Pepper, 1969; Rahe & Arthur, 1968; Rahe, Meyer, Smith, Kjaer, & Holmes, 1964). In these studies anarchy has characterized the selection of events to be covered. Each investigator has developed his own list of events based on common sense, clinical experience, and personal predilection. Nevertheless, there is considerable overlap in the various lists. All include, for example, marriage, birth of a first child, serious injury or physical illness, and death of a loved one. Thus, there appears to be some agreement — at least among researchers — as to what constitutes stressful events.

A number of researchers have attempted to grapple with the problem of how to categorize these events into useful subtypes or to describe critical dimensions on which they vary. Among the proposed categories and dimensions are magnitude of change in usual activities implied by the event (Holmes & Rahe, 1967; Masuda & Holmes, 1967), the extent to which the affected individuals are responsible for the event's occurrence (Brown & Birley, 1968; B. S. Dohrenwend, 1970), whether the event involves the entrance or the exit of other persons into the subject's life (Paykel et al., 1969), and whether most people would consider it a gain or a loss (B. S. Dohrenwend, 1970).

The categories on which we shall focus are traceable to our concern with understanding the high rates of psychiatric symptoms so consistently observed by epidemiologists in members of the lowest socioeconomic class. B. S. Dohrenwend (1970, p. 315) reported finding a significant association between low income level and experience within the last two years of what would generally be considered losses rather than gains. Events categorized as gains included, for example, birth of a first child, a promotion on the job, and making new friends; losses included divorce, being evicted from an apartment, being laid off from a job, and having a car stolen.

Previous studies have shown that subjects with psychiatric symptoms were more likely than those who were relatively free of symptoms to have experienced recent losses (e.g., Brown & Birley, 1968; Murphy et al., 1962) or that gains tended to be followed by decreases and losses by increases in psychiatric symptoms (Dohrenwend & Dohrenwend, 1969, p. 128f.). The relation of gains and losses to income level may, therefore, provide an important piece in the puzzle of how to explain the relatively high rates of psychiatric symptoms reported for the lower class.

There are, however, two alternative processes that could produce the relatively high rate of losses in the lower class, and these alternative processes would fit into different places in the explanatory puzzle. On the one hand, perhaps a higher proportion of chronic "losers" drift into or remain in the lower class, so that the relatively high rate of loss is a consequence of the kind of people who make up that class. On the other hand, perhaps it is the class situation that produces the relatively high rate of events involving loss in the lower class, and losing is not a persistent characteristic of individuals at that level. We shall investigate this issue by examining short-term and long-term data on individual life histories. In particular, we shall ask to what extent an individual's current experiences of events involving gain or loss are a function of his life history of being a gainer or a loser.

METHOD

The data for this inquiry come from two investigations. The first, a cross-sectional study, was an interview survey of 257 adult heads of families, both men and women, married and single, sampled on a probability basis from the general population of Washington Heights, New York City. The aim in selecting the sample was to give equal representation to white Protestants of American ancestry, Jews, Irish, Negroes, and Puerto Ricans. Moreover, the attempt was made to draw the sample in such a way as to balance educational levels within each ethnic group — with partial success. The completed sample is short on poorly educated respondents among white Protestants of old American ancestry and to a lesser extent, among Jews. We are also somewhat short of college graduates among Puerto Ricans and among women who head households in which no husband is present. The 257 interviews secured represent a completion rate of 66 per cent of the respondents designated for interview.

At the end of the interview each respondent was asked, "What was the last major event in your life that, for better or for worse, interrupted or changed your usual activities?" After a pause for an answer, the interviewer used the following probe if no satisfactory response occurred: "For example, events affecting your occupation, your physical health, your living arrangements, your relations with other family members, your friends, or your personal values or beliefs?" This was followed by further probes for dates and other details and an open-ended question about other events almost as important since then. In addition, the interviewer administered a checklist of events that might have occurred in the last twelve months. The checklist was introduced as follows: "Some things happen to most people at one time or another; other things happen to only a few people. Which of these events have you experienced during the last twelve months?" A card was then handed to the respondents which listed these events as shown in the checklist below.

CHECKLIST OF EVENTS

Self	Other		
___	___	a	Engaged
___	___	a	Married
___	___	a,c	Other new love relationship or important friendship
___	___		Widowed
___	___		Divorced
___	___		Separated
___	___		Other broken love relationship or important friendship
___	___	b,c	Pregnancy
___	___	a	Birth of first child
___	___	b	Birth of child other than first
___	___		Miscarriage or stillbirth
___	___		Illness or injury
___	___	a,c	Improvement in health
___	___		Death of a loved one or other important person such as boss.
___	___	a	Started school, training program, etc.
___	___	a	Graduated from school, training program, etc.
___	___		Failed school, training program, etc.
___	___	b,c	Entered Armed Forces
___	___	a,c	Left Armed Forces
___	___	a	Started to work for the first time
___	___	a	Job or own business improved in responsibility, type, location, or some other way.
___	___		Job or own business downgraded in responsibility, type, location, or some other way.

___	___	b,c	Retired from work
___	___		Laid off, fired from job or own business failed
___	___	a,c	Major gain in income not due to change in work
___	___	c	Major loss of income not due to change in work
___	___	a,c	Acquisition of major property
___	___	c	Serious property loss
___	___	c	Arrested, indicted, convicted of other than minor traffic offense
___	___	a,c	Released from prison, acquitted of other than minor traffic offense
___	___	a	Changed residence for better one
___	___		Changed residence for worse one
___	___	a,c	Started new avocation, hobby, or recreational activity
___	___	c	Dropped previous avocation, hobby, or recreational activity
___	___	a,c	Acquired pet
___	___	c	Lost pet
___	___	a,c	Took a vacation
___	___		Other (Describe)_____

a. Gain.
b. Ambiguous as to whether gain or loss.
c. Included in second wave of panel study only.

The other investigation on which this analysis is based is a panel survey designed as a pilot study and conducted in two waves of interviewing, each carried out with a systematic sample of respondents drawn from two census tracts in Washington Heights, New York City. The two census tracts were selected for maximum income heterogeneity within each tract and racial heterogeneity between tracts, thus providing a sample of whites and Negroes over a similar income range. Following procedures described in detail elsewhere (B. S. Dohrenwend, 1970), 97 heads of household were interviewed in the first wave and in the second wave approximately one year later 56 heads of household and, when available, their spouses were interviewed. The questions concerning events that were asked in the cross-sectional study were also asked in both waves of the panel study, with minor variations. In particular, in the first wave interview of the panel study, the period of inquiry concerning events was two years instead of one; on the second wave the event questions were at the beginning rather than at the end of the interview, and the checklist of events was expanded as indicated above.

Responses to the event checklist and to the open-ended questions preceding it provided data on events experienced by respondents in the year or two preceding the interviews in the cross-section and panel studies. A small number of pseudo-events, which were actually subjective experiences of respondents rather than objective occurrences, were eliminated. We then classified each of the objective events in terms of our judgments of whether most people would think of them as representing a gain or a loss, or whether the events might be ambiguous in this respect, with 87 per cent agreement on this three-way classification: 6 per cent of the actual events reported in response to the open question and the checklist were judged ambiguous in the cross-sectional study and on the second wave of the panel study, and 12 per cent were so judged in the first wave of the panel study. You can check our judgment of gain, loss, and ambiguous against your own for the events on the checklist by noting the classification in the list on pages 173–174, on which events that are not marked gain or ambiguous are losses.

We also classified the events into the following substantive types: death, health, occupation, marriage and family, migration and change of residence, and education, with 77 per cent agreement. Most disagreements were over whether an event fitted into any category at all rather than over which of two categories was appropriate.

The interviews also provided data on two sets of antecedent conditions of advantage or disadvantage that we can relate to the contemporary gain-loss data from the stressor questions. The first of these comes from knowledge of the class background of the respondents in the cross-section study gained from the question "When you were about 18 or 19 years old, what kind of work was your father doing for a living?" If the father was not working at the time or had died, his usual line of work was asked about. The second datum on antecedent conditions is provided by the question in the cross-section study "Please think back to how you were brought up — say, up to the time you were about 12 years old. Did you live with both your parents during most of your childhood — up to age 12?"

In both studies, of course, the interviewer also asked about the respondent's education, his occupation, and the family income during the preceding year. It is this last information that we rely on for the index of his class position in this paper. We choose income because of our interest in the effect of earlier life history conditions on the relation of class position to contemporary gain-loss events. Given this problem, we want an index of class that is not itself an antecedent condition. Family income during the preceding year was chosen, therefore, over educational level and usual occupation, both of which usually preceded it in time.

RESULTS

We first examined whether the relation of family income to gains and losses found in the previously reported study (B. S. Dohrenwend, 1970) was replicated with the larger sample used in the cross-sectional study. The answer is provided in Figure 1.

These results include only respondents who reported at least one event in the last year that was unambiguously either a loss or a gain. In this study, perhaps because the questions concerning life events came at the end of a long interview, 33 per cent of respondents reported no events occurring within the last year. Although there is a trend for the proportion reporting no events to be highest at the lowest income level, the relation between reporting or not reporting events and income is not significant ($\chi^2 = 8.83$, $df = 7$). Moreover, the trend is far too slight to play much part in the association between a high rate of psychiatric symptoms and low income.

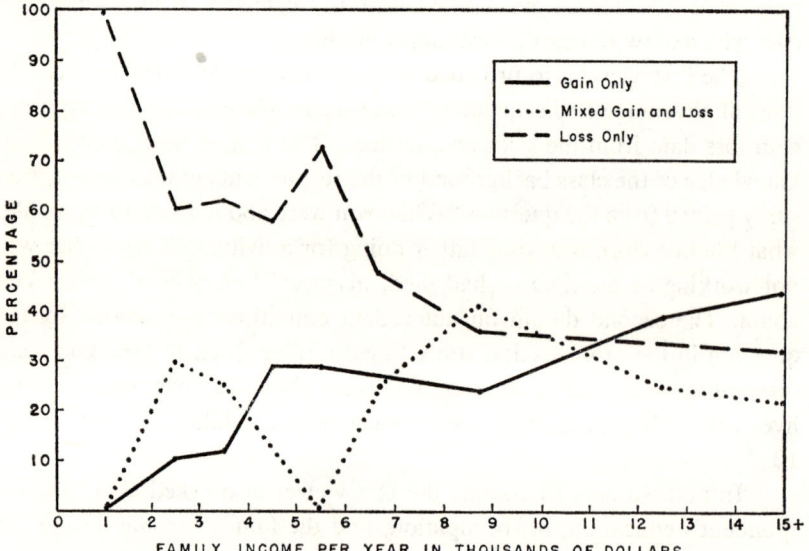

Figure 1. Direction of change in events occurring in the last year according to family income of respondents in cross-section study: 7 respondents earned less than $2,000; 10, $2,000–$2,999; 16, $3,000–$3,999; 14, $4,000–$4,999; 14, $5,000–$5,999; 23, $6,000–$7,499; 34, $7,500–$9,999; 38, $10,000–$14,999; 9, $15,000 or more. For gain versus mixed gain and loss versus loss times income, $\chi^2 = 28.56$, $df = 16$, $p<.05$.

By contrast with the relative lack of difference in proportions reporting no events, Figure 1 shows that the proportion of respondents experiencing losses decreases, and the proportion experiencing gains increases as family income increases, and that the relation of family income to the direction of events is statistically significant. For the purpose of subsequent analysis we have combined the eight income levels in Figure 1 into three groups in such a way as to maximize the difference among them in proportions of respondents experiencing loss only or gain only, and to place enough respondents in each group to permit further breakdowns. The income categories thus formed are less than $4,000 per year, $4,000 to $7,499, and $7,500 or more.

Further evidence concerning the difference in events experienced in these three income groups is seen in Table 1, which shows the distribution of events of various substantive types according to the cross-sectional respondents' current income. Particularly striking is the class difference in the proportion of extreme losses in the form of deaths, with the highest proportion in the lowest class and the lowest proportion in the highest class. In contrast, the proportions of other types of events vary much less among the three income groups. Thus, not only do members of the lower class suffer more losses, but in addition, their losses disproportionately take the extreme form of deaths of persons who are important to them.

We then determined whether factors in the life history of members of the lower class are related to their experience of extreme and excessive loss compared to members of higher classes. Family income is the most contemporary indicator we have of the respondent's social class, and the

Table 1. Relation between Current Income Level and Substantive Events Reported for Last Twelve Months[a] [b]

Substantive Event	Income under $4,000	Income $4,000–$7,499	Income $7,500 or More
Death	34.4%	22.7%	4.5%
Health	23.0	29.5	34.8
Occupation	18.0	27.3	34.8
Marriage and family	3.3	5.7	9.7
Migration	11.5	13.6	5.8
Education	9.8	1.1	10.3

[a] Percentages are based on the total number of events reported, which were 61 for the lowest income group, 88 for the middle, and 155 for the highest.

[b] Excluding respondents who reported no events in the last 12 months, there were 34 respondents in the lowest income group, 52 in the middle, and 84 in the highest.

occupation of his father while he was growing up is the most remote. As the top of Table 2 shows, his father's occupation, even grossly categorized into white collar, blue collar, and farm, is significantly related to the cross-sectional respondent's current experience of gain or loss.

However, the bottom of Table 2 shows, as would be expected, that there is a significant relationship between our respondents' present family income and their fathers' occupation during the respondents' early years. Perhaps, then, present income can account for the relationship between the father's occupation some years back and the respondent's current experience of gains and losses.

This hypothesis is examined in Table 3, with the lowest income group excluded since there were only five respondents at this income level whose fathers were in white-collar occupations. For the remaining cases, introduction of current income as a control reduces the strength of the re-

Table 2. Relation of Father's Occupation to Respondent's Current Gains and Losses and Current Income

Recent Events and Income	Father's Occupation		
	White Collar	Blue Collar	Farm
Direction of events in last 12 months[a] [b]			
Gain only	43.1%	19.7%	15.4%
Mixed gain and loss	20.7	26.8	38.5
Loss only	36.2	53.5	46.2
Current income level[c] [d]			
Less than $4,000	5.9	22.2	44.4
$4,000 to $7,499	32.9	34.3	26.7
$7,500 or more	61.2	43.5	28.9

[a] $\chi^2 = 10.64$, $df = 4$, $p < .05$.

[b] There were 58 respondents whose fathers had white-collar jobs, 71 whose fathers had blue-collar jobs, and 13 whose fathers were farmers, excluding respondents who reported no events or only ambiguous events in last 12 months and 10 respondents who did not answer the question about father's occupation. This question required information on father's occupation at the time the respondent was 18 or 19 years old. The instruction to the interviewer read: "If respondent replies 'not working at that time,' get and record regular line of work. Record if respondent's father was dead at the time and ask questions about his 'usual' occupation. If respondent did not know his father, record this and ask questions about the 'breadwinner,' noting who this was."

[c] $\chi^2 = 29.04$, $df = 4$, $p < .001$.

[d] There were 85 respondents whose fathers had white-collar jobs, 108 whose fathers had blue-collar jobs, and 45 whose fathers were farmers, excluding 10 respondents who did not answer the question about father's occupation.

Table 3. Relation of Father's Occupation to Respondents' Gains and Losses over Last Twelve Months, Controlled for Current Income[a]

Current Income[b] and Direction of Recent Events	Father's Occupation	
	White Collar	Blue Collar
$4,000 to $7,499[c]		
Gain only	33.3%	24.0%
Mixed gain and loss	0.0	32.0
Loss only	66.7	44.0
$7,500 or more[d]		
Gain only	47.4	21.2
Mixed gain and loss	28.9	27.3
Loss only	23.7	51.5

[a] Excluding respondents who reported no events or only ambiguous events in the last twelve months, respondents who did not answer the question about father's occupation, and 25 children of farmers, too small a group to divide by current income.

[b] $N =$ Lowest income group excluded since there were only five respondents at this income level whose fathers were in white-collar occupations.

[c] $N = 15$ whose father's occupation was white collar and 25 blue collar.

[d] $N = 38$ whose father's occupation was white collar and 33 blue collar.

lationship between father's occupation and current experiences of gain and loss, but does not eliminate it. We note that respondents at both current income levels whose fathers were in white-collar occupations were more likely than those whose fathers were in blue-collar occupations to report only gains. For those in the higher current income bracket, those with a white-collar background were also less likely than those with a blue-collar background to report only losses. These trends encourage us to look further for evidence of life history factors that distinguish those who are currently experiencing losses.

An early experience in the life history of some respondents was separation from one or both parents for most of their childhood — that is, for the majority of the time before they were twelve years old. Are people who suffered this early loss more likely than others to suffer later losses as well? Table 4 shows that, for the higher income groups, cross-sectional respondents who experienced early parental separation are no more likely than those who did not to have experienced only losses recently. We are impressed, however, given our particular interest in understanding the basis for the high rate of loss in the lowest class, that in this income group there

Table 4. Relation of Early Separation from Parents to Current
Gains and Losses by Current Income Level[a]

Current Income Level	Gain Only	Mixed Gain and Loss	Loss Only
Under $4,000			
Lived with both parents to age 12	14.3%	23.8%	61.9%
Separated from parent before age 12	0	18.2	81.8
$4,000 to $7,499			
Lived with both parents to age 12	25.0	17.5	57.5
Separated from parent before age 12	30.0	10.0	60.0
$7,500 or more			
Lived with both parents to age 12	37.5	28.1	34.4
Separated from parent before age 12	18.8	43.8	37.5

[a] There were 21 reporting events in the lowest income group who lived with both their parents before age 12, 11 who did not; 40 in the middle group who did, 10 who did not; and 64 in the highest group who did, 16 who did not.

is a tendency for early separation to be associated with a disproportionate rate of contemporary loss.

Up to this point we looked for people who were losers over a considerable span of time. The panel study was designed to supplement and extend the cross-sectional investigation by providing a set of data for a shorter period of time. On both waves of the panel study, as in the cross-sectional study, members of the lowest social class, those with an income of less than $4,000, were significantly more likely than other respondents to report only losses. This consistent group difference over the three years covered by stressor questions in the panel study suggests the possibility of individual consistency in experiencing gains and losses for this relatively short period.

Table 5 shows the shifts in gains and losses between the waves of the panel study for respondents reporting at least one event that was unambiguous with respect to gain and loss on both waves. Note first that there was a shift toward more reporting of gains from the first to the second wave. This was true of all respondents as well as the category who reported unambiguous events on both waves, and seems to be due to the addition to the event checklist used in the second wave of a number of positive events not included in the event checklist in the first wave, as well as to an overall

Table 5. Relation of Direction of Events Reported on First Wave to Direction of Events Reported on Second Wave[a]

Events Reported on Second Wave	Events Reported on First Wave[b]		Total[c]
	Gain Only	Loss Only	
Gain only[d]	66.7%	40.0%	51.6%
Mixed gain and loss[d]	25.0	46.7	38.7
Loss only	8.3	13.3	9.7
Direction of first-wave events[e]	38.7	48.4	...

[a] There were 12 respondents who, on the first wave, reported gain only, 4 who reported mixed gain and loss, and 15 who reported loss only. The 4 who reported mixed gain and loss are excluded because of the small number. In the second wave, 2 of them reported gain only, and 2 again reported mixed gain and loss. Excluded are 11 re-interviewed respondents who reported either no events or only events that were ambiguous with respect to loss and gain on one wave.
[b] Covering previous two years.
[c] For all respondents.
[d] Two respondents reported mixed gain and loss on the first wave.

increase in number of events reported on the second wave. The latter increase probably resulted from the fact that the stressor questions were asked at the end of the first wave interview and at the beginning of the second wave interview. To allow for the shift in the proportion of gains when testing for individual consistency in losses and gains we divided the respondents into approximately equal groups on both waves and determined whether the 48 per cent who reported only losses on the first wave were the same individuals as the 48 per cent who reported either losses only or mixed loss and gain on the second wave. This division indicates that 61 per cent of the respondents were consistent from one wave to the next. However, in the lowest income group the consistency is largely due to losers, whereas in higher income groups it is largely due to gainers. Thus, these short-run results are like those observed over the longer run. The difference is again in the direction expected on the hypothesis that some individuals in the lowest income group are consistent losers.

DISCUSSION

Until the opportunity to contribute to this volume on life history research in psychopathology provided us with the incentive to examine an alternative, we had tended to assume without serious question that in cause-and-effect equations relating individuals' symptoms of psychopathology to the contemporary environment, social stressors could almost always be placed on the side of environmental causes. In particular, we had become quite fond of the notion that the high incidence of losses in the lower class implied that much of the excess of psychiatric symptoms observed in this group was an effect of stressful contemporary events and, hence, not dissimilar to combat reactions on the part of previously normal soldiers. The situation no longer seems so clear-cut.

In the present paper we asked whether those who are experiencing contemporary events that signify loss, particularly those in the lower class, have a life history of being losers in this sense, and the answer is not clearly negative. Our results raise the possibility that, at least for some individuals, loss events do not fit the role of class-linked environmental causes, but rather are themselves a function of something analogous to accident proneness. We are not ready to commit ourselves to this reinterpretation, however, unless we can establish firmly that the small but persistent association of recent with more remote losses that remained when we controlled contemporary social class holds for larger samples and for a wider variety of antecedent loss events. If we find this to be so, we expect that the nature of the earlier events that are more than coincidentally associated with consistent later losses will help us to understand how an individual becomes a loser in life. We hope that they will also suggest how this condition can be prevented.

COMMENTARY

GUZE. My question is a methodological one and has to do with the likelihood of being able to give a gainer response instead of a loser response. If it's true that lower income people are more likely to complete education, start work, and have families earlier, is it perhaps the case that for many of your low-income people these events (that could have been counted as gains) took place much earlier in their lives and so they had fewer possibilities for giving a gainer response than someone from a higher level?

BARBARA DOHRENWEND. Part of the answer to that does not come directly from the data that I've reported here. I mentioned that the rate of reporting of gains increased in the second wave of the panel study. This happened in part because we asked the stressor questions at the beginning of the interview rather than at the end of the interview, and also, because we expanded the list of events that were suggested on the checklist. The kinds of things that we included in the second wave were such things as taking a vacation, acquiring a pet, making new friends. These didn't seem to be limited to any particular period in the life-span. Rather, this new list brought out even more sharply the contrast in the amounts of gain between the higher and the lower classes. So I don't have the impression that one could explain the class difference in terms of age-linked events.

ROBINS. One of the things that I'm concerned about is what the correlation between income and age might be, and therefore the exposure to some of the variables. For instance, as people get older they experience more and more deaths, and if they also get progressively poorer, as census figures seem to indicate, you may be showing that experiencing death is associated with age rather than income.

BARBARA DOHRENWEND. We have found no relation between age and gain or loss in any of the three sets of data we're talking about here. As a matter of fact, when I eliminated the oldest group in one set, I actually increased the strength of the class relationship, though I think that was probably a fluke.

MYERS. We're doing a similar study in New Haven — a longitudinal study of 938 people who were interviewed in 1967 and then re-interviewed two years later. Although we have called our two categories desirable and undesirable, they are similar to your gain and loss categories. We found the same class pattern as you — that is, the higher the class the more likely one is to experience what you call a gain or what we call a desirable event. With people who have experienced multiple events, then we found, as you did, that as social class status declines, disproportionately more people experience more unpleasant than pleasant events. That is, the ratio of unpleasant to pleasant events increases as we move from higher to lower status. Thus, our materials support your findings, including the lack of relationship between class and total number of events experienced.

VAILLANT. I have a methodological concern regarding how, in interpreting stressor events, you can tell the optimists from the pessimists. It's been said that the optimist who got a Christmas stocking full of manure was delighted and told every one that Santa Claus had brought him a pony. In talking about gainers and losers your figures suggest that people with high income experienced an average of 1 death per 14 people and the poor experienced 2 deaths per 3 people. If taken literally, this means that the poor experienced ten times as many stressful deaths as the rich. I would think that you would need to study those deaths and see why the poor should report so many more stressful deaths than the rich. You probably need some kind of objective control for what really is happening in a person's life rather than their subjective perception.

MYERS. We asked about events in terms of whether the event occurred in the past year, not as a result of an open-ended question. The class factor in deaths is a difference of family size. There are more people to die as you go down the social class scale, since families are larger.

BARBARA DOHRENWEND. We have not looked at these deaths in detail, but I can give you some impressions from what I know. For some of the lower-class people, deaths which have an impact are not limited to the family. They may be, for example, the man a cleaning woman has worked for for ten years. So there may be an added vulnerability for some lower-class persons.

In addition to asking about past events, we asked our respondents about anticipated future events. I haven't analyzed these answers thoroughly, but as far as we've gone there are no class differences in the gain-loss of anticipated events. Everybody, even poor people, think good things are going to happen to them in the future.

THOMAS. A question that comes up often in studies involving lower-class populations is the fact that the lower income group is not homogeneous at all. There's a vast difference between the stable working-class family with continuity and stability of living arrangements, and the type of lower-class family so often studied — the disorganized family to whom all kinds of things happen all the time. For example, we followed a Puerto Rican population that is stable, though lower class, and lives in public housing projects, and we didn't get any greater incident of events such as divorce and death in the family or even any dramatic difference in the incidence of behavior disorder than we did in a middle-class population. If one studies a disorganized lower-class family structure, the outcome could be very different.

BARBARA DOHRENWEND. I think this is a quite reasonable comment. Of course, our group is heterogeneous, and more analysis needs to be done.

MYERS. One thing we've done is to record the person's subjective reaction to the occurrence of the event in addition to the actual occurrence. In preliminary analyses we've found a high correlation between the results, whether we use the objective event or an individual's subjective perception of it. Originally we thought that perhaps the individual's subjective perception of what happened to him rather than the objective event itself would be important. So far, this has not been the case, although we haven't gotten far into the analysis. We get no difference in the reporting of these events over a time period for the first or second six months in which they occurred. The number of the events that are reported are, I think, being accurately reported. We have recorded events in terms of whether they happen to the respondent, to a member of his immediate family, to an extended family member, or to a significant other person, so it is possible to answer your question empirically as to whether it makes a difference to whom the events occurred.

REFERENCES

Brown, G. W., & Birley, J. L. T. Crises and life changes and the onset of schizophrenia. *Journal of Health and Social Behavior*, 1968, 9, 203–214.

Dohrenwend, B. P., Chin-Shong, E. T., Egri, G., Mendelsohn, F. R., & Stokes, J. Measures of psychiatric disorder in contrasting class and ethnic groups. In E. H. Hare & J. K. Wing (Eds.), *Psychiatric epidemiology: Proceedings of the international symposium held at Aberdeen University 22–5 July 1969*. New York: Oxford University Press, 1970. Pp. 159–202.

Dohrenwend, B. P., & Dohrenwend, B. S. *Social status and psychological disorder: A causal inquiry.* New York: Wiley, 1969.

Dohrenwend, B. S. An experimental study of the effect of payment on respondent cooperation. *Public Opinion Quarterly,* 1970, 34, 621–624.

———. Social class and stressful events. In E. H. Hare & J. K. Wing (Eds.), *Psychiatric epidemiology: Proceedings of the international symposium held at Aberdeen University 22–5 July 1969.* New York: Oxford University Press, 1970. Pp. 313–319.

Holmes, T. H., & Rahe, R. H. The social readjustment rating scale. *Journal of Psychosomatic Research,* 1967, 11, 213–218.

Masuda, M., & Holmes, T. H. Magnitude estimations of social readjustments. *Journal of Psychosomatic Research,* 1967, 11, 219.

Murphy, G. E., Robins, E., Kuhn, N. O., & Christensen, R. F. Stress, sickness and psychiatric disorder in a "normal" population: A study of 101 young women. *Journal of Nervous and Mental Disease,* 1962, 134, 228–236.

Paykel, E. S., Myers, H. K., Dienelt, M., Klerman, G. L., Lindenthal, J. J., & Pepper, M. P. Life events and depression. *Archives of General Psychiatry,* 1969, 21, 753–760.

Rahe, R. H., & Arthur, R. J. Life-change patterns surrounding illness experience. *Journal of Psychosomatic Research,* 1968, 11, 341–345.

Rahe, R. H., Meyer, M., Smith, J., Kjaer, G., & Holmes, T. H. Social stress and illness onset. *Journal of Psychosomatic Research,* 1964, 8, 35–44.

Selye, H. *The stress of life.* New York: McGraw-Hill, 1956.

Tyhurst, J. S. The role of transition states – including disasters – in mental illness. In *Symposium on preventive and social psychiatry.* Washington, D.C.: Government Printing Office, 1957. Pp. 149–169.

D. H. STOTT] *The Congenital Background to Behavior Disturbance*

IN GENERAL, scientists yield to the cultural pressures of their times. For every Galileo who resists, a hundred do not dare to propose and pursue what they really think. To cite just one example from psychology, in a behaviorist generation Tolman (1938) toyed with the notion of consciousness. He was soon to recant it as "no doubt a silly idea." In his anxiety for acceptance he lost his chance of enduring greatness.

Nineteenth-century Darwinism and Galtonism dictated that the scientists of the succeeding generations find a genetic explanation of individual differences, based on an oversimplified natural selection. In regard to intelligence, this approach was heavily attacked during the late 1920's and 30's by the Iowa foster-home studies. The Scottish Mental Survey (Scottish Council for Research in Education, 1953) failed to confirm the eugenicists' prediction of a fall in IQ owing to the greater fecundity of the presumed unintelligent.

The pendulum has now swung against innateness. Our democratic ideals have virtually dictated that we find environmental reasons for individual differences. The idea that some are born better than others is culturally unacceptable.

When it comes to behavioral disturbance, the present state of affairs is that most specialists in this area sedulously avoid the issue. During the 1940's a group of neo-Freudians made determined efforts to build an etiology of psychopathy on early deprivation. But Spitz was discredited by his refusal to reveal the sources of his data, and by Pinneau's (1955) demonstration from internal evidence that his longitudinal data referred to different children. The work of Goldfarb (1943, 1945) — admitted by Ainsworth (1962) to be the only study demonstrating the long-time effects of early deprivation — rested on the assumption that there were no congenital differences between children put out for adoption at under six months and those retained in the institution until their third birthday. When Bowlby (with Ainsworth, Boston, & Rosenbluth, 1956), notably failed to confirm his own theory of the etiology of the "affectionless character" in his study of young children who had been some months in a tuberculosis sanatorium, he turned to the ethologists' work on imprinting. But the search for critical periods in human personality development has been unrewarding. It is highly important for the chicks of water birds to follow closely behind their mother, and since the mother, for all practical purposes, is the only moving object within sight after hatching, it is not necessary to evolve any finer discrimination about the object to be followed. The human babe's survival does not depend upon a single reaction during one short phase of his development. He has to be an appealing object to receive and give out signals of affection, over many years of childhood. He also has to learn to switch his affections and to develop group attachments. Schaffer (1964), although not wishing at that time to commit himself to drawing congenital conclusions from his studies, cut the ground away from the critical-period hypothesis. He showed that the time of development of the child's attachment responses was independent of the warmth of the mother's interaction with the child. His work should have put an end to the search for ever more subtle and scientifically unreachable differences in maternal handling which have been postulated as the origins of enduring individual differences.

Meanwhile, some progress was being made from quite a different quarter. Pasamanick and Knobloch (1960) found that among a test population of over 1,000 children exhibiting deviant behavior there was three times as much prematurity, and 25–50 per cent higher rates of pregnancy complications, depending upon race, compared with randomly selected controls. The highest associations were with behavior disorders of the hyperactive and disorganized types. Burton (1964) found a much higher incidence of pregnancy stress among accident-prone children. Prechtl and Stemmer (1962) found a high incidence of neurological symptoms among children referred for behavior disabilities and poor schoolwork. In half of them the mother's pregnancy was complicated by toxemia, severe bleeding, and so forth, and in 60 per cent there was postnatal illness. Birch (1964) and Eisenberg (1964) have drawn attention to the behavioral and social consequences of the inhibitional failure which is characteristic of brain-damaged children. They and Chess view the resulting tiresomeness and uncontrollability, to use popular terms, as the starting point of a vicious circle of deteriorating parent-child relations, an observation which I would endorse from my own studies. The hostility and antisocial behavior of older maladjusted and delinquent children could be a secondary formation originating in a primary neurological failure of adaption.

It is of interest that in one of her latest statements Chess (1969) speaks of "the role the child's own *temperament* plays in the development of behavioral disturbance and its symptoms" (my italics). She is careful not to attach any etiological significance to the word *temperament* and insists that there is at present no empirical support for any of the rival theories of the etiology of behavior disturbance. Nevertheless, the word *temperament* implies something that is part of the person's individual constitution, that is to say, something that he is born with. The term is valuable and realistic. Parents cannot fail to notice the differences in temperament of their children from birth. Murphy (1962), with her gift for observation and empirical enquiry, noted differences in temperament within the same family, without being able to find significant differences in the way the children were reared. Adamson (1961), in an equally acute study of the three cubs of Elsa the lioness, was able to note consistent differences in temperament from a day or so after their birth, which persisted during their cubhood.

I find it highly gratifying that Chess identifies two types of temperamental impairment which parallel my own observations. The first is an inability to adapt to new stimuli — what she calls the "slow-to-warm-up" child. I have named this *Unforthcomingness*; it may be defined as a lack of that natural assertiveness and desire for mastery which normally induces a child to overcome his apprehensiveness of strange situations and new tasks. I am quite sure that, as Chess points out, much of the academic incompetence which results from this retreat from difficulties is construed, both by teachers and psychologists, as "dullness." I am beginning to believe, also, that some mental defect is really extreme Unforthcomingness.

Chess suggests no name for her second type of temperamental impairment, but describes the unorganized, restless, distractible, attention-demanding child. I have termed it *Inconsequence* because, owing to his failure to inhibit primitive impulsive responses, the child does not carry out the cognitive rehearsal of an action which would allow him to foresee the consequences.

It behooves me, if I am not to be accused in turn of sitting on the fence, to state the position at which I currently find myself with regard to the etiology of behavior disturbance. I say "currently" because over the years I have tended to reverse my position. In the early 1950's I was, emotionally rather than intellectually, a convinced environmentalist, and in my study of the origins of delinquent behavior I laid much stress upon maternal deprivation. My doubts arose during subsequent case studies of mentally subnormal children (Stott, 1956). Of the 25 who up to the age of 4 years had been separated for at least 10 weeks — actually averaging 72 weeks, or a third of their lives — 8 were Unforthcoming children. But there were just as many with this temperamental impairment among those who had not been separated. Five might be described as Unsettled, and four as maladjusted. However, the last group suffered from contemporary rejection, disloyalty, or painful lack of family which was sufficient to account for their antisocial behavior without our having to postulate an effect from their early lives. Finally, there were eight stable, affectionate, sensible children, despite long separation from the mother.

The oustanding feature in the case histories of the total sample of 102 mentally subnormal children from which these 25 were drawn was the large amount of serious, nonepidemic illness suffered by them during their first three years of life. As the data accumulated I began to see this as one of the major causes of mental subnormality. At the same time, because of the known effects of rubella and the possibility of other teratogenic agents, I recorded the pregnancy histories. Once again there was, compared with the mentally normal controls, a preponderance of maternal ill health — mostly stress diseases such as toxemia, ulcer, asthma — and of events and circumstances likely to cause shock, distress, and harassment. So frequent were these that I came to regard pregnancy complications as a second but independent cause of mental subnormality. When, however, the data were tabulated and analyzed, a highly significant relationship emerged between the pregnancy complications and the morbid childhood conditions (Stott, 1957a). It was equally significant among the normal controls, although the incidence both of pregnancy complications and of early nonepidemic illness was much lower.

I should like to say something in parenthesis here about the value of retrospective studies such as the one quoted here. The fashion is now to reject these out of hand because, as it is roundly claimed, mothers' memories are unreliable. In fact, the accusation of bias can be turned against the critics. They take a standpoint without regard to the empirical findings, and because of this ruling attitude it has become extremely hard to gain a hearing for retrospective studies. Overlooked are the gains made through such studies — for example, the observations which led Gregg

(1941) to discover the noxious effects of prenatal rubella were of a retrospective character; it was nearly twenty years before Manson et al. (1960) confirmed them in a prospective study. If we reject retrospective investigation, important areas of knowledge, notably in the etiology of psychopathic conditions, will remain closed indefinitely. The chief drawback in the prospective, or anterospective, study is the large number of cases needed when one does not know in advance which will come to show the handicap. Rubella, for example, is a comparatively rare antecedent of mental retardation or malformation and would certainly never have been discovered anterospectively.

To take a case in point, Chess, who has recently come out in strong criticism of retrospective studies, has only 136 in her anterospective one, of whom the usual 10 percent were disturbed. It is difficult to see trends, let alone to reach definitive conclusions, with 13 or 14 children, whose disturbances would inevitably be varied in character.

A second major disadvantage of the anterospective study is that the investigators have to know what to look for before they begin. They cannot go back to collect data relating to new insights without becoming retrospective. The usual history of prospective, long-term studies is that before they are complete, new findings come to light which render them out of date. The only guarantee against this is to gain prior insight into the real state of affairs, by all the methods that are available, so that the role of the anterospective study becomes one of confirmation or — as in the case of rubella — of precise epidemiology.

Retrospective studies play an important part in the progressive reduction of uncertainty which is the aim of an empirically minded scientist. They have the immense advantage of being able to start with the result, even though the individual cases may occur only rarely. They give comparatively speedy answers (or, shall we say, hypotheses) because they can telescope to within a few months what has taken place over a generation. They are flexible and do not presuppose an a priori omniscience: false starts can be corrected, and hints can be followed up. In sum, careful retrospective studies are a necessary preliminary to the anterospective, and to undertake the latter without them is to be epistemologically naive.

Nevertheless, we all recognize the unreliability inherent in retrospective studies, and the value of the anterospective study as the most satisfactory way of demonstrating an effect. But the need for retrospection as the first phase of any investigation in broad areas of human life and development should compel us to examine in detail this element of reliability with a view to reducing it to tolerable proportions.

There are a number of studies of the reliability of anamnestic data which enable us to do just this. Chess (1969) quotes two studies, Robbins' (1963) and her own, which highlight some elements of unreliability in maternal memory. If one questions mothers about their child-rearing practices, as these workers did, it is only to be expected that they will claim they did the right thing — whatever that may have been considered to be at the time. Nor is it unexpected, as Robbins found, that mothers cannot state accurately the time of the beginning of such ill-defined phases as weaning and toilet training.

The other side of the coin is that 88 per cent of the same mothers remembered their children's birth weights to within half a pound, and over 80 per cent accurately recalled whether the child had ever sucked his thumb. Lotter (1966) compared the birth weights as reported by mothers with hospital records and found a mean discrepancy of less than 1 oz. There was a difference of only .2 of a month in the age of walking given by the mother over a 6 ½-year interval. In fact a number of studies have shown that, if mothers are asked about facts of the whether-or-not type, their memories are remarkably reliable. Haggard (1960) and his associates found a reliability coefficient of .80 for maternal memory of what he classified as hard facts. In my own study of 102 mentally subnormal children (Stott, 1957b) I was subsequently able to obtain from the vaults of the City Health Department contemporary public health nurses' records of their visits to the homes. Mothers' and nurses' reports tallied in 72 per cent of the illnesses. The mothers actually reported more fully than the nurses, who missed some of the illnesses because of the irregularity of their visits. When the mothers were reinterviewed in order to discover why they had not mentioned certain illnesses, all but one spontaneously mentioned them. It was concluded that such unreliability as there had been in their reporting was due, not to their memories, but to the technique of the interview. In a recent spotcheck against contemporary family physicians' records of information regarding their pregnancies and their children's early health given by mothers of 5-year-old children, we found that with carefully trained interviewers who gained the confidence of the mothers, the reliability of maternal memory reached virtually 100 per cent. The only discrepancies were due to known defects in the doctor's records, or illnesses not severe enough for him to be consulted.

I have devoted quite a little space to this digression into the reliability of maternal memory because it is central to the progress of our understanding of the etiology of behavior disturbance. We just cannot afford to abandon retrospective studies. It is a question of developing a technology which concentrates on those areas of information which can be elicited reliably, at the same time using research designs in which such unreliability as remains counts against the significance of our results.

I would like to refer to an even greater barrier to progress in our search for the causes of behavior disturbance. This is the achievement of satisfactory classification of its manifestations. Until we have this, we have nothing objective to relate to any other variable or to present to the geneticists as a phenotype. I cannot here discuss all the difficulties and complications of such classifications. Briefly, one has to decide what is similar behavior. Kagan's (1965) concept of heterotypic continuity — that is to say, a diversity of manifestations through time of a basic condition — is obviously useful here. But we are thrown back on what we mean by a basic condition. If we take a biological-evolutionary view of the value of behavior to the organism, we arrive at the idea of classification by outcome: that is to say, the change, to the organism's advantage or disadvantage, that the act brings about. Behaviors can thus be classified as similar if they have similar effects.

In the original publication of the Bristol Social Adjustment Guide (Stott & Sykes, 1956), this principle was applied only inconsistently. The method used represented a halfway house in the shift from phenomenological to conceptual-outcome criteria of classification. In the revision upon which we are now working, we believe that we have a classification in terms of the types of relationship which the individual achieves with his environment.

It is doubtful whether we should expect a syndromic arrangement to emerge. A syndrome presupposes a general major factor such as a virus, or a particular deficiency or lesion. In our review of the results for nearly 2,500 schoolchildren in Ontario, certain groupings do in fact come out clearly and consistently for all age groups. These are: *Unforthcomingness*, already defined as an unwillingness to cope with strange situations or presumed difficult material; *Withdrawal*, indifference to or defensiveness against establishing personal relationships; *Hostility*, behavior calculated to destroy or prevent the establishment of a good personal relationship; and *Depression*, a refusal to respond to normal challenges.

Inconsequence is throughout contaminated with aggressive, quasi-hostile behavior. This can be, in fact, one aspect of the failure to inhibit primitive impulses: among these are attack upon meeting frustration, or unreflecting dominance over other children. On the other hand, it can be true hostility in answer to the rejection which the Inconsequential child often brings upon himself. In short, we have what seems to be a primary, neurological form of behavior disturbance complicated by a secondary hostility. The extent to which this hostility or disturbance occurs depends upon the patience of those who have the care of the child. Such an interaction of an original impairment of temperament with a wide variety of human environments would yield not a syndrome but a continuum, at one end of which would be predominantly Hostility, at the other predominantly Inconsequence. We would expect to find a middle zone of Inconsequence (inhibitional failure) combined with aggressive-hostile symptoms (failure to inhibit primitive attack-responses); and this is in fact the picture that emerges.

The upshot is that where we have a comparatively clean syndrome then — for lack of any convincing postnatal determinant — there is a presumption of congenital origin. But the lack of the traditional syndromic clustering does not necessarily weigh against a congenital origin. It may result from an interaction of diverse influences, some of which may be congenital.

One form of direct evidence for a congenital factor would be a significant relationship between the condition and events before birth. Sontag (1941, 1944) was a pioneer in this field. In the early 1940's he reported a relationship between anxiety and tension in the mother and increased fetal activity, followed by gastrointestinal disturbances in the infant. The affected individuals later showed what he termed social apprehensiveness. In some cases this persisted as a temperamental defect for over twenty years (Sontag, 1962). I have found Unforthcomingness to be related to pregnancy stresses occurring more in the later stages of pregnancy. In a small nursery school population, one of my students found a deficiency of effectiveness-motivation (another way of conceptualizing Unforthcomingness) to be similarly related to stressful pregnancy. In experimental biology, the findings of W. R. Thompson (1957), confirmed by Ader and Belfer (1962), were that the offspring of rats subjected to fear of shock during pregnancy showed an apprehensiveness in emerging from the protection of their box and in exploring their run which exactly parallels the behavior of the Unforthcoming child.

Our latest studies have been of Inconsequential children. From those cases referred to the Centre for Educational Disabilities at the University of Guelph, we isolated 29 who met the criterion of eight indications of this syndrome. They were matched with controls of nearly similar birth date from the same school system. With combined samples the correlation between Inconsequence and prenatal stress was .44 ($p<.001$). Twelve indications of hyperactivity, impulsivity, and inhibitional failure in the preschool years showed a nearly similar correlation of .41, with the same level of significance. The correlations were higher with those stresses occurring in the second and third trimesters of pregnancy.

I should add, however, lest it be thought that I am plugging one more monolithic explanation, that these relationships cover only a small part of the variance. The effect of congenital insult upon behavior seems to be to produce a heightened vulnerability to postnatal stress. In a stable environment this may become manifest only in the form of sensitivity, apprehensiveness, irritability, or distractibility within a quasi-normal range. In a stressful environment it may mean a general behavioral disintegration. On the other hand an extremely stressful situation may fail to upset the stability of another individual. The congenital and postnatal environmental influences are interdependent.

This concept of a congenital vulnerability is well demonstrated in Drillien's (1964) follow-up study of premature children and controls of normal birth weight. The mean Bristol Social Adjustment Guide (BSAG) scores — that is, the number of indications of behavior disturbance as recorded at seven years by the children's teachers — fell into the reasonably stable category (6 for the prematurely, 5 for the maturely born) where there were no pregnancy or delivery complications and no significant postnatal stress. With congenital complications and still no postnatal stress, the scores went to 11 for the prematures and 8 for the controls; where there were severe family stresses as well, to 20 for the prematures and 16 for the controls. The congenital insults rendered the affected children markedly more vulnerable to family difficulties.

Indirect evidence of a common factor of congenital insult is seen in the close positive relationship, in children of all ages, between chronic morbidity and behavior disturbance. Children with even a mild chronic health condition score on the average twice as high as the healthy; in the case of girls nearly three times as high. Children with two distinct health conditions were found to have a thirteen times greater chance of being maladjusted than the healthy (Stott, 1966). We can propose a law of multiple impairment covering mental retardation, health, physical defect, and behavior: a child found with one form of impairment has a somewhat greater chance of having a second; a child with two has a still greater chance of having a third; and so on in geometrical progression. It is hard to explain such findings except by postulating a common congenital antecedent for the statistically related but physically distinct conditions.

At this late stage I should explain more fully what I mean by congenital. The dictionary definition is "that which originates from or before birth." Our studies of etiology have been dogged by a false dichotomy: inherited or environmental. *Congenital* defines the time of the influence rather than its nature. It includes the genetic, but also the prenatal-environmental and the effects of the birth process. In fact, work in experimental biology has lent a new significance to the term. Landauer and Bliss (1946) found that the effect of prenatal insult in chickens was dependent upon the genetic constitution of the strain. Clarke Fraser (1954) found the same in the prenatal administration of cortisone to mice. In one variety it invariably produced cleft palate in the offspring, in another none at all. When he crossed the strains he got intermediate incidences of cleft palate. In human beings the nonfamilial type of cleft lip and palate is sensitive to pregnancy stress, the familial or purely genetic type is not (Drillien, Ingram, & Wilkinson, 1966). Except for a very few malformations which seem to follow a straight Mendelian pattern, the general rule is of a genetic predisposition that remains unexpressed unless triggered by prenatal stress (Warkany, 1947).

We know from the work of Marshall et al. (1962) on twins that there is a small genetic factor in all common childhood illnesses. At the same time, from my own work, it would appear that following a seriously stressful pregnancy, some 40 per cent of male infants but only 25 per cent of female infants suffer from nonepidemic illnesses in the first three years of life (Stott, 1957a). The sex differential suggests a genetic factor, and indeed, we know from several other studies that male children show a much higher incidence of morbidity than females.

There are reasons to suppose, when we review the evidence for genetic determinants on the one hand and prenatal-environmental determinants on the other, that human impairments are the result of the same type of interaction between the two as have been demonstrated for animals. We are dealing with relatively frequent conditions, conditions which, in primitive tribal communities, result in the culling out of about a quarter of the infants born during their first year. We have to ask why, if there is a genetic factor operating, it has not been eliminated or rendered exceedingly rare by natural selection. One answer might be that the genes responsible for insults which are lethal under primitive conditions, and thus of no survival value for the individual, must have survival value for the group. The only value that I could think of is that they serve to keep population down to a size that would ensure against starvation. In times of food shortage, apart from undernutrition itself, there would be long treks, incursions by other tribes, anxiety, and a multitude of stresses. If the fetus is vulnerable to such stresses experienced by the mother, and if fewer infants survived under such conditions, this would act as an automatic regulator of population numbers. I was agreeably surprised, when I looked into the literature, that the field biologists knew all this already with regard to animal populations (Stott, 1962). Moreover, they reported that in times of high population many of the yearling animals showed behavioral aberrations that would be detrimental to their survival — loss of fear of human beings, mass wanderings and emigrations culminating in drowning or other virtually certain death — all of which have analogies with the irrational, self-immolatory behavior of the emotionally disturbed delinquent. In sum, it could be that we have to seek the ultimate origins of behavior disturbance in genetic mechanisms which, by interaction with the pre- and postnatal environment, result in the production of maladjusted individuals.

COMMENTARY

MEDNICK. If pregnancy complications do lead to Unforthcomingness, then how do you explain the fact that so many of these children are hyperactive?

STOTT. As far as we can see, there is absolutely no evidence that a particular type of pregnancy complication will produce a particular form of insult in the child. I have to agree with Dr. Pollack that there is a genetic explanation here — in one family there may be the potentiality for Unforthcomingness, in another Inconsequence, in another cleft lip or palate (though that would be something earlier in pregnancy), and in others, there is no genetic propensity and hence no effect. As a matter of fact, the parents of inconsequential children are always telling me "Well, his father was like that" or "I was like that" or something of that sort, and I strongly suspect that there may be something of this sort in hyperactivity.

MEDNICK. Can you distinguish between delivery and pregnancy complications? You said that they're highly correlated in some sense. Can you make any distinction?

STOTT. In our studies of behavior disturbed children, the delivery complications did not come out as significantly related to the behavior disturbances. In my earlier study (Stott, 1957a) involving mentally subnormal children, the delivery complications — they're not all prematurity —

seemed to be so closely connected with the pregnancy complications that the defective factor couldn't be isolated. Drillien (1964) mentioned that there do seem to be certain types of delivery, like breech delivery, that are notably related to later defects.

QUESTION. Do you suspect possibly any other types of behavior which may come about as a result of this?

STOTT. All the types of behavior disturbance in our classification showed themselves as related to minor neurological dysfunction such as motor disability. The overreacting types were more so than the underreacting, and among the overreacting the relationship was closest for Inconsequence.

REFERENCES

Adamson, J. *Living free*. London: Collins & Harvill, 1961.
Ader, R., & Belfer, M. L. Prenatal maternal anxiety and offspring emotionality in the rat. *Psychological Reports*, 1962, 10, 711–718.
Ainsworth, M. D. The effects of maternal deprivation: A review of findings and controversy in the context of research strategy. In *Deprivation of maternal care*. Geneva: WHO, 1962. Pp. 97–165.
Birch, H. G. (Ed.) *Brain damage in children: Its biological and social aspects*. Baltimore: Williams & Wilkins, 1964.
Bowlby, J., Ainsworth, M. D., Boston, M., & Rosenbluth, D. The effects of mother child separation: A follow-up study. *British Journal of Medical Psychology*, 1956, 29, 211–247.
Burton, L. Three studies of deviant child development. Ph.D. thesis, Queen's University, Belfast, 1964.
Chess, S. Genesis of behavior disorders. In J. G. Howells (Ed.), *Modern perspectives in international child psychiatry*. Edinburgh: Oliver & Boyd, 1969.
Drillien, C. M. *The growth and development of the prematurely born infant*. Edinburgh: Livingstone, 1964.
———, Ingram, T. T. S., & Wilkinson, E. M. *The causes and natural history of cleft lip and palate*. Edinburgh: Livingstone, 1966.
Eisenberg, L. Behavioral manifestations of cerebral damage in childhood. In H. G. Birch (Ed.), *Brain damage in children: Biological and social aspects*. Baltimore: Williams & Wilkins, 1964.
Fraser, F. Clarke, Kalter, H., Walker, B. E., & Fainstat, T. D. Experimental production of cleft palate with cortisone and other hormones. *Journal of Cellular and Comparative Physiology*, 1954, 43, Suppl. 1, 237–259.
Goldfarb, W. Effects of early institutional care on adolescent personality. *Journal of Experimental Education*, 1943–1944, 12, 106–129.
———. Effects of psychological deprivation in infancy and subsequent stimulation. *American Journal of Psychiatry*, 1945–1946, 102, 18–33.
Gregg, N. McA. Congenital cataract following German measles in the mother. *Transactions of Opthamological Society of Australia*, 1941.
Haggard, E. A., Brekstad, A., & Skard, A. G. On the reliability of the anamnestic interview. *Journal of Abnormal and Social Psychology*, 1960, 61, 311–318.
Kagan, J. Information processing in the child. In P. H. Mussen, J. J. Conger, & J. Kagan (Eds.), *Readings in child development and personality*. New York: Harper, 1965.
Landauer, W., & Bliss, C. I. Insulin induced rumplessness of chickens. *Journal of Experimental Zoology*, 1946, 102, 1–22.
Lotter, V. Epidemiology of autistic conditions in young children. *Social Psychiatry*, 1966, 1, 163–173.

Manson, M. M., Logan, W. P. D., & Loy, R. M. *Rubella and other virus infections during pregnancy.* London: H.M.S.O., 1960.

Marshall, A. G., Hutchinson, E. O., & Honisett, J. Heredity in common diseases: A retrospective study of twins in a hospital population. *British Medical Journal,* 1962, 1–6.

Murphy, L. B. *The widening world of childhood.* New York: Basic Books, 1962.

Pasamanick, B., & Knobloch, H. Brain damage and reproductive casualty. *American Journal of Orthopsychiatry,* 1960, 30, 298–305.

Pinneau, S. R. The infantile disorder of hospitalism and anaclitic depression. *Psychological Bulletin,* 1955, 52, 429–452.

Prechtl, H. F. R., & Stemmer, Ch. J. The choreiform syndrome in children. *Developmental Medicine and Child Neurology,* 1962, 4, 119–127.

Robbins, L. C. The accuracy of parental recall of aspects of child development and of child rearing practices. *Journal of Abnormal and Social Psychology,* 1963, 66, 261–270.

Schaffer, H. R., & Emerson, P. E. The development of social attachments in infancy. *Monographs of the Society for Research in Child Development,* 1964, 29 (3, Serial No. 94).

Scottish Council for Research in Education. Social implications of the 1947 Scottish mental survey. London: University of London Press, 1953.

Sontag, L. W. Significance of fetal environmental differences. *American Journal of Obstetrics and Gynecology,* 1941, 42, 996–1003.

―――. Differences in the modifiability of fetal behavior. *Psychosomatic Medicine,* 1944, 6, 151–154.

―――. Fetal behavior as a predictor of behavior in childhood. Paper presented at the meeting of the American Psychiatric Association, St. Louis, 1962.

Stott, D. H. The effects of separation from the mother in early life. *Lancet,* 1956, 1, 624–628.

―――. Physical and mental handicaps following a disturbed pregnancy. *Lancet,* 1957, 1, 1006–1012. (a)

―――. The reliability of data on early life. *Case Conference,* 1957, 4, 67–74. (b)

―――. Cultural and natural checks to population growth. In M. F. A. Montagu (Ed.), *Culture and the evolution of man.* New York: Oxford University Press, 1962.

―――. *Studies of troublesome children.* London: Tavistock; New York: Humanities Press; Toronto: Methuen, 1966.

―――, & Sykes, E. G. *The Bristol Social Adjustment Guides.* London: University of London Press; San Diego: Educational and Industrial Testing Service, 1956.

Thompson, W. R. Influence of prenatal maternal anxiety on emotionality of young rats. *Science,* 1957, 125, 698.

Tolman, E. C. The determiners of behavior at a choice point. *Psychological Review,* 1938, 45, 1–41.

Warkany, J. Etiology of congenital malformations. *Advances in Pediatrics,* 1947, 2, 1.

GEORGE E. VAILLANT
CHARLES C. MC ARTHUR

A Thirty-Year Follow-Up of Somatic Symptoms under Emotional Stress

DURING the last decade many psychiatrists have wondered what has happened to the promising hypotheses of the 1940's regarding the etiology and the specificity of psychosomatic symptoms. Much research and many publications during the 1940's and 1950's were devoted to suggesting that individuals under emotional stress often experienced psychological disturbances in "target" organs. Controversy arose as to the personality types and the emotional conflicts that were reflected by pathology in a given organ. More recently, interest in resolving these conflicts in psychosomatic medicine seems to have waned. The results of our thirty-year study of normal, "healthy" adult males suggests one reason for this decline. Our investigation suggests that the physical symptoms which a given individual reports having experienced under stress vary a great deal over time and correlate very weakly with his psychological well-being.

METHODS

In 1940, their sophomore year, 199 men from a liberal arts college were selected for relative physical and psychological health. At the time of college admission a majority of the men could be characterized as ambitious, intellectually able members of the middle and upper middle class. They ranged from lower-middle- to upper-class social status. At the present time virtually all are members of the upper or highly educated upper-middle class (average income $30,000). During the years 1940–1942

NOTE: This investigation was supported by a Research Scientist Development Award, No. MH-38,798 from the National Institute of Mental Health and by the Grant Foundation, Inc.

these men were intensively studied by internists, physiologists, anthropologists, psychologists, and psychiatrists. They have been followed up at intervals of roughly two years until the present time with virtually no attrition in sample size. Over the years the men's marital, occupational, and medical statuses have been recorded. Areas of specific interest have been the regular collection of data regarding sleeping patterns, subjective perception of health (e.g., excellent, very good, good, fair), days missed from work per year, number of hospitalizations, and drug and alcohol usage.

A complete physical exam including electrocardiograms, blood tests, and urinalyses obtained on the men in the sample showed 5 per cent to be ill without gross disability (e.g., Parkinsonism, diabetes, hypertension requiring treatment, emphysema) and 3 per cent to be physically disabled (e.g., recurrent seizures, myocardial infarction, multiple sclerosis). An additional 13 per cent were classed as "? normal" because their medical report cited asymptomatic lab abnormalities, hypertension, renal stones, multiple minor complaints, or non-disabling bone and joint problems. Thus, 21 per cent were considered to manifest objective evidence of ill health.

Upon initial recruitment into the sample and twice during follow-up (at ages 33 and 47), the men were asked how emotional stress affected them physically. At ages 33 and 47, the question was worded, "When under stress, what do you notice about your physical reactions?" The following answers were offered in a checklist: asthma, palpitation, headache, diarrhoea, insomnia, sweating, indigestion or abdominal pain, smoke and drink more, cold hands and feet, frequent colds, constipation, inability to concentrate, nervousness, irritability, other (please specify). At age 19 the same general question had been asked during the course of the physical examination, but in a less rigid format. The rarity of "other" answers in the questionnaire protocols suggests that the checklist covered the important areas in which this particular sample experienced stress. Of the 199 men, 147 provided complete information at all three points in time. When these men were compared with the 52 men from whom information was obtained at only one or two points in time, there were no significant differences on any of a wide variety of social and medical variables examined.

At the completion of their original intensive study, the men had been given a global rating — A, B, or C — that reflected the interdisciplinary staff's assessment of their "psychological soundness." Between 1968 and 1970, 60 of the men were re-interviewed by Vaillant and dichotomized into the 30 more and the 30 less psychologically "unsound." "Unsoundness" was defined as being *relatively* "emotionally constricted, without friends, with overt psychiatric illness, with unstable marriage, with occupational failure, and/or with drug or alcohol misuse." An independent observer agreed with this dichotomization in 87 per cent of the cases. This variable will be described as "Adult Unsoundness."

CHANGES ACROSS TIME

Where in the body a man would experience stress in adult life could rarely have been predicted from examination of the men at 19. For example, adolescent somatotype did not correlate with choice of the bodily locations for stress sensations in adult life except — not surprisingly — that endomorphy in adolescence was statistically associated with adult obesity. No specific somatotype was correlated with peptic ulcer or characterized adults who experienced pain in their abdomen as the site of sensations of stress. However, the 14 men who at some point in their adult life developed either an ulcer or colitis *were* twice as likely to have reported constipation, diarrhoea, or abdominal pain under emotional stress at age 19 ($p<.01$). A complaint of diarrhoea under stress in 1940 was also correlated ($p<.05$) with irritability and inability to concentrate in adult life.

Nail-biting in college was correlated with none of the measures of adult maladjustment or ill health. For example, it was not correlated with psychiatric visits, with nervousness under stress, or with experiencing a relatively large number of physical symptoms under stress. A puzzling aside is that men who on physical examination were observed *not* to be ticklish in 1940 were statistically more likely ($p<.05$) to report themselves as irritable at ages 33 and 47.

In general, there was no consistent relationship between a given symptom at age 19 and an alternative symptom in adult life. The tabulation on page 202 correlating stress symptoms at ages 33 and 47 also suggests that there was little likelihood that an adult would continue to report the presence of the same symptom under stress. Although these correlations (*$p<.10$; **$p<.05$) are not corrected for attenuation and so underestimate, they are so small that such corrections would not make them impressive. Only the behavioral item "smoke and drink more" is impressively self-consistent.

Reliabilities from age 19 to later ages were even lower. Only "abdominal pain" and "sweating" showed consistencies ($p<.01$). The num-

Smoke and drink more	.63*
Abdominal complaints	.47*
Sweating	.39*
Diarrhoea	.32*
Nervousness	.30*
Inability to concentrate	.29*
Insomnia	.28**
Irritability	.27**
Constipation	.23**
Headache	.15
Palpitations	.11

ber of men reporting a given symptom present at all three points in time was exceedingly small (see Table 1). In interpreting this result, however, it is important to remember that where in his body a person subjectively experiences stress depends greatly on the circumstances and his state of mind at the moment he is questioned. That a given symptom would be present at 19 *and* at 33, or at 33 *and* 47, was more likely than its being present at 19 *and* 47. But even when men were asked these questions at one- or two-year intervals, there was a lack of consistency in symptom specificity. In other words, the lack of correlation over time is not due so much to a consistent and orderly shift in reported symptoms as it is to the fact that subjective symptoms of stress appear to be rather unstable perceptions.

If a man experienced emotional stress in college by suffering from several of the symptoms insomnia, headache, constipation, diarrhoea,

Table 1. Percentage of Men Reporting Each Symptom at Different Ages[a]

Stress Symptom	19 (N=195)	33 (N=151)	47 (N=180)	33 and 47 (N=147)	19 and 33 and 47 (N=147)
Irritability	N.A.	66	76	56	N.A.
Smoke and drink more	N.A.	33	38	27	N.A.
Nervous	N.A.	42	46	26	N.A.
Insomnia	19	28	41	18	6
Headache	4	19	16	5	1
Constipation	19	5	4	1	1
Diarrhoea	37	8	15	4	1
Indigestion or abdominal pain	6	17	17	10	2
Sweating	23	25	26	14	5
Palpitation	24	5	10	1	1
Inability to concentrate	N.A.	12	20	6	N.A.

[a] N.A. = Not Asked.

sweating, abdominal pain, or palpitations, then in adulthood he was more likely ($p<.05$) to have many such stress symptoms. But, perhaps more interesting, he was also more likely to complain of irritability and inability to concentrate. In other words, experiencing emotional stress via many physical symptoms in adolescence predicted experiencing stress via mental symptoms in adult life. It should be noted, however, that we are talking about *symptoms* (subjective perception of discomfort) rather than *signs* (objective physiological response) to distress.

Table 1 suggests that over the life cycle the bodily sites where stress is experienced may shift. Although between the ages of 29 and 47 the men's subjective perception of their own health did not change, the site of symptoms under stress did. Men at 47 were just as likely to describe their health as excellent as they had been at 29, but they were much less likely to complain of constipation, diarrhoea, and palpitation than they had been at 19. Table 1 shows that such symptoms, common in college, decreased over time and were replaced by an increasing likelihood that men would complain of insomnia, headache, inability to concentrate, and abdominal pain. Many of the men in college complained of asthma and hay fever, but at 47 only 3 per cent of the men were so affected, and this stress symptom is excluded from our general discussion.

RELATIONS AMONG SYMPTOMS

In an effort to examine the importance of symptom specificity further, the man who reported a given symptom absent at both age 33 and age 47 was scored 1; the man who reported a symptom present at one of those ages was scored 2; and the man who reported a given symptom at both of those times was scored 3. These scores were used to search for association between the persistence of given symptoms and a wide variety of other variables. Table 2 shows that the correlations among symptoms was relatively weak and did not provide the orderly clusters that the personality theories of investigators of psychosomatic medicine in the 1940's would have predicted. Sweating appeared to be correlated with several symptoms, as was the inability to concentrate. Headache seemed to be correlated with palpitation, but otherwise the correlations seemed surprisingly random.

Men who reported that they drank and smoked more under stress were more likely to take four days or more of sick leave a year, to misuse alcohol, and to have been rated C on psychological soundness in college

Table 2. Correlations between Persistence of Stress Symptoms during Adult Life[a] [b]

Symptoms	Nervous	Insomnia	Headache	Palpitations	Sweat	Inability to Concentrate
Irritability	.16*	.21*				
Nervous		.17*	.17*		.17*	.38*
Insomnia						.20*
Headache				.33**		
Constipation					.20*	
Diarrhoea					.21*	
Palpitations					.25**	.21*

[a] Correlations were calculated by rating an individual 1 if he never reported a given symptom, 2 if he reported it at 33 or 47, and 3 if he reported it at both 33 and 47.
[b] Symptoms for which there were no significant correlations are not included. Those omitted in the vertical list are smoke and drink more, abdominal pain or indigestion, sweat, and inability to concentrate; in the horizontal list, irritability, smoke and drink more, constipation, diarrhoea, and abdominal pain or indigestion.
*$p<.05$.   **$p<.01$.

(all significant at $p<.005$). Men who reported "nervousness" and "inability to concentrate" under stress were men who both in college and at 47 were thought least "sound." After college, they were more likely to visit a psychiatrist and more likely to have unstable marriages (all three $p<.025$). Men who reported constipation under stress were more likely to perceive their current health as below average ($p<.01$) and to perceive their sleep as poor ($p<.02$). Paradoxically, these men were not more likely to suffer insomnia under stress or to have objectively Below Average Health. In contrast, obesity was correlated with no variable, except that fat men perceived their health as relatively better than did their more slender classmates ($p<.03$).

Table 3 contrasts the 47 men who reported the fewest somatic symptoms (insomnia, headache, constipation, diarrhoea, abdominal pain or indigestion, palpitations, sweating, and inability to concentrate) under stress in adult life with the 27 men who reported the most. The table reveals that, when compared to men with little response to stress, men with many physical complaints were subjectively poor sleepers, were more likely to take sick leave, and were more likely to experience nervousness under stress. However, these "somatic symptom" men were not more likely to have reported many somatic symptoms in college or to experience overt psychosomatic illness as adults (i.e., ulcers and colitis or back trouble and arthritis). Of the most interest, however, was the fact that men who experienced stress with many somatic symptoms subjectively perceived their

Table 3. Signs and Symptoms of Physical Health in Men with Many and Few Somatic Symptoms under Emotional Stress

Signs and Symptoms	Frequency in Ss with Few Symptoms ($N = 47$)	Frequency in Ss with Many Symptoms ($N = 27$)	p (χ^2 Test)
Sleep perceived as sometimes disturbed	40%	81%	<.001
10+ visits to psychiatrist	9	30	<.01[a]
4+ days/year sick leave	9	22	<.03
"Nervous" with stress	47	81	<.01
Health Below Average (subjective)	4	22	<.002
Health Below Average (objective)	25	15	N.S.
Nail-biting in college	15	33	N.S.
No reported somatic stress symptoms in college	47	39	N.S.
Ulcers or colitis when adult	6	7	N.S.
Joint pain when adult	4	4	N.S.
Denied adolescent masturbation	13	0	<.09

[a] Significance of this association contingent upon selecting extreme groups for comparison.

health to be less good than their classmates, but the findings on recent medical exams revealed that, if anything, their health was superior. They complained more to psychiatrists (Table 3) but their psychological "soundness" as adults was not rated differently from that of their less symptomatic classmates. An interesting sidelight is the fact that the men who reported fewest somatic symptoms under stress included the minority of men who in adolescence reported (in the course of eight psychiatric interviews) that they had never masturbated.

SUBJECTIVE SYMPTOMS OF STRESS VERSUS OBJECTIVE SIGNS OF HEALTH

There were few subjectively reported symptoms under stress that correlated with our objective signs of adult psychological and physical ill health. These signs had been chosen as both theoretically related to health and capable of being determined objectively with a minimum of ex post facto bias. They included number of medical hospitalizations since college, divorce, college "psychological soundness" rating, number of visits to a psychiatrist, and results of a recent medical examination. In Table 4, by chance alone, two items should be associated at the .05 level of significance and one at the .02 level. Yet only the complaints of nervousness, in-

Table 4. Statistically Significant Associations between Subjective Symptoms of Stress and Objective Signs of Ill Health[a][b]

Symptoms under Emotional Stress	10+ Visits to Psychiatrist	Adult Unsoundness	College Unsoundness	Current Health	Adult Hospitalization
Irritable	...	...	...	...	...
Smoke and drink more	...	...	$p<.025$	...	...
Nervous	$p<.01$	...	...	...	...
Insomnia	$p<.01$	...	...	...	$p<.01$
Headache	...	...	...	...	...
Constipation	...	...	...	...	...
Diarrhoea	...	...	...	...	...
Abdominal pain	...	...	...	...	...
Palpitation	...	...	...	...	...
Sweating	...	...	...	...	...
Inability to concentrate	$p<.01$	$p<.025$	$p<.025$	...	...
Obesity	...	...	...	...	...
Adult somatic symptoms	...	...	$p<.05$	...	...

[a] $p<.05$ by χ^2 test of significance.
[b] All values of significance level calculated by χ^2 test. All significant associations are positive.

somnia, and inability to concentrate under stress seemed even modestly associated with objective variables reflecting physical and psychological health.

Nevertheless, the objective signs of health were powerfully associated with one another. For example, "psychological unsoundness" in college was associated with "psychological unsoundness" in adult life ($p<.001$). Of 60 men rated for adult psychological soundness, 35 never visited a psychiatrist. Of these 35, 24 were in the "sound" group; only 11 fell in the "unsound." Subjectively perceived Below Average Health, objectively determined Below Average Health, and divorce were all associated with Adult Unsoundness ($p<.01$).

Below Average Health (as objectively determined) did not correlate with any stress symptoms, with obesity, with days of sick leave taken, or with Below Average Health (subjectively determined). However, medically determined Below Average Health was associated positively with Adult Unsoundness ($p<0.01$) and with number of psychiatric visits ($p<.001$).

Similarly, the number of times a man was medically hospitalized after college was associated with Below Average Health as reported by a physician but not as felt by the subject. Only 10 per cent of the men who had rarely been hospitalized were divorced, but 31 per cent of the men who had been hospitalized four or more times were divorced. Although the number in the present study is too small to cause such findings to be statistically significant, in a larger sample of these men's college classmates the association between adult medical hospitalizations and unstable or broken marriages was significant ($p<.01$) (unpublished data). All these findings suggest that there is indeed a relation between "physical" and "psychological" health, but it may rest on a different basis than that postulated by the pioneers of psychosomatic medicine.

CONCLUSIONS

Thirty-year follow-ups are rare and, when accomplished, the numbers of cases in them are of necessity small. Methods of data collection undoubtedly affected our answers, and the study sample was confined to intellectually ambitious upper-middle- to upper-class males. The physical symptoms that actually occur during *perceived* stress may be different from those remembered afterward, and many physiological changes can occur without the individual's perceiving himself under stress. Thus, our tentative findings require confirmation via other methods and from other populations, and must be regarded with caution.

Nevertheless, the current study does suggest one possible explanation for apparent failure of the hypothesis of organ specificity to survive. The organ in which stress is experienced appears to vary over time and with the stressor. At least when a sample of non-patients selected for health and followed for decades were studied, the specific site where stress was experienced appeared quite unrelated to theoretically relevant variables. In contrast, the character structure (e.g., obsessive compulsive) of these men was relatively stable.

A moral emerges from this study that has also emerged from long-term follow-up of addicts, schizophrenics, and delinquents (Glueck & Glueck, 1943; Vaillant, 1964, 1966). Namely, in follow-up studies, if one wishes specific correlations and dramatic associations, always look for objective signs of functioning rather than for subjective symptoms. Health is not a will-o'-the-wisp; and if, instead of symptoms like abdominal pain or headache or insomnia, one studies divorces, psychiatric visits, or hospitalizations, then one, indeed, finds that relative states of health and ill health exist. Thus, men observed for thirty years who appear to be impaired in interpersonal relationships will also display objective signs of physical and social ill health. Conversely, the man who subjectively complains of indigestion under stress will also subjectively complain that his health is poor. But there is remarkably poor correlation between verbally reported subjective malfunction and the facts of his life as discerned by others. There is a difference between symptom and function.

COMMENTARY

KNUPFER. I'm not a great advocate of the organ-specific hypothesis, but it seems to me to be a delineation of a certain type of disease; to try to demonstrate it statistically in a loose way is not a test of it. Specifically, I think that lists of physical symptoms really mean at least three or four different things. A large number of physical symptoms would probably be opposite to organ specificity, and therefore if you classify people because they have a number of different symptoms, that would indicate that they are not the type who have concentrated on one organ. Lists of symptoms could mean, for instance, either a kind of hypochondriasis that concentrates on body functions or it could be a kind of anxiety, manifesting itself in various symptoms, not particularly specific but fairly familiar, like sweating, headaches, and cramps. On the other hand, having a specific symptom such as headaches or an ulcer might mean that the person wouldn't have all the others, so that people who have just one symptom don't show up if you use a measure based on having many symptoms.

Secondly, asking people what symptoms they have under stress may be distorting your results a little because they may not know when they're under stress. Also, somatic symptoms in some people are a substitute for anxiety — that is, people who have a lot of symptoms tend to also have a lot of anxiety, but it is also true that there are some people, who, instead of having anxiety, have symptoms. Hence, it might have been better if you asked, Do you have these symptoms? rather than Do you have them under stress?

VAILLANT. I agree with your points, which remind me of one other point that certainly should be mentioned. It is that this is a highly selected group of men. They are better-than-average informants and were selected at one point in history from the high end of the human spectrum, both in health and in intelligence. Therefore, it is risky to generalize from this population.

THOMAS. I think that when one gets results that don't fit in with the conventional wisdom in the field they shouldn't be called disappointing. In terms of the variability of symptoms at different periods of life, this finding certainly fits in with our own studies with children (pp. 35–46). In tracing the developments through early adolescence, at least the nature of symptomatology can shift appreciably from one level of development to another even if the basic behavior disorder and the psychodynamic issues remain similar. Certainly this is what suggests itself to me from this finding that at different age periods — adolescence, early maturity rate, later maturity — the nature of symptomatology may shift in relation to the level of development of the organism, psychologically speaking. It would not be surprising if inability to concentrate appeared to be the most striking symptom in the correlations in this population of men, considering their educational backgrounds and the types of work they do. The particular predominant symptom can correlate very nicely with the environmental issues which constitute the greatest stresses for that particular population, in terms of socioeconomic background and so on. This is a striking finding in our comparisons of the symptoms in a group of middle-class children from professional families with those of working-class children of Puerto Rican families. In New York the nature of the symptomatology was highly correlated with the types of environmental demands, expectations of the families, and the whole environment. Finally, I would not consider the lack of correlation or inverse correlation between somatic and non-somatic symptoms disappointing. This bears on the conventional formulation that with more serious disturbances the individual who is psychotic will not show psychosomatic disease and vice versa; if the individual has a psychosomatic disorder, and this is cured, he is more likely to become psychotic. This has not been the case at all in the group we studied at Bellevue Hospital a number of years ago and also in a report by O'Conner from the Psychiatric Institute at Columbia, who again shows none of this kind of inverse correlation with the more severe disorders.

BARBARA DOHRENWEND. It would be very useful if, in a longitudinal study of this kind with successive measures over time, you would state what questions were asked to elicit the symptoms and whether the questioning procedure was the same at each of these points in time. Also, could you give us your own speculations on the sources of what you're calling the "unreliability of symptom reporting"?

VAILLANT. In 1940 the questions regarding emotional stress were gathered during a complete physical exam. In 1954 and 1967 the information was elicited by a questionnaire item which included a checklist of fourteen symptoms (see p. 200). Thus, in 1954 and 1967 the stimulus was the same.

I have three speculations as to why response to stress is so unstable. One is the firm conviction that there is as broad a shift in the maturation of the human nervous system, in both psychological and physiological terms, between age 18 and age 47 as there is between age 3 and age 15. At different ages, different life issues are important and the person has different styles of perceiving his universe. One has only to look at the shift in politics of many people over 30 from when they were under 30 to get an idea of how the world changes as man ages. The second is the fact that when you ask a question the reply may be 1+ or 4+ constipation under stress; part of the inconsistency arises when the person decides to check yes if a symptom is mild. And the third speculation is that *where* a man feels a symptom in his body has a lot to do with metaphorical language and his most recent health experiences. If under stress he worries about his gut or his heart or his head or his mind, his worry will be shaped by recent experience as well as by sensations from those particular organs.

WINOKUR. Sometimes papers like this function as a resurrection. It has come to my mind that ten or more years ago, a test devised by George Saslow was used here at Washington University. Called the Saslow Screening Test, it dealt with psychological stress symptoms. There must have been virtually thousands of these tests given over the course of a few years to incoming students at Washington University and to incoming patients at various clinics around here. Those tests must now be in a drawer or cabinet. It would be possible to do a very systematic study using this material. The test was a single page, took about five minutes to complete, and could easily be given to a group of people in follow-up in exactly the same fashion. It didn't include, as I recall, questions about masturbation, so we couldn't go from the erection to the resurrection in this case.

REFERENCES

Glueck, S., & Glueck, E. *Criminal careers in retrospect.* New York: Commonwealth Fund, 1943.

Vaillant, G. E. Prospective prediction of schizophrenic remission. *Archives of General Psychiatry,* 1964, 11, 509–518.

———. A 12-year follow-up of New York narcotic addicts, and the natural history of a chronic disease. *New England Journal of Medicine,* 1966, 275, 1282–1288.

RICHARD W. HUDGENS
ELI ROBINS
JON TEK LUM
CHARLES H. MERIDETH ⎦ *The Communication of Suicidal Intent in Psychiatric Illness: A Follow-Up*

STUDIES have established that over two thirds of people who commit suicide and over half of those attempting suicide have communicated their intentions before the act (Dorpat & Ripley, 1960; Robins, Gassner, Kayes, Wilkinson, & Murphy, 1959), and that 94 per cent of suicides have a psychiatric illness, most commonly either primary depression or chronic alcoholism (Robins, Murphy, Wilkinson, Gassner, & Kayes, 1959). Furthermore, DeLong and Robins (1961) reported that over two thirds of a group of patients admitted to a psychiatric hospital had previously communicated suicidal intent (with attempts included among means of communication). Thus, the three phenomena — psychiatric illness, communication of suicidal intent, and completed suicide — are related to one another; but several questions must be answered before the nature of these interrelationships can be defined more precisely. For example, do communications of suicidal intent predict suicidal acts, or are they such frequent accompaniments of psychiatric illness as to be without value as predictors of suicide? Which types of suicidal communication, if any, are most ominous with regard to future suicidal acts? With which psychiatric disorders are suicidal communications most often associated? Do persons who have communicated suicidal intent continue to do so as a "way of life" or are communications temporally associated with other symptoms of psychiatric illness, thus occurring only when people are sick?

A study to answer these questions was begun in 1959, when 87 patients admitted to the psychiatric division of the Washington University Medical Center were investigated by DeLong and Robins (1961) with re-

NOTE: This work was supported in part by U.S.P.H.S. Grants MH-10356, MH-13002, MH-05804, and MH-09247.

spect to psychiatric and social histories and sixteen ways of communicating suicidal intent. In that initial study, in which patients and informants were interviewed separately, 68 per cent of the patients (81 per cent of those with primary affective disorder) were reported to have communicated suicidal intent. Their communications were varied and repetitive, but were not chronic or a "way of life," being predominantly associated with the current episodes of illness. Communications of suicidal intent were rarely regarded by patients or informants as manipulative behavior, but rather as serious expressions of despair.

For adequate investigation of the longitudinal relationships between psychiatric illness and suicidal communication it was necessary to study the original group of 87 patients again after an interval of several years. Accordingly, a five- to eleven-year follow-up was undertaken and is reported here.

METHODS

Initial Study, 1959. The initial group of 87 psychiatric inpatients was selected during July and August 1959 by methods described in the first report of this study (DeLong & Robins, 1961). Patients selected were representative of all persons admitted during the study period to the psychiatric division of the Washington University Medical Center with respect to mean age, sex ratio, prior history of suicide attempts, and diagnoses. Within 24 hours of admission, the subjects were administered a systematic interview covering psychiatric and social history, and they were questioned whether they had ever expressed any of sixteen types of suicidal communication (fifteen specified types plus "miscellaneous" communications; these are listed in Table 2). For each patient at least one informant (usually the spouse) was interviewed separately at the time of admission using the same protocol. Following the interview and review of hospital records, each patient was diagnosed according to specific criteria described in DeLong and Robins (1961).

Follow-Up. Of the 87 patients, 2 died during the index admission in 1959, leaving 85 to be followed up. The patients were located through information about addresses and places of work from the initial study and from more recent records at the Medical Center. Subjects who lived in metropolitan St. Louis were usually approached in their homes without prior announcement that the investigator was coming. Subjects who lived outside the metropolitan area but within 150 miles of St. Louis, received letters requesting that the investigator be permitted to visit them for an interview. Subjects who lived farther away were interviewed by telephone. When initial inquiries revealed that the patients had moved since 1959, and when they could not be located in city directories, further inquiries were made of relatives, neighbors, employers, physicians, credit bureaus, and so forth.

In each case an investigator attempted to interview the patient and at least one informant separately, using the same protocol for both. Before each interview it was explained to the subject that we were talking to people who had been hospitalized in the Medical Center in the summer of 1959 in order to learn of their progress since then and to learn of ways in which we might improve patient care.

The protocol used in the interviews was similar to that used in 1959. There was an unstructured portion concerning interval psychiatric, medical, and social history. Each subject was then asked 93 questions: 15 identifying items; 60 items concerning symptoms, feelings, and mental status; and questions about 16 ways of communicating suicidal intent. The follow-up interview also requested specific details concerning subsequent hospitalizations (psychiatric or other), visits to physicians, job history, disability, changes in social status (economic, marital, retirement, etc.), and changes in social and recreational participation. Each of the events was dated, so that we could assess its temporal relationship to psychiatric disorder and suicidal communication.

Suicidal communication was scored as definite if either the patient or his informant reported it, even if the other denied it. For each communication we asked about timing, frequency, identity of the person(s) to whom the communication was made, and association of the communication with other symptoms of psychiatric illness and with alcohol use. An actual suicide attempt was considered a communication even if the patient had told no one about it at the time.

Following the interviews, letters requesting medical records were sent to every physician and every hospital known to have attended the patients in the interval since the original study. In addition, records of the Medical Center subsequent to 1959 were searched for all patients. Records which contained no positive evidence of suicidal communication were scored as negative in that regard. In the cases of subjects who had died, we requested not only medical records, but also death certificates, autopsy reports, and coroners' records from the appropriate institutions.

After all data had been collected, the subjects were diagnosed in the following manner: The 1959 research interviews and hospital records of the index admissions were reviewed by the first author, who had not participated in the original study. In this review he made use of any new information about the 1959 illness which had been gained during the follow-up period. Using the same diagnostic criteria employed in 1959, this investigator then independently rediagnosed the original sample. The 1959 protocols for the 30 patients concerning whom he had even minor questions about the original diagnosis were given to the second author, who had directed the initial study. The latter blindly rediagnosed the patients from the original data, then discussed the cases with the first author. Of the original sample of 87 patients, there was retrospective modification of diagnosis in 8 cases, only 3 of which are relevant to the analysis of data in this paper. (These 3 are discussed below.) Data gathered in the follow-up interval were then considered, and the patients received a final follow-up diagnosis based on the criteria in DeLong and Robins (1961).

DATA ANALYSIS

In the initial report of the 1959 sample, the 87 patients were divided into three diagnostic groups for purposes of data analysis: there were 48 persons with affective disorders (depression or mania), 9 with alcoholism, and 30 with miscellaneous diagnoses. The patients were divided in this way because of the findings of Robins et al. (1959) that suicide occurs predominantly among people with primary affective disorders and alcoholism. Also this grouping was practical, because none of the syndromes in the miscellaneous group contained enough patients for separate statistical treatment. We also adhered to this basic diagnostic division in analyzing the follow-up data.

We compared these diagnostic groups with one another with regard to clinical outcome and the communication of suicidal intent, including suicidal acts. We compared the incidence of each type of suicidal communication in the initial study with the incidence at follow-up, taking into account whether the data had come from patients themselves, informants, or both sources. We compared patients' and informants' contributions of information about suicidal communication in the group as a whole and within each diagnostic group. By these means we attempted to determine the interrelationships among suicidal communications (including suicidal acts), prior communications, type of psychiatric illness, alcohol use, age, and sex. Statistical significances were calculated by the chi-square test, with the Yates correction.

RESULTS

Follow-Up. Of the 85 patients discharged alive from the index admission in 1959, 10 had died. Of the remaining 75, 73 were located between 1965 and 1970, and 2 were not found. Thus 98 per cent of the total sample was accounted for. At the time of follow-up or death, 48 per cent of the patients lived in the city or county of St. Louis, 13 per cent elsewhere in Missouri, 21 per cent in Illinois, and 18 per cent in other states.

Positive or definitely negative follow-up information about suicidal communication was collected for 80 of the 85 patients, 94 per cent of the sample. Of the 80 (52 women, 28 men), 8 had died — 3 within eighteen months of the index admission, 3 after four years, 1 after six years, and 1 after seven years. Hence, 72 of the 80 were alive when followed up, five to eleven years after the initial study (mean length of follow-up, 6.9 years). The data were from interviews in 79 of the 80 cases (for 49 of whom we had additional interval records from psychiatric hospitalizations or outpatient treatment) and from only psychiatric hospital records in one case. Interviews were carried out with both patients and informants, separately, in 35 cases (a total of 70 interviews), with patients only in 32 cases, and with informants only in 12 cases. Some 87 per cent of the interviews were in person, 13 per cent by telephone. Three quarters of the follow-up informants had also been informants in the initial, 1959 study. We had positive and negative information from at least two sources in 40 cases (patient and informants in 35, patients and psychiatric records in 5) and from one source in the remaining 40 cases.

As for the five patients for whom we did not have data about suicidal communication, two patients were not located, though we collected psychiatric and medical outpatient records on one of them up to four years after the initial study; one patient refused to be interviewed but was known to have had psychiatric care elsewhere in the follow-up interval; and two patients died of organic brain disorders within a year of the initial study. We had complete medical records for the last two, and an interview with the husband of one, but collected no information about suicidal communication.

In all, we gathered some information about 98 per cent of our sample, research interviews and suicidal communication data about 94 per cent. We obtained additional psychiatric hospital outpatient records for 75 per cent of the 65 patients known to have been treated for psychiatric disorders during the follow-up period.

Diagnostic Groupings. As noted above, the follow-up group included

47 patients originally diagnosed as affective disorders, 9 with alcoholism, and 29 with miscellaneous illnesses. When we reviewed the 1959 protocols in the light of follow-up data, new information was gained about the 1959 episodes of illness which led us to change 3 patients from one diagnostic group to another. Two were moved from the affective disorder to the alcoholic group, because we discovered that their heavy drinking had preceded their depressions well before the 1959 admissions. The third patient, originally diagnosed antisocial personality, was moved from the miscellaneous to the alcoholic group, because heavy drinking had preceded and caused his social difficulties and because he had too few symptoms to meet our criteria for antisocial personality.

These changes left 45 patients with affective disorders, 12 with alcoholism, and 28 with miscellaneous syndromes. Of the last group, 14 had an "undiagnosed psychiatric illness" — that is, the clinical picture did not fulfill the criteria for a specific diagnosis and could not be explained by a known medical disorder.

Psychiatric Status during the Follow-Up. The top of Table 1 shows the psychiatric status during the follow-up period for the total sample and for each of the three diagnostic groups. The patients in all diagnostic groups had considerable difficulty after discharge from the index admission. For example, of the patients with mania and depression, disorders generally considered to have rather good prognoses, 62 per cent were rehospitalized within the follow-up period, 34 per cent at least twice. These were not simply rehospitalizations for the initial (1959) episode of illness: two thirds of the new episodes which could be dated accurately occurred more than two years after the index admission. Electroconvulsive treatments were required during the follow-up period by 40 per cent of the patients with affective disorder. Although the total duration of rehospitalization was usually brief (an average of only 2½ months), disability was not limited to time hospitalized. Indeed, 38 per cent of all patients with affective illnesses were severely disabled for more than a fourth of the follow-up period, 21 per cent more than three fourths of the time.

The bottom of Table 1 shows the condition of patients at the time of most recent information. Differences among the three diagnostic groups were not great. In all, 44 per cent of the sample were not disabled at follow-up (three quarters of these were well), 43 per cent were disabled by psychiatric illness and 12 per cent were dead.

Communications of Suicidal Intent. Table 2 shows the proportion of patients who communicated each type of suicidal intent before the index

Table 1. Psychiatric Status during Follow-Up Interval and at Time of Most Recent Information

Item	All Patients	Affective Disorders	Alcoholism	Miscellaneous
Psychiatric Status during Follow-Up[a]				
Treated for psychiatric symptoms	82%	89%	67%	78%
Rehospitalized for psychiatric illness	57	62	58	39
Rehospitalized more than once	29	34	25	23
Hospitalized for nonpsychiatric disorder	51	44	91	46
Psychiatric condition same or worse more than ¼ of follow-up period	41	38	45	44
Psychiatric symptoms severely disabling for ¾ of follow-up period	26	21	20	35
Most Recent Condition (If Ascertainable)[b]				
Well	33	31	18	42
Psychiatric symptoms, but not disabling	11	11	18	8
Ill with same disorder, not in hospital	28	36	27	15
Ill with same disorder, in hospital	13	13	9	15
Ill with other psychiatric disorder	2[c]	0	18[c]	0
Dead	12	9	9	19

[a] Depending on whether or not information on an item was available, the base N varied from item to item: from 77 to 83 for all patients, from 42 to 45 for affective disorders, from 10 to 12 for alcoholics, and from 25 to 28 for the miscellaneous group.

[b] N's are 83 for all patients, 45 affective disorders, 11 alcoholics, and 26 miscellaneous.

[c] At follow-up one alcoholic had organic brain syndrome, and one had depression despite abstinence from alcohol.

hospitalization in 1959 and during the follow-up interval. The means of communication most commonly reported were virtually the same at follow-up as in the initial investigation: 77 per cent of those communicating suicidal intent before 1959 did so in one or more of the first five ways listed in Table 2; this is true of 83 per cent of the follow-up communicators. The frequencies of the various types of communication during the follow-up interval appear lower than in the initial study, but this difference is an artifact. In the initial study information was more often obtained from two sources of information, which increased the number of positive answers. Considering only those persons for whom we had two sources of data (84 in the initial study, 40 at follow-up), suicidal communication of any kind was approximately as frequent during the follow-up

Table 2. Ways of Communicating Suicidal Intent

Form of Communication	Initial Study ($N = 87$)	Follow-Up: Total Group ($N = 80$)	Follow-Up: 2 Sources of Information ($N = 40$)
Desire to die	37%	28%	35%
Better off dead	40	30	38
Family would be better off	37	20	25
Intent to commit suicide	33	18	22
Actual suicide attempt	14	11[a]	10
References to methods	23	16	18
Dire predictions	10	10	13
References to dying before relative	16	5	8
Putting affairs in order	6	6	5
Can't take it; no other way out	22	13	13
References to burial or grave	7	1	3
Afraid (or not afraid) to die	18	13	13
Talk of others' suicides	3	5	8
Insist not buy new things for him	2	0	0
Taunts and threats	7	4	3
Miscellaneous	1	10	10
Total percentage having any communication	68	51	65

[a] Includes two persons who killed themselves during follow-up.

interval as it had been before the index admission. Communication of at least one type was reported for two thirds of the sample at both times. This high frequency of communication during follow-up is not surprising in view of the high prevalence of psychiatric illness and hospitalization during the follow-up period.

Circumstances of Communication. Of the 41 patients reported to have communicated suicidal intent during the follow-up period, it was possible to determine in 38 cases whether or not communication had taken place during times when the patients were psychiatrically ill. In 35 of the 38 cases communication occurred only with illness. Of the other three patients, one young woman with undiagnosed psychiatric disorder continued during the six years after the index admission to fight with her husband, to be provocative, to cry easily, and to have a few chronic physical complaints. It was her custom about twice weekly to say "I can't take it any longer." No other type of suicidal communication was reported for this unhappy person. The second patient was a depressed woman who communicated suicidal intent not only during a recurrence of her illness but also when apparently well during arguments with her husband. The third patient was a middle-aged alcoholic man whose illness remitted after the index admission. During the follow-up interval, he talked about dying before his wife did, made efforts to put his affairs in order, and discussed suicide in talks to AA. In summary, suicidal communication rarely occurred in the absence of other symptoms of concurrent psychiatric illness.

It was possible in 38 of the 41 cases to identify the persons to whom the communications were made: to the spouses in 66 per cent, to other members of the household in 8 per cent, to a psychiatrist or personnel in a psychiatric hospital in 40 per cent, to a nonpsychiatric physician in 3 per cent (one case), and to nonprofessional persons outside the home in 32 per cent. (Figures total more than 100 per cent because communications were to more than one person in 42 per cent of the cases.) Thus, spouses and psychiatric personnel were the major recipients of communication. Nonpsychiatric physicians apparently received and reported few communications.

The presence or absence of alcohol at time of suicidal communication was ascertained for 56 of the 60 communicators in 1959, and for 28 of the 41 communicators at follow-up. Drinking coincided with communication at least once in 20 per cent of the 1959 communicators and 29 per cent of the follow-up communicators.

The possible associations between suicidal communication and other factors which we found significant are outlined below.

a. Importance of having two sources of information. As the tabulation below demonstrates, we received significantly more reports of suicidal communication when there were two sources of information, a patient and an informant, rather than only one ($\chi^2 = 5.0$, $p<.05$). This was especially the case if the patient had *not* been a suicidal communicator in the initial study ($\chi^2 = 4.5$, $p<.05$). Informants were significantly more likely to contribute positive information about suicidal communication than were the patients themselves. Of the 52 informants, 58 per cent said there had been suicidal communication; of the 68 patients questioned, only 32 per cent admitted such communication ($\chi^2 = 6.7$, $p<.01$). In the 40 cases for whom both sources of information were available, there was agreement in 63 per cent on whether or not communication had occurred, and disagreement in 37 per cent. Disagreement was more likely to be in the

	Reports from 2 Sources	Reports from 1 Source
Communication reported at follow-up	26	15
No communication reported at follow-up ..	14	25

direction of the informant giving positive information about communication and the patient denying it (12 cases) than vice versa (3 cases).

b. Influence of diagnosis. At the time of the initial study, suicidal communication was reported for 81 per cent of the patients with affective disorder, 78 per cent of alcoholics, and 43 per cent of the patients with miscellaneous diagnoses. The difference between affective disorders and the miscellaneous group was significant ($p<.01$) with respect to communication, and the alcoholic group was not large enough for separate comparison.

At follow-up, suicidal communication was reported for 59 per cent with affective disorders, 58 per cent with alcoholism, and 33 per cent of the miscellaneous group. Comparing the first two groups with the third, χ^2 was 3.44, not quite significant ($.05<p<.10$). We had two sources of data (patients and informants) for 59 per cent of the combined affective disorder–alcoholic sample and for only 29 per cent of the miscellaneous sample, which in itself might have accounted for a higher yield of positive information in the former group. To avoid this difficulty we considered the responses of patients and informants separately. The accompanying tabulation demonstrates that when patient responses were considered separately, the affective disorders plus alcoholics reported more suicidal communication than the miscellaneous group, though not quite significantly so ($\chi^2 = 3.42$, $.05<p<.10$). When only the informant responses were considered, the difference between groups was not significant.

	Affective Disorder + Alcoholics	Miscellaneous Diagnoses
Information from patients		
Suicidal communication	19	3
No suicidal communication	28	18
Information from informants		
Suicidal communication	24	6
No suicidal communication	18	4

c. Influence of prior communications. Persons who communicated suicidal intent before the index admission in 1959 were more likely to have suicidal communications reported at follow-up. Of the 55 initial communicators who were studied at follow-up, 32 (58 per cent) were follow-up communicators; of the 25 initial non-communicators, 9 (36 per cent) were follow-up communicators. This difference was not significant, and disappeared when only persons with two sources of data (patient and informant) were considered (44 per cent versus 46 per cent).

When we considered patients' and informants' responses separately, we found that suicidal communication in 1959 predicted reports of follow-up communication by the patients themselves ($\chi^2 = 4.4$, $p<.05$), but not such reports by informants. This consistency between initial and follow-up communication occurred only for patients with affective disorders. Among other diagnostic groups, 1959 communication did not predict subsequent statements of suicidal intent.

d. Alcohol use. At follow-up the custom of drinking any alcohol at all, as compared with teetotaling, was significantly associated with suicidal communication in the total group ($\chi^2 = 6.4$, $p<.02$) and in the nonalcoholics ($\chi^2 = 5.4$, $p<.05$). However there was no significant difference between patients with social or medical complications of drinking and drinking patients without alcohol problems, or between heavy drinkers (who drank the equivalent of a pint or more whisky per week) and more moderate drinkers.

e. Influence of sex and age. At follow-up, as in the initial study, age and sex had no significant influence on incidence of suicidal communication for the group as a whole, nor with any diagnostic category, whether patient and informant responses were considered together or separately.

f. Suicide attempts and suicide. Before admission in 1959, 13 of the original 87 patients had attempted suicide. Compared with the 44 who had communicated about but not attempted suicide (and for whom we had data from both patients and informants), the 13 had a higher incidence of all other major types of communication (see accompanying tabulation).

	Attempters	Non-attempting Communicators
Desire to die	77%	48%
Better off dead	77	61
Family would be better off	85	48
Intent to commit suicide	69	45
Actual suicide attempt	100	0
References to methods	46	32

But the difference between attempters and non-attempting communicators in the initial study was significant only with respect to statements that the family would be better off if the patient were dead ($\chi^2 = 4.15$, $p<.05$). At follow-up a statistically valid comparison between attempters and non-attempting communicators could not be carried out, because there were too few follow-up attempters for whom we had two sources of data.

One of the 13 suicide attempters from the initial study died during the index admission, 9 did not attempt suicide in the follow-up interval, 2 did attempt, and a third was a probable suicide.* Of the 74 non-attempters in the initial study, 1 died during the index hospitalization, and we had insufficient follow-up information about 5, leaving 68; 62 of these patients did not attempt suicide during follow-up, 5 did attempt, and a sixth killed herself. Suicidal attempts in the initial study did not predict follow-up attempts to a significant degree, nor did suicidal communication of any other type. Of the 9 persons who attempted or committed suicide during follow-up, 3 had not communicated intent initially (one, manic in 1959, killed herself during a subsequent depression).

On the other hand, diagnosis was of greatest importance in predicting suicidal acts at any time in this group. In 1959, 11 of the 13 attempters had primary affective disorder, and 2 were alcoholics. At follow-up 6 of the 7 attempters and both completed suicides were in the primary affective disorder group, and 1 attempter was an alcoholic. No suicidal act was reported for the miscellaneous group, either initially or at follow-up.

DISCUSSION

In this longitudinal investigation of psychiatric illness and the communication of suicidal intent in 85 persons admitted to a psychiatric hospital, we obtained systematic follow-up information concerning 94 per cent of the patients, an average of seven years after the index hospitalization. Data were obtained concerning approximately the same proportion of patients who had died in the interval as of those alive at follow-up. The patients were representative of those treated at Renard Hospital, a private acute psychiatric facility in the Washington University Medical Center. The modal patient was a white, middle-aged woman from the middle socioeconomic class who suffered from primary affective disorder, a typical patient in this kind of hospital. Recurrent or persistent psychiatric disorder was the rule for this group during the five- to eleven-year follow-up period.

When the patients were studied at the time of index hospitalization in 1959, communication of suicidal intent was reported for two thirds of them. An identical proportion was discovered to have made suicidal communication during the follow-up interval, if we considered those for whom we had two sources of data (patient and informant). In another study at the same institution Stevenson et al. (in press) found that two thirds of the

* This was a man who recovered from his index depression, which later recurred. He communicated suicidal intent during the new episode and was later found dead in his closed garage with the car motor running. We scored him only as a probable suicide, because the coroner recorded his death as natural — no autopsy was performed.

adolescent patients also communicated suicidal intent. Thus, we may expect a recent history of suicidal communication for two of three psychiatric inpatients ever hospitalized at this institution, where primary affective disorder is the predominant syndrome.

There were six common types of communication both initially and at follow-up: actual suicide attempts, statements by the patient that he wanted to die, that he would be better off dead, that his family would be better off, that he intended to kill himself, and references to methods of committing suicide. For practical purposes, specific questioning of patients and informants about those six items should identify almost all serious suicidal communicators in a sample. The same types of communication and comparable incidence for each type were reported for the adolescent group studied by Stevenson et al. (1971). It was rare for a communication to be regarded as a shallow threat for manipulative purposes. In these people, all sick enough for hospitalization at least once, suicidal communications were viewed as serious by patients, relatives, and physicians.

In the initial and follow-up investigation of these patients we studied suicidal communication rather than just "thoughts" or "wishes" about suicide. This was because the occurrence of communications is potentially verifiable by informants, and because suicidal thoughts are commonly thought to occur in almost everyone, and thus may have no special relationship to psychiatric disorder.

Our follow-up investigation has corroborated the findings reported by DeLong and Robins (1961) in the initial study of this sample: that communication of suicidal intent was an important symptom of psychiatric illness, was temporally associated with other symptoms of illness, and occurred very rarely in the absence of obvious psychiatric disorder.

Our results also confirmed the importance of obtaining medical records and questioning a relative concerning patients' suicidal communication. The best sources of data were spouses and psychiatric personnel who had previously treated the patients. Considering our total sample, informants were significantly more likely than patients to give such positive information. Furthermore, with regard to the 40 patients for whom we had two sources of follow-up data (patient and informant), we would have missed 11 of 25 communicators (44 per cent) if there had not been informants or interval psychiatric records. This was also true in the initial study, when we would have missed 17 per cent of persons reported to have communicated suicidal intent in one of the five principal ways. Thus, it seems to us that reliance exclusively on the patients' reports with no other source of data would be methodologically unsound in research of this type. It would also be unsound clinical practice, at least in evaluating patients who are sick enough to be hospitalized.

We believe that our most important findings concern the association of suicidal communications and acts, initially and at follow-up, with chronic alcoholism and primary affective disorder, especially the latter. It was the presence of alcoholism and primary depression (that is, depression in the absence of any pre-existing psychiatric syndrome) which most reliably predicted recurrent suicidal communication over the years, and it was the presence of depression which predicted future acts of avowedly suicidal intent. Only two subjects committed suicide, and both had affective disorder.

Diagnosis was thus of greatest value in determining suicidal risk, whereas age, sex, and the presence of prior communication were by themselves not reliable predictors. Also, use of alcohol during follow-up was significantly correlated with communication, even in nonalcoholics and even if the patient denied drinking at the time of the communication.

Our findings are in accord with those of Robins, Murphy, Wilkinson, Gassner, & Kayes (1959) concerning types of illness in persons committing suicide. They reported that among 134 suicides whose histories were studied by means of medical records and interviews with relatives, 45 per cent had primary depression and 23 per cent were chronic alcoholics. An additional 19 per cent were undiagnosed; many of this last group may have had depression or alcoholism but could not be so labeled because of insufficient information. No other psychiatric syndrome approached depression or alcoholism in importance among the completed suicides — for example, only 5 per cent had chronic brain syndrome, 5 per cent terminal medical illness, and 3 per cent schizophrenia.

It may be said, then, that suicidal communication and behavior are symptoms of certain psychiatric illnesses: such phenomena are most prominently seen in two disorders, primary affective disorder and chronic alcoholism. Among hospitalized psychiatric patients the presence of one of these syndromes seems to be the most important factor in predicting future repetitive suicidal communications, attempts, and completed suicide.

SUMMARY

In 1959, 87 psychiatric inpatients were studied with respect to their illnesses and the communication of suicidal intent (DeLong & Robins,

1961). After an average interval of seven years, the authors followed up 80 (94 per cent) of the 85 who had been discharged alive from the index hospitalization, obtaining systematic clinical data and positive or definitely negative information concerning specific types of suicidal communications and acts.

Suicidal communications preceded the initial 1959 hospitalization in two thirds of the original sample and in 81 per cent of those with primary affective disorder. During the follow-up interval such communications were also reported for two thirds of those for whom there were two sources of data (the patient and an informant). Of the 80 patients, 7 attempted suicide during the follow-up, and 2 others killed themselves. Among the persons followed up, recurrent or persistent psychiatric disorder was the rule, and suicidal communication occurred during definite episodes of illness, very rarely when patients were well. It was not a "way of life" for these persons.

An initial diagnosis of primary affective disorder or chronic alcoholism was of the greatest value in predicting future repetitive suicidal communications and the presence of primary affective disorder in itself significantly determined actual suicidal behavior: at follow-up 6 of the 7 suicide attempters and both suicides had primary depression. Diagnosis was a much better predictor of suicidal communication and behavior than were age, sex, or the presence of prior communications.

Our findings add to the evidence of previous studies that serious suicidal communication and self-destructive acts are principally associated with two widely prevalent psychiatric disorders, primary depression and chronic alcoholism.

COMMENTARY

SCHULSINGER. I want to congratulate you on this study. On the whole it confirms other information about the importance of suicidal communication, but more subtly than many other published studies. I think that it also might be of interest to see what comes out if you study things like that in a different way. For instance, your *S*s did not consist of first timers — some of them had a long history of affective and other disorders. In my department a related study was done by Dr. Egill Jensen, now chief of the alcoholic outpatient services for the city of Copenhagen. In Copenhagen 1 per cent of the whole population is admitted every year (not the same 1 per cent) to one of the psychiatric departments. Among alcoholics in Copenhagen, the frequency of suicide is about twenty times as high as in the average population. In the old days we had a diagnostic category called "acute affective reaction"; this means that people come in, out of their minds, most of them with some kind of suicidal attempt, and they are discharged very quickly. They do not belong, to our best knowledge, to the manic depressive group. We found in 1950 that 5 per cent (96 Ss) of all those admitted to my department upon their first psychiatric hospitalization, had a depressive affective reaction. In 1963, we carried out a follow-up study, without interviewing the Ss because it's easy in Denmark to get information from other sources. After an observation period of thirteen years, only 25 per cent of the 96 Ss had had another psychiatric admission. We also looked at the Ss' social fate, on the basis of the nine-level system devised by the sociologist Svalastoga. The lowest (ninth) level consists of people who are unemployed, hoodlums, shoeshiners, and so on. In 1950 the fathers of those patients had a normal distribution on this scale, which meant that 1 per cent of them were in class nine. Of the patients 3–4 per cent were in class nine in 1950, but in 1963 between 10–30 per cent were in class nine. The women were abusers of hypnotic drugs, prostitutes, or on welfare; the males had become criminals, psychopaths, and so on. Our conclusions from this study were that we should not discharge Ss with affective disorders so quickly as they want themselves discharged.

GUZE. I have a question about the apparent benefit of talking to an informant. Your data are different from the ones we obtained with regard to the diagnosis of alcoholism. We were much more likely to make the diagnosis of alcoholism from talking to the patient than from talking to a relative. In fact, we would have missed 26 per cent of the alcoholism diagnoses if we had limited ourselves to talking with the relatives. We interviewed a relative for 91 per cent of all the men who were reported to have a relative in the geographic area. I wonder, then, whether you have any data that bear on the possibility that the availability of an informant was a function of the suicidal communication — that is, was a relative who had been communicated with more likely to cooperate with the study?

HUDGENS. I think that may have been true. Very often the relative questioned was the person communicated with. Also, it was up to the patient to let us see the relative. If the patient wanted to conceal information about himself as a communicator he might also want to prevent us from seeing the relative.

SCHUCKIT. There is one major group that may be underrepresented with an inpatient population, the hysterics. This group has a high incidence of suicidal behavior and a high incidence of suicidal communication. Murphy et al. (1969), in a study of people who called a suicide prevention center, found that about 20 per cent were hysterics. They would be a group that you missed and probably would have a different long-term prognosis on suicide completion.

HUDGENS. The people with hysteria and other character disorders, with the exception of alcoholism, apparently don't get admitted to a hospital so often for their threats and attempts and therefore would not be included in this study. We tend to admit people with primary affective disorders and alcoholism who make such threats. We perhaps do not take the hysterics and sociopaths so seriously. It would be quite easy to study outpatients in a clinic, asking the first six questions of Table 2.

ROFF. Along this line, several years ago Dr. David Rioch studied an Army population of people who had attempted suicide, probably not sincerely. Have you attempted to distinguish between sincere and insincere suicide attempts? I got the impression that you consider almost all your subjects sincere in their attempts. In Rioch's study, quite a large number were judged to be insincere. Further study showed that the prognosis for further adjustment in the service turned out to be very poor for these men. That group provides an outpatient population that supplements the work you have reported.

HUDGENS. The people we've listed under taunts and threats represent a low proportion of the communications in this study. In a sense, our group has been screened for seriousness because they've been admitted to the hospital. Interestingly enough, the same is true of adolescents — of the 60 adolescents that we studied with this same instrument, 98 per cent of those who communicated did so in one of the five main ways, all considered serious. Only 12 per cent communicated in a taunting, threatening way, and these 12 per cent also communicated in one of the more serious ways at other times. Hence, a hospitalized patient is probably considered a serious communicator by himself, his family, and his doctor. You just don't pick up the taunters and manipulators as inpatients very much.

ROFF. I was speaking not merely of taunts, but of people who actually made an attempt when they thought they'd be found in time to save them.

[Lack of time prevented a response.]

REFERENCES

DeLong, W. B., & Robins, E. The communication of suicidal intent prior to psychiatric hospitalization: A study of 87 patients. *American Journal of Psychiatry*, 1961, 117, 695–705.

Dorpat, T. L., & Ripley, H. S. A study of suicide in the Seattle area. *Comprehensive Psychiatry*, 1960, 1, 349.

Murphy, G. E., Wetzel, R. D., Swallow, C. F., & McClure, J. M., Jr. Who calls the suicide prevention center: A study of fifty-five persons calling on their own behalf. *American Journal of Psychiatry*, 1969, 126, 314–324.

Robins, E., Gassner, S., Kayes, J., Wilkinson, R. H., Jr., & Murphy, G. E. The communication of suicidal intent: A study of 134 successful (completed) suicides. *American Journal of Psychiatry*, 1959, 115, 724–733.

Robins, E., Murphy, G. E., Wilkinson, R. H., Jr., Gassner, S., & Kayes, J. Some clinical considerations in the prevention of suicide based on a study of 134 successful suicides. *American Journal of Public Health*, 1959, 49, 889–899.

Stevenson, E. K., Hudgens, R. W., Held, C. P., Merideth, C. H., Hendrix, M. E., & Carr, D. L. Suicidal communication by adolescents: A study of two matched groups of 60 teenagers in psychiatric and non-psychiatric hospitals. *Diseases of the Nervous System*, in press.

RODRIGO A. MUNOZ
GARY KULAK
SUSAN MARTEN
VICENTE B. TUASON | *Simple and Hebephrenic Schizophrenia: A Follow-Up Study*

SIMPLE schizophrenia is described as a psychosis "characterized chiefly by a slow and insidious reduction of external attachments and interest and by apathy and indifference leading to impoverishment of interpersonal relations, mental deterioration, and adjustment on a lower level of functioning" (American Psychiatric Association, 1968). This description indicates that simple schizophrenia may be diagnosed in the presence of three main characteristics: slow and insidious onset; social detachment accompanied by indifference; lack of full recovery.

Hebephrenia, on the other hand, is noted as follows: "This psychosis is characterized by disorganized thinking, shallow and inappropriate affect, unpredictable giggling, silly and regressive behavior and mannerisms, and frequent hypochondriacal complaints" (American Psychiatric Association, 1968). The characteristics of hebephrenia may then be summarized as formal thought disorder; blunted affect; presence of accessory symptoms, such as delusions and hallucinations.

Nosological tradition has established these two syndromes as separate entities affecting different individuals. We propose that the two conditions may be cross-sectional descriptions representing different degrees of severity rather than stable clinical entities. This concept would generate two testable hypotheses: first, simple schizophrenia is diagnosed in younger patients who may have a different diagnosis at follow-up; second, hebephrenic schizophrenia is diagnosed in older patients with a long morbid course during which they may have shown symptoms common to simple schizophrenia. This study deals with these two hypotheses and discusses their clinical implications.

MATERIALS AND METHODS

The population studied was 29 patients who received the diagnosis of either simple or hebephrenic schizophrenia in the inpatient service of Malcolm Bliss Mental Health Center (MBMHC), St. Louis, Missouri, during the four years between April 1964 and April 1968. The diagnosis was made in each case at a conference attended by the psychiatric residents in charge of the patient, a senior psychiatrist, and paramedical personnel of the same ward.

An initial diagnosis of simple schizophrenia was made for 17 patients, of whom 9 patients received a different diagnosis before discharge from the hospital. The diagnoses of 7 patients were changed to a different type of schizophrenia because of the presence of delusions or hallucinations, and 2 other patients received, respectively, the diagnoses of mental retardation (IQ 56) and antisocial personality (history of persistent antisocial behavior since before the age of 15 years). This left 8 patients with the final diagnosis of simple schizophrenia.

An initial diagnosis of hebephrenic schizophrenia was made for 12 patients. Mental retardation was thought to be a more fitting diagnosis of 3 patients on the basis of a lifelong deficit in intellectual functioning, absence of clear deterioration from a higher to a lower level of intellectual ability, and a tested IQ lower than 65. This left 9 patients with a final diagnosis of hebephrenic schizophrenia.

An intensive effort was made to locate and interview the 17 patients with final diagnoses of simple and hebephrenic schizophrenia, but 5 could not be located. This paper reports on the results of a one- to five-year follow-up interview of the remaining 12 patients, each of whom was examined by one of the authors.

RESULTS

Table 1 shows some of the characteristics of the patients studied and their follow-up diagnoses.

Simple Schizophrenia. All of the five patients who received this diagnosis were under 30 years old. Their ages ranged from 18 to 29 years with a mean age of 23 years. They had been ill from 1 to 6 years. Three patients had had remissions and exacerbations of symptoms so that the duration of the episode before the index admission was shorter than the total duration of the disorder. At follow-up they had symptoms or a history of symptoms compatible with the diagnosis of affective disorder as defined by Cassidy

Table 1. Characteristics of Patients Initially Diagnosed Simple and Hebephrenic Schizophrenics

Characteristic	Simple Schizophrenia (N = 5)	Hebephrenic Schizophrenia (N = 7)
Single	5	4
Married		3
White	5	5
Negro		2
Male	3	
Female	2	7
Age		
Less than 20 years	1	
21–24 years	3	1
25–29 years	1	1
30–34 years		1
35–39 years		1
40–50 years		2
More than 50 years		1
At follow-up		
Recovered	3	2
Unimproved	2	5
Out of hospital	4	2
In hospital	1	5
Follow-up diagnosis		
Simple schizophrenia		
Affective disorder	3	2
Hebephrenic schizophrenia	1	5
Antisocial personality	1	

et al. (1957). One patient had had a progressive clinical course leading to a picture compatible with the diagnosis of hebephrenic schizophrenia. The fifth patient had had lifelong antisocial behavior, which had not been previously apparent. Since his mental status was free of schizophrenic features at follow-up, he was regarded as an antisocial personality. The following are examples of two outcomes: remission in the depressed patient and severe, persistent illness in the schizophrenic patient.

Simple Schizophrenia, Later Diagnosed as Affective Disorder. The patient was a 19-year-old single white male when he was admitted to MBMHC in June 1967. For about 15 months before hospitalization he had abandoned his job, had been withdrawn, and had manifested decreased verbal communications and lack of interest in his family. The symptoms showed minimal change during 4 months of hospitalization. He was discharged in October 1967 when he progressively regained interest in his usual pursuits, obtained a job, and planned on resuming his high school studies. In February 1968 he became depressed and tired, complained about insomnia, feelings of hopelessness and worthlessness, and suicidal ideation. He was readmitted to a mental hospital where he was successfully treated for typical symptoms of depression, including feelings of guilt, feelings of incapacity, difficulty in concentrating, and severe retardation.

Simple Schizophrenia, Later Diagnosed as Hebephrenic Schizophrenia. This single white female was 29 years of age when she was admitted to MBMHC in January 1965. The family reported that she had had symptoms since 1961, when she became withdrawn, uninterested in doing any work or taking care of herself, dependent on her family for support, and indifferent about the future. She did not change after 3 months in the hospital and was eventually referred to the St. Louis State Hospital, where she stayed until October 1967. When she was interviewed at home one year later, she presented marked affective blunting and disconnected speech. She lived in total social isolation, was taken care of by the family, had no plans for the future, and seemed to have lost all drive and initiative. Although she denied delusions to the interviewer, her parents reported that she had expressed the belief that they were trying to kill her.

Hebephrenic Schizophrenia. Five of the seven patients were over 30. Their ages ranged from 21 to 51 years with a mean age of 37 years. The two patients under 30 had had a remitting course and had suffered symptoms of an affective disorder (mania). Both patients had a history of affective disorder or alcoholism in their families. The other five patients had suffered unremitting psychoses lasting for 10 years and longer. At followup they showed symptoms suggestive of hebephrenic schizophrenia. At least two of these chronically ill patients had formerly exhibited a clinical picture identical to that of simple schizophrenia. The following cases are illustrative:

Hebephrenic Schizophrenia, Later Diagnosed as Affective Disorder. This was the youngest patient with the initial diagnosis of hebephrenia. She was a 21-year-old single white female admitted to MBMHC in June 1967. Her mother had suffered a severe episode of depression with spontaneous and complete remission. An older sister had been admitted to mental hospitals twice for episodes of hyperactivity and grandiose ideation, from which she also had a complete remission. The patient's symptoms had started 4 years before the index admission when she lost all interest in friends and outside activities and had trouble thinking and making decisions. She felt depressed, fatigued, sleepless, and unable to work. These symptoms improved after three psychiatric hospitalizations and several courses of electroshock therapy. She was then noted to be unusually gay and happy, moving about all the time, talking rapidly and excessively, and jumping quickly from idea to idea. During the index admission she was childlike in appearance and smiled and laughed unpredictably. The patient was described as more shallow and inappropriate than euphoric. She expressed false ideas that she was a married actress who had twins, was a pilot, and knew fifty-two languages. She was transferred to the state hospital from which she was discharged after two months. At the follow-up interview, she had been asymptomatic for almost a year. She had resumed a normal social life and was free of detectable sequelae, working as a waitress, and supporting herself. The diagnosis at this time was manic depressive illness, in remission.

Hebephrenic Schizophrenia, Early History Suggestive of Simple Schizophrenia. This single white female was the oldest patient in the study. She was 51 years of age at the time of the index admission in February 1967. She had no family history of mental illness. After an uneventful childhood she left the eighth grade at age 13 because she did not care about school, and then remained at home in almost complete isolation with no friends or social life. In her early twenties she made a short and unsuccessful attempt to work at a stationery shop arranging displays. Her relatives committed her to the state hospital at age 25 because of progressive withdrawal, indifference, and inability to support herself. After 18 years without significant change, she was discharged in the care of her father. After his death she was brought to MBMHC by the police because neighbors complained that she dumped garbage on their lawns and wandered about ringing doorbells at night.

On admission, the patient was dressed inappropriately. Though grinning, giggling, and singing, she insisted that her neighbors were planning to take away her house. She was transferred to the state hospital where she stayed for a year. She was then transferred to a nursing home, where she was interviewed for follow-up. The patient showed manneristic behavior and blunted affect. She had forgotten about the neighbors but now felt electric currents going through her body. Her social interaction was quite reduced, and she seemed to be living in a world of her own.

COMMENT

The results support the proposed hypotheses. All of the patients who had the diagnosis of simple schizophrenia were under 30 and had a different diagnosis at follow-up, including affective disorder, hebephrenic schizophrenia, and antisocial personality. Five patients with both initial and follow-up diagnoses of hebephrenic schizophrenia were over 30 and had had symptoms for more than 10 years. Two younger patients with the initial diagnosis of hebephrenic schizophrenia received a different diagnosis at follow-up.

The population studied could be divided into two groups (Table 2). Five patients who were under 30 at the time of admission had affective disorders. Three had suffered protracted periods of atypical depressions ("simple schizophrenia"). Two had suffered attacks of mania that cross-sectionally suggested hebephrenic schizophrenia. Six patients had chronic psychoses that could be diagnosed as hebephrenic schizophrenia. Four of these patients were over 30 and had been ill for more than 10 years. At

Table 2. Follow-Up Diagnosis of Patients Initially Diagnosed as Simple or Hebephrenic Schizophrenics[a]

Characteristic	Affective Disorder ($N=5$)	Hebephrenia ($N=6$)
Age at index admission		
Over 30	5	1
Under 30	..	5
Duration of illness before index admission		
1–2 years	1	..
2–4 years	1	..
4–6 years	3	1
6–10 years	..	1
+10 years	..	4
Duration of episode before index admission		
6 months–1 year	2	..
1–2 years	2	1
2–4 years	1	..
4–6 years	..	1
+10 years	..	4

[a] Excluded is the single case diagnosed antisocial personality at follow-up.

least four had presented clinical characteristics of simple schizophrenia or had received this diagnosis early. These findings are in keeping with those of Brill and Glass (1965), most of whose patients received the diagnosis of hebephrenic schizophrenia after the age of 30, in spite of earlier hospitalizations.

The progression of simple into hebephrenic schizophrenia has already been suggested by Sim (1968) and Slater and Roth (1969). Kraepelin (1919) also mentioned the close relation of simple schizophrenia to other forms of the disorder.

This follow-up study questions the validity of the diagnosis of simple schizophrenia, especially when dealing with younger patients. A history of several months or even one to two years of withdrawal, detachment, and apparent deterioration, may still be compatible with a follow-up diagnosis of affective disorder.

COMMENTARY

MYERS. You said your interviews lasted four hours. Was that a continuous interview session?

MARTEN. Yes.

MYERS. Could you comment on your experience? In my experience most people tire after an hour or an hour and a half. I am curious to know how you were able to keep a constructive interview going for four hours.

MARTEN. Well, perseverance. This may also be the reason that the interviews lasted longer than we would have liked. Many times the patients were very ill, and we went out to the homes. Some of the homes were rather sick too. Many times we took a break, talked to people, walked out, let them get a drink of water or something, and then went on.

GUZE. One might conclude that the negative results are explained by the fact that an inpatient population was studied. Perhaps simple schizophrenia doesn't get into the hospital because of the absence of delusions, hallucinations, and other more dramatic symptoms. We have recently studied a series of 500 consecutive patients in our psychiatry clinic, however, and found no cases who met the criteria for simple schizophrenia. There were patients who showed many schizoid qualities in their life style, but all had other disturbances, such as alcoholism, antisocial personality, or drug dependency. Our findings would thus support Dr. Marten's contention that simple schizophrenia, as an uncomplicated entity, must be quite rare in psychiatric centers.

MARTEN. That's what I think.

WIRT. If you can't turn up even 1 out of 8,000 people after that kind of careful study, then it doesn't exist. We ought to change the diagnostic manual.

MURPHY. I'm a bit concerned about the fact that you started with a discharged population. My impression of simple schizophrenia, which I've seen two or three times in my clinical career, is that once these people get in the hospital they don't get out. First of all, my impression is that simple schizophrenics don't cause anybody any trouble. They just sit at home and go to seed, and the only way they ever get to a psychiatric clinic is if the parents who have been keeping them die or something like that. Then they are put into a custodial situation of some sort or other, possibly a psychiatric hospital. I wouldn't expect simple schizophrenics to be discharged from a psychiatric hospital because there's no place to send them other than possibly to a chronic hospital. You didn't say that all of these discharges were to the community rather than to chronic hospitals, but if they were all to the community I would think this would be a great way to eliminate all the simple schizophrenics. I would wonder if you shouldn't start with admission diagnoses rather than those at discharge.

MARTEN. Well, of course we did collect all the charts that had ever received that diagnosis. We had approximately 29 patients who'd ever gotten either of the two diagnoses. There were 17 patients who had been diagnosed simple schizophrenic at admission, and about 8 of these were changed because something else came up — either they had delusions or hallucinations, so the diagnosis was changed to paranoid schizophrenia; or they turned out to have an antisocial history; or they were mentally retarded. That cut down on the total.

MURPHY. Then I misunderstood the dimensions of your intake — on that basis I agree with you that simple schizophrenia certainly is rare, but

I do think I've seen it. But since I didn't do a follow-up, I could be just as wrong as the other doctors were about that.

WINOKUR. I think that, normally, simple schizophrenia does not exist in the hospital or in the community. It doesn't even exist in the families of schizophrenic probands. We've recently completed a study of 28 schizo-affective probands and 25 schizophrenic probands, including a large family study in which we interviewed all available first-degree relatives. Not a single first-degree relative or proband fit the criteria for simple schizophrenia. There was a considerable number of schizophrenics in the families of schizophrenic probands but they did not have simple schizophrenia; they had either paranoid or hebephrenic-catatonic schizophrenia. I might say that we had a great deal of difficulty differentiating the hebephrenics from the catatonics, but we were able to at least put them into two groups, either paranoid or hebephrenic-catatonic; I think the evidence from our study and the evidence from Munoz et al.'s study put together would indicate that simple schizophrenia is probably not a viable diagnostic entity.

POLLACK. Do you think the mental retardation you speak of preceded the full-blown episode or is it associated with the disease?

MARTEN. These were patients in whom we established the fact that there was a lifelong history of mental retardation — that is, at a very early age they had difficulty in school, were never able to get out of the home, and had to be cared for by relatives. It was certainly something that began very, very early in life and definitely antedated the psychiatric problem that got them into the hospital. I would like to add one thing about family history, after hearing Dr. Winokur. Among our three patients who were initially considered simple schizophrenics but who had depressions and recovered, all had a positive family history for affective disorder. The two patients who went on to develop chronic schizophrenia had no family history, that we could find, of any psychiatric illness. Thus, among the seven the family history varied. Among our hebephrenic schizophrenics, of the five who had that diagnosis at follow-up, three had a family history that suggested a chronic schizophrenic illness in the family. Then, of course, there are affective disorders in the group that had positive family history for affective disorder, the two manics.

REFERENCES

American Psychiatric Association. *Diagnostic and statistical manual of mental disorders.* (2nd ed.) Washington, D.C., 1968.

Brill, N. Q., & Glass, J. F. Hebephrenic schizophrenic reactions. *Archives of General Psychiatry*, 1965, 12, 545.

Cassidy, W. L., Flanagan, N. B., Spellman, M., & Cohen, M. E. Clinical observations in manic-depressive disease. *Journal of the American Medical Association*, 1957, 164, 1535–1546.

Kraepelin, E. *Dementia praecox.* Edinburgh: Livingston, 1919.

Sim, M. *Guide to psychiatry.* (2nd ed.) Baltimore: Williams & Wilkins, 1968.

Slater, E., & Roth, M. *Clinical psychiatry.* Baltimore: Williams & Wilkins, 1969.

JOHN A. O'DONNELL | *Lifetime Patterns of Narcotic Addiction*

THIS PAPER will occasionally touch on the general set of narcotics users, but focuses primarily on the smaller set of narcotic addicts, who may be defined for present purposes as those users who become physically and psychologically dependent on narcotics, and who use the drugs on a daily basis for periods of at least a year or more. For the early stages of addiction it will use the general literature, but for later stages it will rely on follow-up studies, and primarily on the only long-range follow-ups which have been done in this country — my study of Kentucky addicts, Vaillant's study of New York City addicts, and Ball's of Puerto Rico addicts. The paper is therefore restricted to narcotic addicts in the United States. Most of my data are drawn from a series of long-range follow-up studies of narcotic addicts, and since all of them are follow-ups of patients at the NIMH Clinical Research Center (formerly the U.S. Public Health Service Hospital) in Lexington, Kentucky, it might be well to begin by describing the institution.

Congress passed the Harrison Narcotic Act in 1914 and then, with the exception of a few local clinics in the early 1920's, nothing much was done about the problem outside of law enforcement for a number of years. The addicts began to pile up in the federal prisons where they were troublesome to handle, and so in the late 1920's Congress authorized two federal institutions primarily for the treatment of federal prisoners who were addicts. They did add a provision which permitted the admission of voluntary patients and with that, Congress felt it had taken care of the problem. The Lexington institution opened in 1935 and a sister institution at Fort Worth about three years later. The Lexington institution took males from east of the Mississippi and females from the entire United States, whereas Fort Worth restricted itself to males from west of the Mississippi. The admissions over the years came to include more and more voluntary patients. By the postwar period about 90 per cent of all admissions were voluntary, but of course, the prisoners tended to remain there longer. Hence, on any given day the patients consisted of more than half prisoners, and the institution, I think, has been accurately described as more like a hospital than most prisons and much more like a prison than most hospitals. The prisoners of course were selected by the federal courts on varying principles, and the voluntary patients were self-selected. In the early years patients were mostly from non-minority groups, with increasing percentages of Negroes until in the postwar years roughly half of the patients coming in were Negro or Mexican. Up to 1967, when the mission of the institution changed, it was nominally a psychiatric institution and usually had anywhere from eight to twenty psychiatrists on the staff, but since admissions ranged up to 4,000 a year and there might be 1,200 or 1,300 patients there at any given time, obviously individual psychotherapy did not play a major role in the treatment program. In length, treatment might range from two or three days (after which many of the voluntary patients signed out) to two or three years as the prisoners served out their sentences. There were undoubtedly wide variations in treatments offered to patients, but these were more or less accidental and got buried in individual case folders.

The vast bulk of studies described addicts up to the point in time at which they are incarcerated, or enter treatment, or otherwise become available to the investigator. Addicts who are treated repeatedly or who are elderly when they first enter treatment can provide some data on almost the full life history of the addict, but of course they present biased life histories since they have continued to be addicted. But such elderly and recidivist addicts are in the minority; it has been noted for forty years that most addicts who become available for study are young, often in their twenties or thirties, rarely in their forties or older (Winick, 1965). Most of the available data, therefore, refer to the onset and early years of addiction. Follow-up studies extend the time coverage, but usually not to any great extent; most have followed their subjects for only a year or two. It will be argued below that some longstanding beliefs about addicts are wrong, and wrong precisely because they have extrapolated from the limited histories and findings that were available.

What would be desirable would be to identify a group of addicts and follow them until death. No study meets this desideratum, but three come close enough to reveal patterns which are missed by short-term follow-ups.

The Kentucky study took as its universe the 1,013 white residents of Kentucky who were admitted to the Lexington hospital for the treatment of narcotic addiction, from the opening of the hospital in 1935 to the end of 1959. There were only 50 nonwhites admitted in these 25 years. A stratified random selection procedure gave a sample of 266 patients, for whom an interview with the patient or a death certificate were secured in all but two cases. In addition relatives, physicians, and others were interviewed, for an average of two such interviews per case, and a variety of records were checked, so that in no case was information obtained from fewer than half a dozen reasonably independent sources. Since fieldwork was done in 1961–1963, the minimum length of follow-up was about 3 years, the maximum about 27. More than half of the subjects had died by the time of follow-up, and the living averaged 54 years in age. Thus, data covered the full life history of many subjects, and most of it for the remainder. The mean number of years from first admission to death was 9 years for the deceased males and 16 years from first admission to interview for those still alive, with slightly lower figures for females. Since median age at onset was about 30, and at first admission about 42, the follow-up data covered a period averaging 23 years after the onset of addiction (O'Donnell, 1969).

Vaillant's sample was quite different. He studied 100 male patients randomly selected from New York City admissions to the Lexington hospital in 1952, of whom half were black and 30 per cent Puerto Rican. He also included a secondary sample of 32 addicts who had been at least 28 years old at their 1952 admissions, to bring to 50 those who would be at least 40 years old in 1964, when his field work began. Of his sample 98 per cent were followed for 10 years after admission, and 96 per cent were followed until 15 years after the start of their addiction (Vaillant, 1966a–e, 1969, 1970).

Ball studied the entire universe of 243 residents of Puerto Rico who were hospitalized at Lexington between 1935 and 1962, the fieldwork being done in 1962–1964. Post-hospital information was secured for 97 per cent of subjects. Of the 112 still living in Puerto Rico, all but 3 were interviewed. More than 20 years elapsed between hospital discharge and interview for some cases, but because the bulk of admissions had been in recent years, the interval was only 3 years or less for two thirds of the sample. As in the other two studies cited, data were obtained from a wide variety of records and other sources, in addition to the subjects (Ball, 1965, 1967, 1969a&b, 1970).

The differences among the samples are evident — small town Kentucky residents, WASP's, older than the other samples, with addiction histories going back as far as 1897 and as recently as 1959, whose social status covered the entire range and averaged at least as high as the Kentucky population; as against younger New Yorkers, largely Negro and Puerto Rican, whose drug use was almost entirely postwar; as against Puerto Ricans in Puerto Rico, again covering the entire social status range and a long time period, but bulked in recent years and in younger, more deprived persons. These differences obviously pose difficulties in making comparisons, and in this sense constitute a weakness in the data.

On the other hand, the same differences constitute a strength. Findings which are invariant across three such different samples may tentatively be taken as suggesting universals for addiction. It will be seen below that some differences, taking others into account, may suggest interpretations which hold for all the studies.

Pre-addiction Characteristics. It would be theoretically and practically of great importance if we could, on the basis of early characteristics, predict who would fall into various groups: those who never use narcotics, those who experiment with narcotics but do not become addicted, those who become addicted but rather quickly become and remain abstinent, and those who enter into the cyclical pattern of addiction, abstinence, and relapse which is the focal concern here. Chein et al. (1964) have found that even in the areas of high narcotics use it is only a minority who experiment with narcotics, though a few biographies and as yet unpublished studies suggest that in a few periods of time and a few areas it may be a sizable minority and perhaps even a majority. We know from the work of Robins and Murphy (1967) that perhaps a majority of those who use heroin regularly enough to be classified as addicts are found, a few years later, not to be using the drug.

In short, the hard-core addict who has been most intensively studied is the residue after several sifting processes, but we know almost nothing about those processes. It is true that almost all investigators infer from their findings that something was wrong with these persons before they became addicts, but the agreement on what was wrong is not impressive. Negative findings are perhaps best established; there seems to be no evidence that those destined to become addicts are any less intelligent, or any less healthy, than the groups from which they come. Positive findings tend to vary from study to study. For example, Vaillant found among his addicts a preponderance of youngest children, reared in environments culturally disparate from those in which their parents had been reared. His findings were not replicated among the Kentucky addicts, though the cultural disparity finding is consistent with plausible evidence that among white addicts of forty to sixty years ago, there was a disproportionate number of United States–born children of immigrants (Dai, 1937; Lichtenstein, 1914). This finding should be interpreted with some caution because such addicts were not compared with the then current proportion of first-generation Americans in the communities where the addicts lived.

One finding common to the Vaillant and Kentucky studies was loss of a parent in childhood, and especially before the age of 6. It may be highly significant that in the Kentucky study this finding was even more marked among women than among men, in view of the universal finding that for the past fifty years or more women have been much less likely than men to become addicts.

Another finding common to the two studies was that most of the future addicts showed a history of difficulty in achieving an adequate adult role. In Vaillant's sample, where the average age at first addiction was 23, this showed up primarily in poor employment records and in excessive dependency, as indicated by the fact that as late as age 30, almost half were still living with a female blood relative. Because of the age at onset, this might be viewed as an effect rather than a precursor of addiction, but the same finding was repeated in Kentucky, before the onset of addiction. The poor employment record was also repeated in Kentucky, and in addition, among those with military service before addiction, the number of dishonorable, undesirable, inept, and psychiatric discharges was high.

An area in which various studies seem to disagree, but can be interpreted to agree, is the criminal behavior of addicts before their addiction. There are wide variations in the proportion reported to have prior records of criminal behavior. The major factors which reconcile these discrepancies seem to be (a) age at onset of addiction and (b) date of the study. If the onset is quite early — say before age 20 — the addict is quite likely to have escaped a formal record of prior criminality. But this seems to mean mainly that arrest and conviction rarely follow first offenses. Those who have studied addicts with early onset uniformly agree that there was prior criminal behavior, or signs such as truancy and delinquent associations which make criminal behavior predictable (Finestone, 1957; Meyer, 1952).

As for the dates of the studies, there is clear evidence from the Kentucky study, and from comparison of early studies with later ones, that over the last 30 to 40 years there has been an increasing tendency for addicts to have prior criminal records. It is a safe inference that today addicts are primarily drawn from among delinquent or criminal subgroups. The causal chain is probably both sociological and psychological; those who have criminal connections are more likely to be exposed to narcotics, and those who have been deviant in one way are more ready to experiment with other forms of deviance. In line with the latter observation, narcotics are rarely the first drug abused. In a recent series of Lexington admissions, heroin was preceded by marihuana in 75 per cent of cases, by alcoholic excesses in from 81 to 95 per cent of cases, with the alcohol almost invariably preceding the marihuana. Finally, almost all observers agree that psychiatric or personality difficulties are detectable in the histories of most addicts before their drug use. Unfortunately, there is little agreement on what these difficulties are — schizoid personalities and depression are frequently mentioned, and even more often "antisocial personality" or an equivalent phrase.

There are, then, numerous indications of premorbid characteristics among addicts. In the present state of knowledge, however, these are best seen not as findings, but as suggestions for further research. The most needed direction of research is a comparison of addicts with appropriate controls from the subgroups from which they come. For the most part we have no firm basis to conclude that the characteristics noted are either more frequent or more severe among those destined to become addicts than among their peers. One of the few controlled studies, which does indicate such differences, may be found in Chein et al. (1964).

Roads to Addiction. This subject can be dismissed briefly. Historically, there have been three major roads to addiction: onset in the course of medical treatment or self-treatment, onset as treatment of alcoholism, and onset within peer groups in the search for kicks. The first two roads were still common in the Kentucky sample, among those addicts whose use had started before the 1940's. The alcoholism route has almost entirely disappeared (though as noted above, alcoholic excesses are still a frequent precursor of addiction), and the medical route has greatly diminished in importance. For practical purposes, narcotic addiction today can be seen as arising within peer groups, almost invariably for the express purpose of seeking kicks, though of course the basic reason may be group pressures of varying kinds.

CORRELATES OF THE ADDICTION CAREER

It may well be true that those who merely experiment with narcotics, or even become addicted for only a short time, suffer few ill effects from their drug use. We simply do not know, since such users have been little studied. But for those whose addictive careers span at least a few years, effects or correlates can be noted in a number of areas.

Involvement in a Drug Subculture. Perhaps the most important factor, even more important than the drug use itself, is that the addicts tend to form or join an addict subculture. The initial motivation seems to be that this is necessary to achieve or maintain regular access to drugs. Its importance, however, lies in the fact that it becomes a learning environment, in which new skills, attitudes, and values are developed and in which the addict becomes increasingly alienated from society at large. Indeed, some have suggested that it is this narrow world, in which he can be accepted and win status, rather than the drug effects, which attracts many to addiction.

The subculture facilitates what Lemert (1951) has referred to as secondary deviance, and others as fixing one's self-concept as an addict, in which being an addict becomes one's master status to which all others are subordinated. To an outsider, the daily life of the addict seems a dismal one. He is constantly scurrying for his drug or money for it, in constant danger of being cheated, or being arrested, or dying. He can trust few, if any, of his fellows. As tolerance to the drug increases, the enjoyment he gets from it decreases, perhaps to the vanishing point. The negative aspects of his life are so great that almost all addicts at times want to quit their drug use and find another way of living, and may account for the fact that over the years some succeed. The addict life is so demanding, so much a young man's game, that it may force older or less competent addicts out.

But not all is negative. Several students of the street addict's life have emphasized its positive aspects. At the minimum, addiction gives a purpose in life to many who have never had a purpose, even if it be no more than getting the next shot. Even its demands become sources of pride, in that one can succeed in meeting them, and win the respect of others for this success (Feldman, 1968; Preble & Casey, 1969).

Whatever the pleasures or pains of the addict life, it tends increasingly to render the addict unfit for any alternative life. He takes on the antisocial attitudes of his friends, and loses the attitudes of his family and earlier friends. Work and the eight-hour day are for squares; a hustle is his only source of pride or of the funds he needs but is incapable of earning legitimately. To give up the use of drugs is not simply to give up drugs. It is also to give up the only way of living one knows, has been successful in, has taken pride in, with the simultaneous need to find a new way of living, which has been devalued and despised, and in which one has few skills.

Involvement in the drug subculture clearly must be related to most other variables in the addiction career, including abstinence and criminality. The importance of this involvement has been recognized by many theorists in the field. We need to develop operational measures of it. One such measure, developed for the Kentucky study but needing elaboration to be useful for other addict groups, among whom the degree of involvement will average much higher, was found to be related to most of the other variables considered.

Health and Mortality. Numerous studies testify to an increased incidence of disease among addicts, especially diseases transmitted by unsterile techniques of administering the drug (Cherubin, 1968; Nelson, 1966). In addition, the death rate among addicts seems to be 2.5 to 3 times as high as in the general population. These were the ratios of observed to expected deaths found for males and females in the Kentucky study, but they are confirmed in a number of others (O'Donnell, 1969; Retterstol & Sund, 1964; Vaillant, 1969).

To some extent, these excess deaths are attributable to the health hazards touched on above. Some are directly due to what are commonly called overdoses, the mechanism of which is as yet imperfectly understood. True overdoses are included, but some "overdose" deaths may be due to adulterants rather than the drug. It also seems necessary to postulate some unknown, third mechanism, since these deaths seem to be almost as common among heroin addicts in Great Britain, where the purity of the drug is assured and where one would therefore assume the dose is accurately known. In addition to these deaths, there is an excess of unnatural deaths from homicides, suicides, and accidents. Students have speculated for years why so few addicts over forty are found in hospitals or incarcerated, given the numbers known to be addicted in their twenties. Clearly, one reason, though not the major reason, is that many have died in the interim.

Criminality. The stereotype of the young innocent who somehow becomes addicted, and then as a result becomes a thief, a pimp, or a prostitute, has few counterparts in real life. As was noted above, the large majority of addicts were well embarked in criminality before their drug use. But that addiction causes an increase in crime seems to be well documented. This increase occurs in a number of ways. First, there is the obvious point that there is a large increase in technical drug offenses, such as possession, sale, importation, and conspiracy. This is not an increase from zero — since a sizable minority sell drugs before they use them — but necessarily approaches 100 per cent after the onset of addiction. Second, among those with no criminal records before addiction, some begin to commit property offenses as the need for money to buy drugs increases.

Third, and probably most important, those who were already criminal and from whom more crimes would normally have been expected, commit more offenses than would have been probable had they not become addicted. Although they would have stolen, they would not have needed to do so as frequently if they had not been hooked on one of the most expensive commodities for sale. Further, the addiction almost certainly extends the period of criminal activity. It is known that most delinquents settle down to a possibly marginal, but essentially noncriminal working-class way of life as they emerge from adolescence. But if in the interim they have become addicted, they cannot afford this and must continue and expand their criminal activities.

The literature is in almost universal agreement that the crimes of addicts are property offenses, not offenses against the person or crimes of violence. The findings in Kentucky suggest that this point needs further study, and perhaps reformulation. It was true in Kentucky that the ratio of property offenses to offenses against the person increased after the onset of addiction, but this seemed to be due to a very large increase in the former, not to any reduction in the latter. The mass media and public opinion hold that many armed robberies, and ensuing murders and injuries, are committed by addicts. They may well be correct. The pharmacological effect of narcotics is tranquilizing, and may be assumed to reduce the probability of impulsive assaults and similar offenses, other things being equal. But the point is that other things are not equal. The need for the drug or money for the drug, the whole way of life described above, may motivate other offenses against the person to a degree which more than offsets the tranquilizing effects of the drug.

Employment. Here we can be brief. All studies agree that addicts — aside from physician and nurse addicts, and what is probably no more than a handful of wealthy or highly paid workers — have extremely poor employment histories, markedly worse than before they became addicted.

It is not, of course, that the drug itself prevents them from working satisfactorily. One contrary example would be enough to destroy that contention, and the exceptions above are all contrary examples. Further, small numbers of relatively older addicts can be located who have learned to hold their daily intake of drugs to small, though still addicting dosages, and who can earn enough in skilled labor to avoid crime.*

But the fact is that most addicts cannot afford to work at legitimate jobs. Whether because of minority group status, or lack of education, or failure to learn work skills or habits, or a devaluation of these skills and habits, or from more deep-seated personality problems, they do not have the capacity to hold high-paying jobs. They can expect to learn less than their habit costs, so a job is no solution. They need a hustle, an illegitimate but high-paying source of income. A further factor is that most regular jobs do not give them the time they need to make connections for drugs, and the time and privacy for injecting them. Most addicts today use the intravenous route of injection, and this implies usually more than two shots per day. Those who do manage to hold down a legitimate job for any length of time while addicted are likely to have, in addition to fairly high pay and a fairly small intake, a stable source of drugs, which usually means a medical source, and to use a long-acting narcotic, by the oral or subcutaneous route.

When addiction ends, or if there is a long period of abstinence in the addiction career, there would seem to be no reason why the addict cannot work. This seemed to be true of a few cases in the Kentucky study, but on the whole the subjects were so old when addiction ended, or it was followed by alcoholism in so many cases, that a stable work life did not emerge. It did appear in Ball's Puerto Rico study, however, and in Vaillant's New York study. It is not completely clear how the causal connection runs. Vaillant does not interpret his findings as indicating that the end of addiction permits the appearance of a stable work performance, but seems inclined to see the reverse — or perhaps more accurately, a feedback relation in which success on a job, often required by parole regulations, establishes a social bond which makes abstinence easier, and this, in turn, facilitates further success on the job.

However, the relationship is interpreted, it seems to be close enough to warrant the inference that if the subject in a follow-up study is working

---

* Personal communication from W. C. Capel, Visiting Assistant Professor of Epidemiology, School of Public Health and Tropical Medicine, Tulane University, New Orleans.

regularly, he is probably not using narcotics or at least not to the point of addiction. We could well use further documentation of this, because if true it suggests that larger-scale follow-ups could be done, and more cheaply, by using Social Security or similar employment records, rather than the expensive personal follow-ups of the past.

Marital Histories. Another area in which role performance seems to be markedly affected by addiction is that of marriage and children. In Kentucky there were more men who never married than would be expected, but the majority of men and almost all women did marry. The same holds for Vaillant's sample, counting common-law marriages. In both samples, the striking finding was multiple marriages, with well over half of them ending by divorce. Again in both samples, despite the many marriages there were fewer children than expected — under two children per subject, about two thirds of the expected number in Kentucky, and probably a slightly higher ratio in New York, where the expected number would be smaller because of metropolitan-rural differences in fertility, and the differences expectable because the Kentucky subjects went through the reproductive years several decades earlier.

Relapse and Abstinence. The numerous studies of addicts at one point in time almost always reveal histories of repeated periods of abstinence and relapse, except for those whose addiction is so recent that they have not had time to become abstinent and relapse. Data from institutions where addicts are treated or incarcerated naturally reveal histories of relapse in those who are readmitted. On the basis of such data, it was natural even if not rigorously logical to assume that all addicts relapse. The assumption was reflected in the popular stereotype "Once an addict, always an addict," and in at least one theoretical formulation a "tendency to relapse" was built into the very definition of addiction (Lindesmith, 1968).

The short-term follow-up studies of addicts seemed to confirm this assumption. With few exceptions, and these usually the least methodologically sophisticated studies, they showed large proportions relapsing, usually within a few weeks or a few months after the index period of abstinence. It was easy to make the further assumption that the few who were not found to have relapsed might merely have concealed the fact, or that they soon would relapse.

But the long-range follow-ups clearly establish that, though relapse is highly probable after any given period of abstinence in an institution, or any relatively short period of voluntary abstinence, over time the percentage abstinent increases at a fairly steady rate. The first such study was the Duvall et al. (1963) follow-up of 453 subjects for 5 years after discharge from Lexington. At 6 months after discharge, only 9 per cent of subjects were voluntarily abstinent; at 2 years 17 per cent, and at 5 years 25 per cent were voluntarily abstinent.

The Kentucky study showed a similar pattern: the percentage abstinent from narcotics kept increasing for at least 10 years after first discharge from Lexington, and probably for 20 years, though this was less firm because only small numbers had been discharged early enough, and had lived long enough, to be observed so long (O'Donnell, 1969). Vaillant's pattern was identical for a period of observation of at least 12 years, as was Ball's for a shorter period.

In the Kentucky study, abstinence from narcotics often involved a shift to other drugs, primarily alcohol. This may, however, reflect the prior history of alcoholism in many subjects, the fact that the career of abusing alcohol or narcotics covered most of their adult lives, and that they were much older when abstinence from narcotics was achieved, relative to other studies. In the younger samples studied by Ball and especially Vaillant, the shift to alcohol was also frequent, but was temporary. Once a stable pattern of employment, noncriminality, and abstinence from narcotics was fixed, the alcohol use was reduced. The findings of both Ball and Vaillant suggest that when the pattern of abstinence has been stable for three to four years, it is rarely broken.

The major question that remains is, What accounts for this increase in abstinence over time? What are the determinants of abstinence and relapse? A wide variety of variables have been found to be associated with eventual abstinence in the long-term follow-ups, but so far there are not many which have been duplicated. In Kentucky the major reason for abstinence seems to have been the decreasing availability of narcotics, which in turn was traceable to increasingly effective controls over the legal channels of distributing narcotics and to improved standards of medical practice. This factor was so important that it left little room for other variables to show an effect. Despite the fact that other variables explained relatively little of the variation in drug use patterns, and were not efficient predictors of these patterns, a number of variables were significantly associated with addition:

a. The less the involvement in the drug subculture, the more probable was eventual abstinence.

b. Self-concept, as a patient using medicine or as an addict seeking kicks, was indirectly related to abstinence. For those with self-concept as patients, the determining factor was their physicians; if the physicians continued to prescribe, the subjects continued to be addicted, whereas if they refused to prescribe, the subjects became abstinent and did not use other drugs or substitutes. For those whose self-concept was of addicts seeking kicks, addiction tended to continue if narcotics were available, and if they were not available, subjects tended to shift to substitute drugs.

c. Criminal record was mildly predictive of post-hospital drug patterns. The greater the number of sentences after the onset of addiction, the greater was the probability that men would show a pattern of continued addiction to narcotics or of addiction to substitutes. Abstinence was found mainly among men with no sentences, or with only one or two sentences.

d. Several variables connected with employment were associated with abstinence. Those in the health professions showed the largest proportion in the abstinence patterns, and those in illegitimate occupations showed the smallest. Those whose work patterns had been steady before addiction began were somewhat more likely to be abstinent from narcotics, but were about equally likely to be addicted to narcotics. The real difference was that they were less likely to spend much time in prisons or other institutions, and to have shifted to other drugs.

e. Men with no history of alcoholism before addiction showed post-hospital patterns either of addiction to narcotics or of complete abstinence. Those with early histories of alcoholism were no more or less likely to show a pattern of complete abstinence, but were more likely to show patterns of addiction to substitutes than to narcotics.

f. Variables recorded at the time of first hospitalization — such as prognosis; status as voluntary, probationer, or prisoner; length of hospital stay; and psychiatric diagnosis — were not found to be predictive of post-hospital drug patterns.

The decreasing availability of drugs noted in Kentucky did not hold for the other studies, where the major source of narcotics has been the illicit market, rather than the legal drugs which were the major source in Kentucky. But if the Kentucky finding is stated at a slightly higher level of abstraction, that those who became abstinent did so involuntarily, it is strikingly confirmed by Vaillant. The core of his data on this point is that his subjects were involved very frequently in short periods of hospitalization, short and long periods of imprisonment, and fairly long periods of imprisonment followed by parole. Of these four types of events, only the last was frequently followed by long periods of abstinence. Ball's finding that periods of abstinence of three years or more normally followed imprisonment for several years is not identical, but is analogous. More direct support for the importance of parole is found in studies by Diskind and Klonsky (1964) and in the experience of the California program for addicts (Kramer, 1970).*

The association between stable employment record preceding addiction and later abstinence was also confirmed by Vaillant, as it has been in a European follow-up by Retterstol and Sund (1964). Vaillant did not find, however, an association between criminal record and later abstinence. This seems puzzling, since almost any theoretical formulation would be likely to predict such an association. It may be that there was not enough variation in criminality in Vaillant's sample to show an effect.

Vaillant also suggests several psychiatric variables as predictors of eventual abstinence, but these seem to be impressionistic rather than formally defined and measured. There are also indications in all studies that idiosyncratic events like a marriage or religious conversion seem to account for abstinence in individual cases. No one has yet reported any empirical support for Winick's (1962) hypothesis that maturation accounts for abstinence, but it remains a plausible hypothesis, which probably needs testing by a variety of indicators. It may not be maturation in the sense of increased psychological maturity, but the aging process, with increased difficulties in meeting the demands of addiction, which accounts for some cases of abstinence. Self-concept has not been examined in enough studies, but one suggests it may not be self-concept so much as the acceptance of this concept by significant others which makes the difference (Ray, 1964).

In short, aside from the highly suggestive finding that abstinence is rarely voluntary among the subgroup of narcotic users who are firmly addicted for some time, we do not as yet have many well-documented findings on the differences between those who become abstinent and those who do not, or on why abstinence begins when it does. More important, we have no good theoretical or speculative answers to these questions.

The best data we have come from the long-term follow-up studies, but for once it seems justified to avoid the suggestion that we need more research of this type. Such studies are expensive and slow, and addictive patterns may well change more rapidly than studies could accumulate.

* Although Kramer criticizes the California program, and advocates major changes in it, he notes that one in three treated patients remains in good standing on parole (which implies abstinence) after one year, and one in six after three years. In the field of treatment for addiction, these are excellent results.

More important, such studies have inherent limitations. To be practical, they must be restricted to fairly small samples, so the number of cases restricts analysis to two or three variables at a time, rather than the multivariate analyses which are needed to sort out causal connections and permit the examination of interactions among independent variables. Most important of all, such studies, which necessarily are largely retrospective, meet great difficulties in precisely dating events in history, so that the analysis of data tends to be cross-sectional in nature, or in analysis of data over time, the time intervals tend to be huge. Becoming abstinent from narcotics, like becoming addicted to them, is almost certainly better conceptualized and better studied as a process, in which events have effects not in themselves, but in their temporal connection with other events.

Process studies have become possible in just the last few years. California, New York, and now the federal government have large-scale rehabilitation programs for addicts which include an initial period of institutionalization and three or more years of close supervision. The initial period of institutionalization will permit the collection of historical data up to that time, and a host of baseline measurements. The insitutionalization and ensuing supervision will easily lend themselves to experimental designs to permit the testing of different treatment models, and the after care will furnish detailed monthly reports not only on outcome, but on those intercurrent events and changes which may affect outcome. The mass of data will permit us to use powerful methods of analysis like multiple regression or discriminant function analysis where we have previously been restricted to chi-squares and similar statistics. And the precise dating of events will permit us to study processes, and to use complex models, including feedback models, where we have been restricted to short and simple one-way causal chains.

COMMENTARY

THOMAS. Dr. O'Donnell has covered a number of very basic issues in studies of the addiction problem, briefly and succinctly but, I think, quite accurately. In addition, his point about the patterns of addiction changing more quickly than the studies can accumulate is very pertinent because certainly in the recent period with the tremendous increase in addiction — especially heroin addiction in some of the major metropolitan centers — the type of population involved in addiction is beginning to shift quite rapidly from that involved in the past. So the relevance of the findings of previous follow-up studies to the present groups would have to be substantiated by new follow-up studies and analyses of characteristics of the present groups. I'm not so sanguine as Dr. O'Donnell about what will come out of the civil commitment procedures, at least in New York state, because this program has been, to put it conservatively, a dismal failure as far as what it has done for the addict. It is being radically modified at the present time in a direction which we may hope will eliminate most of this procedure, which tended to treat the addict, in the state institutions which dealt with addiction, primarily as a prisoner rather than as a patient. The addict's having a motivation for living and functioning in terms of being part of the addict subculture was very accurately stated by Dr. O'Donnell. This we see all the time in New York, where addiction becomes a way of life. Sometimes the attraction of this insidiously strikes not only those whom we might consider marginal individuals in life as regards their level of adjustment in society as a whole, but also many youngsters of even middle-class and affluent families who may also feel they have no purpose in life. Looking for immediacy of experience, they turn to drug subculture, including many other drugs besides heroin. Then an involvement in that subculture becomes more and more established as a way of life. We see now, in terms of at least short-term follow-ups, a number of addicts who come to the hospital because they've reached a state of desperation, because life eventually for many of them becomes so difficult. This is the pattern of life that Dr. O'Donnell described: it may have been an attractive style of life and may have made addicts part of a subculture, sometimes for a number of years; but eventually, for some of them, this life becomes grim, so unhappy, and so fraught with miserable consequences — not only day by day but hour by hour — that they plead to stay in the hospital for a few days, if not longer, for even the briefest of respites. Unless the situation changes drastically, we'll see more and more of this reaction to the addictive way of life. This reaction has also resulted in a marked increase in the suicidal risk among addicts. Just as an addendum to Hudgens et al.'s paper, addicts are a new group in which suicidal risk has to be taken with great concern, at least in the geographical centers where addiction has become common. Finally, on the question of treatment, it's probably just as well Dr. O'Donnell didn't mention the various approaches through psychotherapy because they've been uniformly unsatisfactory and disappointing — the latest being the group psychotherapy and group living set-ups through New York City's Phoenix houses, where now the overall results appear to be little, if any better, than if no treatment at all were offered. The most promising approach is through methadone, probably in combination with psychological and social help. Here again, follow-up for at least a few years will be required before we know how sustained its success is, how many addicts will require long-term maintenance on methadone, and how many can be taken off after a time without relapsing into heroin addiction.

O'DONNELL. I certainly agree that addiction is a young man's game. After a while addicts just can't take the demands of the addict's life anymore. This probably accounts more than treatment does for those who do manage to quit.

VAILLANT. My message is that most long-term follow-ups reflect only two points on the graph, and from two points you can only make a straight line. If there's one thing better than long-term follow-ups, it is repeated, long-term follow-up of the same sample. This makes a much more interesting graph. We need to follow up groups of people who have been well studied in the past.

As for Dr. Thomas's comment about the changing suicide pattern of heroin addicts, the more older literature I read about addiction, the more I'm impressed that much less has changed than anybody thinks. For example, the suicide rate in addiction has always been as high as in manic depressive psychosis over the last fifty years. What I want to do is to summarize what happened by 1970 to the 100 addicts who had been well for at least 3 years when I did a 12-year follow-up on them in 1964. Only one of these by 1970 appeared to have relapsed. Excluding the abstinent and the dead, there were 49 addicts (average age 35) still at risk in 1964. To find out what happened to them in 1970 provides a clue to what happens to addicts over 40. Of the 49, 17 had probably been clean for between 5 and 13 years. Thus, at age 40, out of 100 addicts who were initially addicted at an average age of 21: 18 were dead, 44 were probably alive and abstinent for five years, 1 was institutionalized, and 37 remained actively addicted. One point is that the death rate of young addicts is very much higher than that of the population as a whole. When one starts putting more follow-up points on the hypothetical graph, one learns that as addicts get older the likelihood of their killing themselves through misuse of drugs seems to go down. Furthermore, as Hudgens pointed out earlier on, between 20 and 30 per cent of all patients admitted to Renard Hospital were readmitted to psychiatric hospitals within the next seven years. Of the 100 drug addicts in our study, in spite of having severe "ego" problems and personality disorders, only 10 were ever hospitalized for mental illness: 2 for schizophrenia, 2 for psychotic depression, and the others for characterological reasons. None was hospitalized more than once or for more than a few weeks. So addicts over 40 do not go into mental hospitals.

O'DONNELL. I don't want to attack the long-range follow-up. After all, we're taught these days to let each man do his thing. But I think we've too long thought in terms of dichotomies — relapsed and abstinent, broken home or no broken home. Just as we need to conceptualize the onset of addiction as a process in which different events have different values and valences depending on the context within which they occur, it seems to me obvious that becoming abstinent must be seen as a process. Therefore, it should not be studied at two widely separated points in time but continuously. This is what the civil commitment programs can give us. Even if they don't cure anybody, at least they can supply some data on what happens. This is where I would see some hope.

BRUCE DOHRENWEND. You mentioned that the evidence showed that the criminal careers of addicts begin before the onset of addiction. You also mentioned that control data from the general population were frequently lacking for many patterns of addict behavior. I found your statement about addiction and criminality an interesting and important generalization. Can you tell me a little more about the data on which it was established? Were there, for example, control data from the general population?

O'DONNELL. I think that one of the bits of evidence is the dates of the studies, which give data on the incidence of criminal behavior before addiction. The early studies invariably report low percentages, or if they report large percentages, it's because they're studying prisoners who had to get arrested in order to be counted. The more recent studies are universally in agreement. They don't always give data on how many arrests and sentences had occurred before addiction but Chein in New York and Finestone in Chicago, in particular, certainly describe prior delinquency even among those who begin very young. Chein's heroin users began at 16, and he describes a pattern of delinquent behavior or what he interpreted as obvious predictors of delinquency. That's one item on which I would base the inference. Another was that in the Kentucky study we covered a wide range of people — some had become addicted as early as 1895 and others as late as 1959. Breaking the data down by decade of onset and looking at the percentage with prior criminal records produce a beautiful linear increase over time. This concatenation of evidence is what I base that inference on. Granted, in this field, most inferences are based on data rather than provided by them.

BRUCE DOHRENWEND. Do you feel this is a strong inference? I had considered this a rather controversial issue.

ROBINS. It's hard to get good evidence, but one study that sheds some light was done by the California Youth Authority (Roberts, 1967). Youths arrested for non-opiate drug offenses for the first time had prior arrest records in 42 per cent of the cases, certainly a higher rate than for the general population. More interestingly, those with prior offenses were more likely to have subsequent non-drug offenses than those whose drug use was the first offense. But in both groups, subsequent non-drug arrest was common (89 per cent with a prior non-drug arrest; 69 per cent without). One could argue both that delinquency leads to drug use and that the drug use leads to delinquency.

REFERENCES

Ball, J. C. Locating and interviewing narcotic addicts in Puerto Rico. *Sociology and Social Research*, 1965, 49, 401–411.

―――. The reliability and validity of interview data obtained from 59 narcotic drug addicts. *American Journal of Sociology*, 1967, 72, 650–654.

―――. The long-term social correlates of opiate addiction. *Social Problems*, 1969, 17, 225–234. (a)

———. A test of the maturation hypothesis with respect to opiate addiction. *Bulletin on Narcotics*, 1969, 21, 9–13. (b)
———. Onset of marihuana and heroin use among Puerto Rican addicts. In J. C. Ball & C. D. Chambers (Eds.), *The epidemiology of opiate addiction in the United States*. Springfield, Ill.: Thomas, 1970. Ch. 10.
Chein, I., Gerard, D. L., Lee, R. S., & Rosenfeld, E. *The road to H.* New York: Basic Books, 1964.
Cherubin, C. E. A review of the medical complications of narcotic addiction. *International Journal of the Addictions*, 1968, 3, 163–175.
Dai, B. *Opium addiction in Chicago*. Shanghai: Commercial Press, 1937.
Diskind, M. H., & Klonsky, G. *Recent developments in the treatment of paroled offenders addicted to narcotic drugs*. New York: State Division of Parole, 1964.
Duvall, H. J., Locke, B. Z., & Brill, L. Follow-up study of narcotic drug addicts five years after hospitalization. *Public Health Reports*, 1963, 78, 185–193.
Feldman, H. W. Ideological supports to becoming and remaining a heroin addict. *Journal of Health and Social Behavior*, 1968, 9, 131–139.
Finestone, H. Narcotics and criminality. *Law and Contemporary Problems*, 1957, 22, 69–85.
Kramer, J. C. The state versus the addict: Uncivil commitment. *Boston University Law Review*, 1970, 50, 1–22.
Lemert, E. M. *Social pathology*. New York: McGraw-Hill, 1951.
Lichtenstein, P. M. Narcotic addiction. *New York Medical Journal*, 1914, 100, 962–966. Reprinted in J. A. O'Donnell & J. C. Ball (Eds.), *Narcotic addiction*. New York: Harper, 1966.
Lindesmith, A. A. *Addiction and opiates*. Chicago: Aldine, 1968.
Meyer, A. S. (Ed.) *Social and psychological factors in opiate addiction*. New York: Bureau of Applied Social Research, 1952.
Nelson, A. S. Medical problems associated with addiction to opioid drugs. *International Journal of the Addictions*, 1966, 1, 50–61.
O'Donnell, J. A. *Narcotic addicts in Kentucky*. Washington, D.C.: Government Printing Office, 1969.
Preble, E., & Casey, J. J. Taking care of business — the heroin user's life on the street. *International Journal of the Addictions*, 1969, 4, 1–24.
Ray, M. B. The cycle of abstinence and relapse among heroin addicts. In H. S. Becker (Ed.), *The other side*. Glencoe, Ill.: Free Press, 1964.
Retterstol, N., & Sund, A. *Drug addiction and habituation*. Oslo: Universitetsforlaget, 1964.
Roberts, C. F. *A follow-up study of the juvenile drug offender*. Sacramento, Calif.: Institute for the Study of Crime and Delinquency, 1967.
Robins, L. N., & Murphy, G. E. Drug use in a normal population of young Negro men. *American Journal of Public Health*, 1967, 57, 1580–1596.
Vaillant, G. E. Parent-child cultural disparity and drug addiction. *Journal of Nervous and Mental Disease*, 1966, 142, 534–539. (a)
———. A 12-year follow-up of New York narcotic addicts: I. The relation of treatment to outcome. *American Journal of Psychiatry*, 1966, 122, 727–737. (b)
———. A 12-year follow-up of New York narcotic addicts: II. The natural history of a chronic disease. *New England Journal of Medicine*, 1966, 275, 1282–1288. (c)
———. A 12-year follow-up of New York narcotic addicts: III. Some social and psychiatric characteristics. *Archives of General Psychiatry*, 1966, 15, 599–609. (d)
———. A 12-year follow-up of New York narcotic addicts: IV. Some determinants and characteristics of abstinence. *American Journal of Psychiatry*, 1966, 123, 573–584. (e)
———. The natural history of urban narcotic drug addiction. In H. Steinberg

(Ed.), *Scientific basis of drug dependence.* London: J. & A. Churchill, 1969. Pp. 341–361.

―――. The natural history of narcotic drug addiction. *Seminars in Psychiatry,* 1970, 2, 486–498.

Winick, C. Maturing out of narcotic addiction. *Bulletin on Narcotics,* 1962, 14, 1–7.

―――. Epidemiology of narcotics use. In D. M. Wilner & G. G. Kassebaum (Eds.), *Narcotics.* New York: McGraw-Hill, 1965.

GENEVIEVE KNUPFER] *Ex–Problem Drinkers*

THE LIFE history of problem drinking has been very little studied. This statement may seem strange when we consider that one of the classics in the field of alcohol studies is Jellinek's (1952) description of the phases of alcohol addiction. But that classic itself has been a factor in the lack of interest in life history. It has contributed to freezing our thinking on the subject into a model of an unalterable progression toward an increasingly malignant state (Room, 1970). Other ideas concerning "arrested" cases and different types of alcoholism (Jellinek, 1960) which do not follow the classic model, have not really freed us sufficiently so that studies of the epidemiology of the life history of problem drinking have been planned. Other factors in this "freezing" have been the doctrines of Alcoholics Anonymous. Although AA has been of more practical benefit to alcoholics than psychiatry or any other resource, its contribution to science has been of doubtful value.

The present study can make only a modest contribution to the description of life history. One of its advantages is that it is based on data from two general population surveys. This type of sample can provide a different perspective from that given by samples of hospitalized, jailed, or otherwise specially selected alcoholics. (There have been many follow-up studies of alcoholics — e.g., Pfeffer & Berger, 1957; Rakkolainen & Turunen, 1969; Robins, 1966; Room, 1970; Rossi et al., 1963). The data we have comparing lifetime and present drinking patterns are retrospective because the longitudinal study has not yet been carried out; plans are now under way to follow these respondents, funding having at last been obtained.

In general, the picture of disease we get from population samples, as compared with samples derived from people who apply for treatment,

NOTE: The research of which this paper is a part was partially supported by Grant MH-09226 from the National Institute of Mental Health.

tends to give a wider range of severity of disease, sometimes even revealing the existence of hitherto unknown mild and arrested forms of diseases. We have found more cases than we expected to find of people who cut down more or less spontaneously (i.e., without treatment) and people who now drink "socially" or "normally," whereas their pattern at one time looked like an addictive, or diseased pattern.

In evaluating treatment methods for a variety of diseases, a frequently used research design is to look for the characteristics of those patients who benefit more than others from particular treatment modalities. In most cases, such characteristics actually define a relatively mild form of the disease. For example, studies of the results of sympathectomy in the treatment of hypertension show that the best candidates were those who had fewer cardiac and ophthalmologic signs. It is also true that drug therapy for hypertension is most likely to succeed in patients who have no eyeground changes. Mastectomy has better results in cancer of the breast if the cancer has not metastasized. Psychoanalysis and other types of psychiatric treatment work best for patients whose mental illness is not too serious. The schizophrenic who has a sudden acute episode of mental aberration is more likely to get well after shock treatment, phenothiazine treatment, or psychotherapy. He is also more likely to get well spontaneously.

What this means, I think, is not that treatment is useless, but that we should recognize that we may be working with a mild form or with a malignant form of the disease. In the former situation, we have an ally: the strength of the recovery potential of the patient. In the latter situation we are working with an enemy: the malignancy of the disease. The measure of the mildness may be the spontaneous recovery rate. This does not mean that intervention cannot help; it means that intervention should not be given undue credit.

Although the reasoning about what constitutes a malignant form of the disease seems circular, there is some justification for it empirically. Those cases of any disease which are resistant to treatment for whatever reason (physiological or psychological) and which get progressively worse are termed malignant, even though we must grant that the malignancy is usually ascertainable only after the fact. The only error lies in using the malignant form of the disease as the archetypal model for all its forms.

In the present paper the term *problem drinkers* (PD) is used instead of *alcoholic* to avoid some of the controversy about the "true" nature of "real" alcoholism. The approach of Jellinek and others to this difficulty, which is to distinguish different types of alcoholism, is fairly satisfactory, but there is something about the word *alcoholism* that seems to lead people to choose up sides and dig in their heels. Also, I like to think in terms of degrees of severity in this area (Knupfer, 1967), although many people tend to think that alcoholism is like pregnancy: either one is or one isn't. Of course there are still problems of value judgment and interpretation, even with the term *problem drinking*. If a person chooses to spend a lot of his time in a state of intoxication, who is to say that that is a problem? My position is that if either he thinks it is a problem, or his wife does, or his boss does, or he gets arrested for drunkenness, then it is a problem. I also reserve the right to decide that it is a problem, even without those conditions, if he drinks, say, a fifth of whiskey a day. As used here, then, "problem" includes the problematic — behaviors which put the respondent at substantial risk of social or medical damage.

The first objective of this paper is to compare current problem drinkers with ex-problem drinkers as to certain childhood characteristics and personality traits, using data from two interview surveys of different samples of the adult population of San Francisco. Although I am contending that there are many varieties of problem drinking, far more than, for example, Jellinek's five types, I have, of course, had to make some arbitrary definitions. The data are presented in terms of dichotomies: HPD (i.e., high problem-drinking) scores versus not HPD scores and ever versus current HPD. However, I hope to be able to show some of the variety in types of problem drinking in the discussion of cases. The discussion of cases will be used in connection with the second objective of this paper, which is to describe how ex-problem drinkers are drinking currently, how they drank in the past, and what caused them to change.

METHOD

Samples. Two different samples are used in the tables below. Sample A consists of 970 respondents ages 21 or over, based on a 1962 probability sample of San Francisco adults and reinterviewed in 1964. There were several changes between the 1962 and the 1964 sample: half of the light drinkers and abstainers and all of the heavier drinkers were reinterviewed, and in addition the spouses of all married respondents were interviewed. Some attrition also affected this sample — we were able to interview only 70 per cent of the chosen respondents. The sample was weighted for the purpose of these tables to reconstitute a sample representative of the San

Francisco population (Knupfer & Room, 1970). Although it was a second interview, no comparisons over time of the extent of problem drinking are possible because questions about problem drinking were not asked in the first interview.

Sample B, consisting of 786 respondents, was a probability sample of white males aged 21–59, living in San Francisco and interviewed in 1967. This group was chosen because it was sure to have a higher proportion of problem drinkers than the previously described sample, which included both sexes, all races, and all ages over 21. Furthermore, its greater homogeneity promised to give clearer meaning to correlates of problem drinking, and finally, our experience of interviewing blacks and orientals gave us the impression that such interviews were less reliable than the others. We felt that we should devise special selection and training methods for interviewers of minority groups.

The Problem-Drinking Score. The general idea was to effect some sort of compromise between clinical and survey techniques. I am afraid the survey technique got the upper hand, especially in the 1967 interview. Thus, there is some artificiality about the scores, which were made by adding up points given for problems in eleven different areas: Police Trouble, Job Trouble, Amount of Drinking, Number and Length of Prolonged Binges, Reasons Given for Drinking (e.g., to feel less tense or to forget problems), Addictive Symptoms, Trouble with Family, Trouble with Friends, Health Difficulties, Financial Difficulties, Belligerence When "under the Influence." Differences between scoring in the two samples result from differences in the interviews. The 1964 interview contained much more open-ended material that had to be rated; there were fewer questions about complaints from relatives and friends, and there were no questions about financial and health difficulties. On the other hand, only for the 1964 sample was information from police and hospital records obtained (see Knupfer, 1967, appendix).

The questions referred to current as well as past drinking and problems resulting therefrom. For each problem area a score of 1 was given for a "mild problem," a score of 3 for a "moderate problem," and a score of 6 for a "serious problem." A classification as a high score on problem drinking, which was defined as a score of 16 or more, might thus result from any one of the following: 3 or more serious problems, or 2 serious problems and 1 moderate and 1 mild, or 2 serious and 4 mild, or 5 moderate and 1 mild, and so on.

The categories of ex–problem drinkers shown in Tables 1–4 (the second and third columns) are called "decreased" and "reformed." A respondent having a score any time in his life which added up to what we have called *high score* on problem drinking, whose current problem score is less than 10 points, is called "reformed." Those whose current scores are between 10 and 15 points are called "decreased," and those whose current scores are still 16 or over are called "still high" (see first column in Tables 1–4). In addition, those currently "virtual abstainers" (defined in Knupfer & Room, 1970, p. 12) are included among the "reformed."

SOME CORRELATES OF REFORM

Childhood Factors. For each category of past versus present problem-drinking scores, Table 1 shows the proportion high on the characteristic named at the left. The top half of the table is based on data from Sample B; it is a weighted sample, for reasons that were explained earlier. The bottom half of the table is based on data from Sample B. That sample included white men aged 21–59, but in the table we have included only white men aged 35–59, thinking in this way to get a more homogeneous sample and one with more time in which to cut down. All of the childhood factors represent some experience or characteristic presumably unfavorable to mental health or to adjustment. Although the data are retrospective, they nevertheless refer to a period considerably before the onset of heavy drinking. The figures in the table are all percentages of men in that particular drinking problem category who scored high on the characteristic at the left. Thus, nothing adds up to 100 per cent because each percentage is independent of the others. With one exception — the childhood delinquency factor — the "reformed" in both samples are proportionately lower on these unfavorable characteristics than are the "still high." The position of the "decreased" varies. Most of them, with only three exceptions, have percentages that are in between those of the "still high" and the "reformed." The resemblance between the "decreased" and the "reformed" is much stronger in Sample B, probably because the slightly different definition of "reformed" in the second interview was an improvement. For Sample B we included in the "reformed" not only those whose scores were currently lower — that is, currently not more than 9 points — but also those who were currently light drinkers or abstainers despite higher scores. This allowed us to include as reformed some current abstainers who had a relatively high "current" score because they said "I am an alcoholic." In the PD score for Sample A such statements were given 6 points on the self-perception score.

Table 1. Past versus Current Problem Drinking Typology by Childhood Factors (in Percentages)

Childhood Factor	Ever High				Ever Medium		
	Still High	De-creased	Re-formed	Ever Medium Medium	Still Medium	Now Low	Always Low
Sample A[a]							
Lived with both parents to age 16 (no)	56	50	45	39			34
Father's education (no high school)	59	42	40	53			51
Parents' marriage (other than very happy)	80	79	46	63			42
Drinking problem in family when a child (yes)	34	46	14	21			17
Childhood stress score (high)	40	49	14	22			19
Childhood delinquency score (high)	55	62	65	25			13
Sample B[b]							
Lived with both parents to age 16 (no)	38	15	24		15	16	7
Father's education (no high school)	67	57	58		51	67	59
Parent's marriage (other than very happy)	66	76	47		38	50	50
Drinking problem in family when a child (yes)	38	15	24		15	16	7
Childhood stress score (high)	45	20	26		25	24	19
Sent to principal for acting up (yes)	53	40	56		30	34	26
Childhood happy (no)	28	5	5		17	11	13
Sure of parent's love (no)	45	19	31		28	21	19

[a] $N = 42$ Still High, 33 Decreased, 27 Reformed, 163 Ever Medium, and 706 Always Low.
[b] $N = 58$ Still High, 21 Decreased, 19 Reformed, 66 Still Medium, and 73 Ever Medium Now Low, 212 Always Low.

I have not included tests of statistical significance primarily because they are less persuasive. The most important test of significance is the test of replication, which we do have here. The most striking differences in both parts of Table 1 between the Still High and the Reformed are found in relation to parents' marital happiness, drinking problem in family when growing up, and childhood stress scores.

The fourth column, "Ever Medium," means that at some time the respondents had problems from drinking of such a nature as to obtain a score which we have labeled medium — that is, between 5 and 15 points, but no higher score in their lifetime. "Always Low" means that the respondent reported no period in his life which rates a score of more than 5. It will be observed that in every case percentages in the "Ever Medium" column are lower than those in the "Still High," and the percentages in the "Always Low" column are lower than those in the "Ever Medium."

The exception among these factors to the general comment that the Reformed have more favorable childhood experiences in general than the Still High is the delinquency score. In Sample A a delinquency score was constructed from three true/false items: playing hooky as a child, being sent to the principal for acting up, and wanting to run away from home. In Sample B this factor is represented by only the second of the three items. The Reformed appear to have been no more docile children than the Still High, although less docile than the Always Low. This finding confirms the results reported by Robins (1966) on child psychiatric patients grown up (her point being that childhood antisocial behavior, or the capacity to get into trouble, is a powerful predictor of adult problems, including drinking problems, but that childhood behavior does not predict who will recover from these adult problems). Our results suggest, similarly, that those who have little or no history of rebelliousness or impulsivity are less likely to get into drinking problems at all. However, the eventual fate of those who do display some rebelliousness in childhood, and who do get in trouble with drinking at some time in their life, is partly determined by the nature of their other childhood experiences: relatively little childhood stress (i.e., an unbroken home, secure feelings about being loved, absence of parental drinking problems) tends to influence them in middle age to settle down and to be able to give up their excessive drinking.

There are exceptions of course. A good illustration of such an exception is the case of a man interviewed in 1964. This respondent (#01641) had a particularly miserable childhood and drank to excess for several years, yet at the time of the interview, when he was 41, was definitely a controlled drinker and had been for some time. Describing his childhood, he says, "What I seen of that marriage was enough for me — continuous fight, day and night. He was a fifth-a-day man, and she did pretty good herself. I was just a piece of furniture. There wasn't any meals cooked; I had to shift for myself. I was ashamed all the time, thinking that the kids in school would know." (The parents' marriage ended in divorce before he was fully grown.) Of his heavy drinking period, he reports: "I was in the Merchant Marine. All during the war [the war is a common excuse; he continued until 1951], it was wild. Every night and day on shore we'd drink a week or ten days straight. We drank like it was going out of style. We drank till we fell on our face. We never ate, we never slept. I was down to 92 pounds." He also drank on the job and several times was punished for it. Although this could, I suppose, be regarded as a pattern more determined by environment than by addiction, it is likely that had he been seen at that time, he would have been regarded as an alcoholic, with not too bright a prognosis. He also stated that he was lonely and had no friends. One day he decided to quit this whole life. He wanted a home, he wanted to save money to buy one. So he became a cook in a cafeteria, a job which he continues to hold. He bought a home, he enjoys having it. He enjoys his neighbors and a few friends, but does not seem to be really intimate with anyone. He drinks once or twice a week — never less than four drinks, usually six. He says he never drinks on work nights, but by this he means he doesn't take more than one drink, and then only to oblige a friend. For example, "there was a death in the person's family. I had to calm him down a bit. He was all upset. He's an Irishman, and I guess they supposedly drink to the spirits. I just had one drink. He was disappointed because he wanted to go 'all out.'" On New Year's Eve he had eight or nine drinks, just to go along with the crowd, but he was sorry the next day because he wasn't up to working in his garden.

Aside from showing that improvement can occur even when the childhood was not too benign, this man's history also exemplifies an important addendum I think we can make to the, by now, well-documented fact that some — although relatively few — former problem drinkers are able to drink socially. This social drinking does not necessarily mean never getting drunk or drinking just a glass or two of wine, but may include fairly heavy drinking which, in fact, in many segments of our urban society *is* regarded as "social drinking."

Current Maladjustment or Dysphoria. In Table 2 the relation be-

Table 2. Past versus Current Problem Drinking Typology by Dysphoria Indexes (in Percentages)

Dysphoria Index	Ever High				Ever Medium			Always Low
	Still High	De-creased	Re-formed	Ever Medium Medium	Still Medium	Now Low	
Sample A[a]								
Anxiety-depression (high)	58	46	17	38	32	30		30
Serious symptoms (high)	30	24	11	4	4	3		4
Somatic symptoms (high)	28	40	50	25	50	53		29
General maladjustment (high)	60	57	36	30	21	22		20
Guilt (high)	28	23	14	14	11	7		7
Lack of self-confidence (high)	63	51	36	50	20	15		53
Need for approval (high)	57	42	55	35	20	15		42
Most of the time feel happy (true)	40	50	70	65	35	45		68
Euphoria (high)	58	61	79	68				72
Zest (high)	47	82	73	64				67
Sample B[b]								
Anxiety-depression (high)	62	38	42					22
Serious symptoms (high)	38	5	16					5
Somatic symptoms (high)	31	33	37					53
General maladjustment (high)	64	24	32					21
Guilt (high)	43	14	5					5
Lack of self-confidence (high)	55	24	37					15
Need for approval (high)	65	24	37					15
How happy are you these days (very)	20	34	40					47

[a] $N = 42$ Still High, 33 Decreased, 27 Reformed, 163 Ever Medium, and 706 Always Low.
[b] $N = 58$ Still High, 21 Decreased, 19 Reformed, 66 Still Medium, 73 Ever Medium Now Low, and 212 Always Low.

en the categories of past and current problem drinking scores and various measures of dysphoria is shown. It is no surprise to find that there are large differences between Still High and the Reformed — the Reformed being generally happier, less distressed, and less symptomatic than the Still High. These results might be dismissed as merely tautological, but I suspect there is more to it than that. Many of the items suggest relatively enduring personality patterns, especially the items composing the guilt score, the lack of self-confidence score, and the need for approval score.* It therefore seems to me likely that there are pre-existing personality differences between those who are Reformed and those who are Still High. Our data not being longitudinal, however, they cannot be construed as unequivocal support of a hypothesis about greater pre-existing mental health among the reformed.

An exception to the general pattern in Table 2 is the somatic symptoms score. This does not differentiate between the Still High and the Decreased and Reformed groups. In fact, in Sample B, those who were never HPD have higher proportions of high somatic scores than those who were HPD at some time. There are several possible interpretations. Maybe it takes a stronger constitution to be a heavy drinker. Or possibly the somatic symptoms are a substitute defense mechanism.

Sociability Factors. Table 3 shows the proportions high on five sociability scores. The isolation score is made up of behavior items such as visiting with friends, living alone, belonging to a church, and so forth. The others are made up of attitude items. The introversion score is a version of the Myers-Briggs instrument (1962). The only result showing a difference between Still High and Reformed in both Samples A and B is the introversion score — in both samples, the Reformed group is much lower in proportions high on introversion than the Still High, and the decreased group percentages fall in between. Results for the other sociability scores differ for the two samples, and we are inclined therefore to write them off as random effects or at least as of doubtful reliability.

* Items listed below are for Sample A. A shorter list of the most effective items, marked with an asterisk, was used for Sample B.

Guilt score: (a) I waste time and spend it uselessly.* (b) I often start things I never finish. (c) I seem to do things I'm sorry for afterwards, more often than other people. (d) I often feel as though I have done something wrong or wicked.

Lack of self-confidence score: (a) I am certainly lacking in self-confidence.* (b) I would be willing to describe myself as a pretty "strong" personality.

Need for approval score: (a) I hardly ever argue or talk back. (b) I get very tense when I think other people disapprove of me.* (c) I often cannot stand up for myself. (d) I am tender and soft-hearted. (e) I'm very eager to please others. (f) I am touchy and easily hurt.*

Table 3. Past versus Current Problem Drinking Typology by Sociability Factors (in Percentages)

Sociability Factor	Ever High				Ever Medium			
	Still High	De-creased	Re-formed	Ever Medium	Still Medium	Now Low	Always Low	
Sample A[a]								
Gregariousness score (high)	20	23	47	20		15	31	29
Isolation score (high)	43	40	25	30		21	26	32
Distrust score (high)	35	26	40	15		9	12	20
Intimacy score (high)	25	26	4	24		26	27	23
Introversion score (high)	50	46	28	28		27	22	31
Sample B[b]								
Gregariousness score (high)	31	29	21					25
Isolation score (high)	31	19	37					28
Distrust score (high)	22	14	26					15
Intimacy score (high)	24	24	26					22
Introversion score (high)	35	19	16					16

[a] $N = 42$ Still High, 33 Decreased, 27 Reformed, 163 Ever Medium, and 706 Always Low.
[b] $N = 58$ Still High, 21 Decreased, 19 Reformed, 66 Still Medium, 73 Ever Medium Now Low, and 212 Always Low.

Table 4. Past versus Current Problem Drinking Typology by Aggressivity and Impulsivity Scores (in Percentages)

Aggressivity or Impulsivity Score	Ever High			Ever Medium			Always Low
	Still High	De-creased	Re-formed	Ever Medium Medium	Still Medium	Now Low	
Sample A[a]							
Noncompliance score (high)	85	63	82	49			21
Impulsivity score (high)	70	54	72	49			32
Aggressiveness score (high)	50	55	43	40			23
Toughness score (high)	70	73	75	62			48
Daring score (high)	53	55	68	50			30
Masculine interests score (high)	52	55	57	48			25
Rigidity score (high)	28	24	40	40			56
Sample B[b]							
Noncompliance score (high)	74	48	63		44	41	30
Impulsivity score (high)	90	52	53		39	22	28
Aggressiveness score (high)	57	48	32		42	41	33
Toughness score (high)	36	14	32		26	29	20
Masculine interests score (high)	50	38	37		41	41	47
Rigidity score (high)	14	24	11		24	29	45

[a] $N = 42$ Still High, 33 Decreased, 27 Reformed, 163 Ever Medium, and 706 Always Low.
[b] $N = 58$ Still High, 21 Decreased, 19 Reformed, 66 Still Medium, 73 Ever Medium Now Low, and 212 Always Low.

Impulsivity and Aggressiveness Score. The personality scores in Table 4 are efforts to measure aspects of masculinity and undercontrol, both presumably related to heavy drinking. The scores for Samples A and B are constructed slightly differently, generally by omitting some items in the second sample. "Daring" is omitted altogether in Sample B.

The noncompliance score is composed of both attitude and behavior items, including those mentioned above as part of the delinquency score.* As was true for the childhood delinquency score in Table 1, there is little difference in the percentage high on this factor among the Still High, the Decreased, and the Reformed, although there is a very large difference between those who are Ever High and those who are Always Low. This applies to Sample A. In Sample B there is some decline in percentage high among the Decreased and the Reformed compared with the Still High. The Always Low do not have percentages quite so small as Sample A, probably because there are no women and no older people in Sample B. This score was originally thought of as an antisocial score, but it appears to be fairly mild. It indicates attitudes of nonconformity which seem to be very important for ever getting into problem drinking but not necessarily decisive in getting over it.

The other personality scores show different results in the two samples. In Sample A a sizable percentage difference between the Still High and those who improved shows up only on the rigidity score. In Sample B the Decreased and Reformed groups are lower in noncompliance, impulsivity, aggressiveness, and masculine interests. Since the results in the two samples do not agree, we regard them as indecisive. The difference may, of course, be due to the different composition of the two samples, although no particular explanation comes to mind of why the fact that Sample B is composed of white men aged 35–59 should cause the difference.

RATES AND TYPES OF RECOVERY FROM PROBLEM DRINKING

In this section I shall discuss rates and types of recovered problem drinkers. This will involve some evaluation of what is a recovery, and therefore we must first deal with the question of abstinence versus social drinking among ex-alcoholics.

The Question of "Normal" Drinking among Ex–Problem Drinkers. A storm of controversy was raised by Davies's (1962) publication show-

---

* Details about the construction of the scores may be had on request from the University of California School of Public Health, Social Research Group, 1912 Bonita Avenue, Berkeley, California 94704.

ing that some recovered alcoholics can drink normally. Among the reasons for the resistance to this idea is that in the treatment of alcoholics, it is often difficult to convince them that they cannot drink; many insist that they can "handle it," which is usually an excuse not to give it up. Also, the concept of an incurable, constitutional abnormality as the cause of their trouble has some value in enhancing the self-esteem of alcoholics and is part of the AA program. Nevertheless, there is a lot of evidence to substantiate Davies's findings. Davies himself (1969), to demonstrate that it is not only mild cases who can drink normally, described several cases of people with alcoholic psychoses who recovered and drank normally. Cain (1964) advanced the idea that the ability to drink normally is the real test of cure. Rakkolinen (Rakkolinen & Turunen, 1969) investigated a series of labeled alcoholics in Finland, who had died, and found that several of them had become social drinkers before their death. Shea (1954) described one case who, after psychoanalysis, was able to resume normal drinking. Mukasa (1963), feeling that in Japan the demand for abstinence was cruel and unnecessary owing to the importance of drinking in the culture, devised a form of pharmacological treatment which would allow the alcoholic to drink a limited amount of sake every day but which provided that unpleasant effects would follow exceeding that amount. Several other authors have reported return to normal drinking by former alcoholics (Drew, 1968; Kendell, 1965; Kendell & Staton, 1966; and Pathson et al., 1968).

It seems likely that the proportion of ex–problem drinkers who can drink normally is quite small. Several series have indicated a rate of around 8 per cent. Therefore, the phenomenon may not be of great importance to most alcoholics. However, it is theoretically very important, disproving as it does the notion that alcoholics are so constituted that even a very small amount of alcohol in their system will create an irresistible craving that will send them off into uncontrollable drinking. Mendelson (1962) confirmed in lab experiments with alcoholics that craving occurs only following large intake.

Rates of Recovery. From the totals in Tables 1–4, we see that in Sample A there were 102 Ever High PD's, of whom 27 were Reformed and 33 Decreased. In Sample B there were 98 Ever High PD's of whom 19 were Reformed and 21 were Decreased. Not shown in the tables is the total 1967 sample of white males 21–59. This total sample consisted of 786 respondents of whom 168 were Ever High PD; 30 (18 per cent) were Reformed at the time of interview, 38 were Decreased (23 per cent). The rate of decrease and reform is obviously higher in Sample A. That this is not due to the women and men over 60 is shown by the fact that if we take only men 21–59 in Sample A, we find that the proportion Reformed is about the same — 30 per cent. Facts which could contribute to the difference in results between the samples are: (a) that the duration of reformation was required to be longer (3 years) in the social problem areas for Sample B; (b) that currency was not always specifically asked, and thus was somewhat less determinate, for Sample A; (c) that current self-perceived problems even of non-drinkers were included in current problems for Sample A. All these factors are mitigated in the clinical case review described below.

As far as estimating the rate of reform goes, we can say, from the two samples, only that the rate appears to lie somewhere between 19 and 30 per cent. Two cautions are indicated in assessing these estimates: first, that the "reformation" applies to the time of the interview and we cannot tell without follow-up studies how permanent the reform is; second, that the definition of "reform" was made quite mechanically and might look different from a study of each interview.

Because of the arbitrary way in which problem drinkers and ex–problem drinkers were defined, it seemed of interest to read over the interviews of Decreased and Reformed HPD with the idea of asking myself whether there was some doubt that these people did once have a serious problem or some doubt that they were currently recovered. I had trouble making up my mind about this, and I realized finally that it was because I was trying to test the case against several inconsistent or divergent criteria. If a respondent stops drinking because he has been told it is bad for his health or because his wife threatens to leave him, some purists would say that he was never truly addicted. On the other hand, Mark Keller, who feels strongly that social consequences have nothing to do with addiction, also states that if a man has two arrests for drunkenness, that is sufficient evidence of addiction; if he were not addicted, he would stop after one arrest since it is not rational to continue behavior that gets one into trouble (personal communication, January 26, 1967). When I came to evaluate the reform of the Reformed and Decreased respondents, then opposite views beset me. Thus, one set of alcohologists might deny that these people were reformed, whereas another set might deny that they ever had a problem.

We reconsidered all cases classified as Decreased and Reformed and, on the basis of apparent stability and non–problem-causing nature of their current drinking patterns, reclassified some of them as Recovered. Almost all of the Reformed and a number from the Decreased categories qualified as Recovered. The accompanying tabulation shows the proportion of High PD's who were classified as Recovered and as Spontaneous Recoveries — to be discussed shortly — for three samples. Samples A and B are the same as in the previous tables; Sample C consists of the total 1967 sample — not just those over 34. As thus revised, the rates of recovery are similar in the different samples, varying only between 26 and 33 per cent. These are minimal figures, since a few of the Still Heavy cases not reviewed in detail might also have qualified as no longer having serious problems despite continued heavy drinking. Following are two examples of persons whose current drinking, though not very light, appears to be still within social norms and reasonably well controlled and thus qualifies them as Recovered.

	Total Recovery	Spontaneous Recovery	Total No. Ever PD's
Sample A	33%	28%	102
Sample B	26	20	98
Sample C	31	25	168

Case #0591. This 45-year-old electronics instructor drank heavily from age 25 to 40 — at least a fifth of fortified wine daily, sometimes more. He was arrested for drunkenness several times, lost at least one job, and is not sure whether the break-up of his first marriage was a cause or a result of his drinking. Two years before the interview, he married his present (second) wife. For her sake he cut down on his drinking, and he did not find this difficult. He says he would not miss alcohol at all if he had to stop. He drinks some beer almost every day — sometimes as much as a quart. The most he drank in the last year was eight highballs at a party.

Case #0834. A 41-year-old teamster who was for 16 years a "typical boozehound," he says. His wife did not object: "she was alcoholic too." At present he drinks one or two beers after work, and got drunk on two occasions in the last year — his birthday and New Year's Eve. His present (second) wife drinks very little, and he has changed jobs, which partly accounts for the change. He himself says he just decided to cut down because it cost too much, and he was afraid it was bad for his health.

Although practically all of the respondents in the Ever High Problem Drinking group did have a serious drinking problem at some time, some had far more serious problems than others. We examined recovery rates for the ten with the highest and the ten with the lowest scores among the High PD's in Sample A. The ten highest scores ranged from 41 to 69 points. Of the high scores, only two were Recovered, and both were currently abstinent. The ten lowest scores were all either 16 or 17 points. Of the ten lowest scores, 7 were Recovered and only 2 of the Recovered were total abstainers. Thus, there may be evidence here for believing the "true" alcoholic is unlikely to recover and must abstain totally to do so. The milder case may be the one able to become a social drinker in time.

The Routes to Recovery. From the cases in our samples, there seemed to be two routes to controlled drinking: some problem drinkers abstain for a few years and then find they can drink a little without losing control; others just cut down gradually as they get older or as their circumstances change.

In "Alcoholism as a Self-Limiting Disease," Drew (1968) advanced the thesis that "a significant number of alcoholics pass spontaneously beyond the phase in which health, productivity, or happiness is impaired by alcohol." In evaluating the "spontaneity" of recovery, Drew contributes some important ideas and data about the doubtful value of the various therapeutic modalities that have been tried. Just because a patient has been exposed to hospitalization, psychiatry, or AA doesn't mean that these were the deciding influences in bringing about change.

We reviewed our cases of "recovery" in order to find out how many of them were "spontaneous." The classification had to be made by exclusion: those whose recovery appeared to have been mediated by either a serious involvement in AA, a religious conversion, the discovery of a serious physical disease, or prolonged psychiatric treatment were excluded from the "spontaneous" category. The second column in the tabulation on page 271 shows the proportions in each sample who were spontaneous recoveries. The rates are about 25 per cent, which represents at least three fourths of all recoveries.

Spontaneous or not, the motivation for the recovery is usually to a large extent mysterious. In explaining "why they quit" respondents often give strangely trivial reasons. One man, after 17 years of drinking a fifth of whiskey daily, said, "I seen it wasn't doing me no good, so I quit." Another began going with a woman (his future wife) and was ashamed for her to see him drunk. Another walked into his favorite bar one day (after many years of excessive drinking and a variety of problems), and the bartender began telling him about the new, fancy sports car he had just purchased. The respondent thought to himself, indignantly, "He's buying that car with my money, goddamn it, and what have I got?" Then and there he decided to quit. He states that his wife did not believe he was serious and did not expect him to persist in this resolution, but he did. Thus, there is a certain mystery about the precipitating factors in the change of this type. Even when we consider the kind of "turning point" popular in AA theory — that is, "hitting bottom" — we find that it is not so clear-cut as it appears to be. Some hit bottom once before they change, some many times, some just see themselves about to do so at the time when they make their crucial decision. In Davies's (1969) series of alcoholic psychoses, for example, some reformed after their first hospitalization for psychosis, some only after several such hospitalizations.

There are many problem drinkers who are told that they have cirrhosis of the liver, or who experience alcoholic psychosis, or just DT's, and who are not thereby motivated to change, just as one sees people whose limbs have been amputated because of Burger's Disease, yet who continue to smoke.

William James's speculation on what happens in religious conversion seems relevant here (5, pp. 195ff.). He speaks of some persons in whom "motives ripen in silence," of a "subconsciously maturing process." (Incidentally, one of the cases of conversion he describes is that of a drunkard.) Although he is speaking of religious conversions rather than of the type of thing most of our respondents exhibit — that is, a sudden decision not accompanied by religious fervor — his idea of a subconscious or subliminal incubation of the sudden decision seems pertinent although it does not suffice, of course, to explain very much. It merely points the way to the area where one might seek explanation. As we shall see from the cases discussed in detail, some have a rather practical motive which is denied by the respondent or at least played down by him; but from other sources, we find good evidence that it was probably the motivating factor.

Case #05021. This is a 50-year-old married bartender who quit 6 years ago. He used to drink 10–20 shots every day. He says he never got into trouble; indeed, we have no record of any police or hospital contact, although he has lived in San Francisco for many years. He states, "I'm the happiest guy in the world (when drunk), never got in trouble. I was just happy; I was a good drunk." He has been on 4- to 7-day binges many times. He used to stay out all night, drinking and gambling, which bothered his wife. His friends suggested he lay off, his wife complained, but he had no trouble on the job. As a matter of fact, he could stand the drunks in his business better when he was drunk than now, when he is sober; but that is the only difference. He seems to imply that he just quit because he thought it would be better for his health; whereas his wife makes it clear that he can't drink two drinks now without getting sick. Apparently he had an ulcer, and his doctor must have told him something, but he claims that he quit without any help at all and found it not at all difficult.

His control appears to be very good. He said that people have stopped urging liquor on him because he only has one or two — usually one — and very rarely maybe three or four when he is out hunting. This case, incidentally, underlines another semantic problem: Just as "drinking" often means drinking a lot rather than one or two drinks, so also "quitting" seems to mean for some people quitting excessive drinking. For example, this man says, "I just quit," by which he means "I quit drinking so much."

Case #0904. Interviewed at age 35. At ages 23-25 he was in the Army, had a desk job stateside, drank a fifth of whiskey daily "because he hated the service." Was disciplined several times, went on 3-day binges several times, had blackouts, drank first thing in the morning, parents were upset about his drinking, friends worried about him, and he was afraid he was an alcoholic. When he left the service he wanted to go to school, and he didn't have much money so he gave up drinking, except for beer occasionally. Now he has a job he likes, as a commercial artist, considers he has no drinking problem, drinks 4-5 drinks almost every day. It's easy to say from the perspective of 10 years that he never was really addicted, but what would we have said had we studied him 10 years ago? Or would some say he is still addicted?

Case #07821. His longest drunk was for four months, which occurred about 15 years ago. (This was just before he got married.) He used to drink a pint or more every day until 5 years ago. He had arrests, criticisms from friends, trouble on the job, symptoms, and so forth. He was never hospitalized for alcoholism. He quit entirely for four years and then found he could have a drink of wine without doing himself any harm. He states he had one glass of beer and one whiskey in the last year. Concerning the most he drank this year, he had several bottles of champagne on the occasion of a party at his home. The guests had brought champagne and, when they left, several bottles were left over which he proceeded to consume by himself. He says, "I used to be an awful boozehound." He worries a good deal about getting back into drinking.

He does not say why he quit; he is not completely frank. His wife stated that he had seizures and that this really made her start to worry that it might "harm his brain." He says he had no help from doctors or AA, just did it on his own.

Case #01561. A 49-year-old sales engineer of Irish and German ancestry. His first experience of drunkenness was at 16 years of age, his first blackout was at 17. His father was alcoholic, but his parents' marriage was allegedly happy. He was first married to an alcoholic. His present marriage is of 4 years' duration, but it was seriously threatened by his drinking. He lost his job and his wife filed for divorce. After 30 years of excessive drinking, 10 years of drinking about one quart of spirits a day, he gave it up 2½ years ago. His wife describes the change: "He was without a job, money, or a wife, so he called AA. And he, this whole month, he spent it at those meetings and was sent to a very good doctor who saw me and said that he felt Bill would be about to take up with a normal life. I told him he didn't know Bill. During that time the papers were served. I met him one time and we went home to where we were living, and nothing was right. Then this doctor arranged for us to get together once more, so a week later I met him again, and something struck the both of us at the same time, and we went home, made up, and lived happily ever after, just like in the movies. [Interviewer: Something struck you?] Bill, who is closer to religion than I am, thinks it was God. We just both felt as though we were changed people at the same instant, and both knew it was happening to both of us at the same time. And everything has been completely different ever since."

CONCLUSION

The proportion of persons in a metropolitan community who have had fairly serious problems with drinking is a good deal higher than most previous epidemiological estimates have indicated. Indeed, even our figures are an underestimate since our sample excluded homeless and institutionalized persons. True, many of these problem drinkers do not conform to classical concepts of alcoholism but, on the other hand, it is not easy to distinguish operationally (at the time the person is at the height of his drinking) whether he is a classical case or not. The recovery rate is rather high — around 30 per cent on cross-section — which means it would probably be higher if a cohort were examined at the end of their lives, when the young men sowing wild oats have had time to recover. Most of the recoveries were spontaneous.

The great majority of our HPD's are people who are motivated to function socially and who are able to feel concern about their health. For example, 90 per cent of those in Sample B are employed, more or less — that is, they may have lost several jobs, or have been partially employed, or have more periods of unemployment than non-HPD's, but they are basically earning a living. Very few of them have "hit bottom" in the AA sense. Most of them are not willing to see themselves as hopeless bums. I think there are at least two types of drive to get drunk: One is to get intoxicated but still remain able to navigate and carry on (which is possible to a relatively extreme degree if you are a bartender, for example, or an army clerk). The other is the drive to get comatose or essentially helpless. Many drinkers with the former drive are really playing with fire. They think they can get away with it, and often they can. But sometimes when someone describes their behavior in humiliating terms or when they realize what is going on, they change. They realize that they are *not* getting away with it.

Though recognizing the existence of spontaneous recovery and social drinking among former alcoholics, one must be cautious about overgeneralizing in this new direction. Many people do not recover from alcoholism, and not all of those who do become able to drink socially again.

In comparing the Recovered with the Still High, we found that among the Still High the proportion was greater than among Recovered for the following characteristics:

    Childhood Stress   Anxiety-Depression
    Unhappy Childhood   Maladjustment
    Broken Home   Guilt
    Parents' Marriage Not Happy   Need for Approval
    Drinking Problem in Family   Introversion
        While Growing Up   Severity of Alcoholism

There were no differences in childhood delinquency, sociability, and gregariousness; for daring, masculine interests, and impulsivity, differences were variable and uncertain.

COMMENTARY

GOODWIN. I want to comment on your findings because they are close to the ones that Dr. Guze and I came up with in our follow-up study of alcoholic criminals. We started with a population of convicted felons and did an eight-year follow-up; more than half could be called alcoholics in the sense that they had serious problems at some time or other from drinking. About 40 per cent were in "remission," defined as not having any problems from drinking for the two-year period preceding the follow-up. Very few of them were abstinent. Most were still drinking, but according to their wives and themselves, they were working and not having troubles. The majority were still drinking — some to the point, perhaps, of getting drunk once a week. But the mysteriousness of the remissions impressed me the same way it did Dr. Knupfer. Sometimes the most trivial explanations were offered. At any rate, the spontaneous remission rate appeared to exceed the remission rate following therapy. I don't know if that necessarily means that therapy is harmful. I hate to draw that conclusion. You start with a different population when you do therapy. You start with people who come to you for help.

KNUPFER. They came to therapy because they never got a spontaneous remission.

GOODWIN. I suppose so. At any rate, in our study there were only two of those in remission who ever worked with a psychiatrist. The largest follow-up study I know of came out a year or so ago, starting with some eight clinic populations. It was found that internists had better success than psychiatrists in producing amelioration of the problem. Perhaps the internist is in a somewhat better position. He can say to the man, "Look, you're not going to be with us much longer. Your liver is enlarged and it's too bad to see a man your age die so soon, so you'd better cut down." The internist is in a position to do this with great authority, and I think the psychiatrist, on the other hand, sits and listens and often not much happens.

ROFF. If you have a man who has been confined for four or five years so that his pattern is broken forcibly as in the case of some of the drug cases, what happens? Does that eliminate his alcoholism or his problem with drinking when he gets out?

GUZE. We found that many felons who were alcoholics before they were incarcerated came out of prison and continued to drink as heavily as they had before. We haven't analyzed the data in sufficient detail yet to be able to give a percentage, but many of them do.

I'd like to make one other comment to corroborate your findings further. We did a survey on our general medical wards a number of years ago and found that a substantial proportion of the patients on the general medical wards met our criteria for alcoholism. A third of them were in remission. In these patients, the most common reason given for remission was medical. That is to say they reported that their doctors had told them that they had to stop drinking or that their illnesses made the consequences of drinking too unpleasant. So I think a lot of alcoholics do go into spontaneous remission.

The alcoholics who come to psychiatrists are different from the alcoholics on medical wards. Alcoholics frequently come to psychiatrists when depressed. We found in our clinic study that over 50 per cent of the alcoholics presented depression as the reason they came to the psychiatric clinic. It would be unfair and misleading, therefore, to compare results that psychiatrists get with those of general physicians.

KNUPFER. If the figures I have on degree of enthusiasm and euphoria are anything but temporary, it might indicate that cases of spontaneous remission are less depressed than the others.

SCHULSINGER. I don't know if the problems with alcoholics are very different in the United States and Denmark. When I drink with Americans, I have the feeling that alcohol acts about the same way. But I think there's a problem when you compare criminal alcoholics and just ordinary alcoholics. A colleague of mine, Dr. K. Arentsen, made a survey some years ago in a municipal outpatient clinic for alcoholics in the town of Arhus, Denmark. This clinic also served the criminals — either those who got a conditional sentence (the condition being that they go for treatment) or people who were released on parole under the same condition. Surprisingly enough, results after the treatment (the usual thing — Antabuse, social assistance, and a little conversation) were considerably better for the criminal group. You might debate that that was because the criminal group, so to say, had the whip over them and if they started drinking again they would be in trouble. But I don't think so. Rather, it might be a question of age. Criminality, at least in Denmark, culminates around the age of thirty-five, after which the criminal career starts to decrease. Some of those people were convicted in their twenties but it's very difficult to get alcoholics in their twenties to go for any voluntary treatment. That's a big problem with alcoholics. You can't get them in for any treatment until they are forced by their wives or by somebody else. So I think that when you compare criminal alcoholics and ordinary alcoholics, you have to take the age problem into consideration.

BABAGIAN. We learned by experience in Monroe County that the best way to motivate an alcoholic for rehabilitation is to provide a nonpunitive and accepting facility for withdrawal without too many hurdles. After withdrawal, outpatient groups and other programs are suggested to some and a hostel-like rehabilitation and work adjustment program to others. Many do not want any program, so they go out and keep coming back for withdrawal periodically. Eventually some ask for further care, and this is when their chances for rehabilitation are best.

The Continued Care Unit for alcoholics of the Monroe Community Hospital is a hostel-like facility in the same building complex where detoxification is carried out. Many alcoholics with arrest records and no immediate family and some with conditional discharge from the court are treated. They take Antabuse and participate in a work adjustment program and group therapy. This program's results are currently being studied, but our impression is that about half of the patients have been working regularly and have few or no arrests since their rehabilitation.

QUESTION. You mention a general population sample. What general population does the sample you studied represent, and how did you establish your contacts with them?

KNUPFER. They're both samples of a San Francisco population 21 years old and over; 21 was chosen instead of 20 because that's an age when drinking is legal. There was some feeble idea, which I think was quite wrong, that you would have trouble getting people to talk about their drinking if it were illegal, but that's part of the timidity of the interviewers; you eventually find out you can ask anything. The first sample was of everybody in the population including, with no restrictions, all races, both sexes, and all ages. The second sample was restricted to white males 21 to 59. It was drawn with the use of more or less standard probability methods. I don't recall the exact details, but the first one was based almost entirely on a list of all census tracts from which some tracts were chosen randomly, from which blocks were chosen randomly, from which houses were chosen randomly, from which the member of the family was chosen randomly by a system of random numbers that the interviewer was given to pick the adult interviewee. With the second one the same procedure was used, but of course it was more complicated because we had to eliminate all those households that did not contain a white man of the right age; it still required enumerating the entire family in order to find out if it did contain the right age and color.

QUESTION. Do you have the incidence figure?

KNUPFER. Oh yes. In the first sample it's 11 per cent, and in the whole group of white males aged 21 to 59, it's 27 per cent. That's in San Francisco. We have done studies comparing San Francisco with national central cities, finding that the rate is probably not much higher; rather, it's probably underestimated in other cities.

REFERENCES

Cain, A. *The cured alcoholic.* New York: Day, 1964.
Davies, D. L. Normal drinking in recovered alcohol addiction. *Quarterly Journal of Studies on Alcohol,* 1962, 23, 94–104.
———, Scott, D. F., & Malherbe, N. Resumed normal drinking in recovered psychotic alcoholics. *International Journal of Addiction,* 1969, 4, 187–194.
Drew, L. Alcoholism as a self-limiting disease. *Quarterly Journal of Studies on Alcohol,* 1968, 29, 956–967.
James, W. *The varieties of religious experience.* New York: Modern Library.
Jellinek, E. M. Phases of alcohol addiction. *Quarterly Journal of Studies on Alcohol,* 1952, 13, 673–684.
———. *The disease concept of alcoholism.* New Haven, Conn.: College and University Press, 1960.
Kendell, R. E. Normal drinking by former alcohol addicts. *Quarterly Journal of Studies on Alcohol,* 1965, 26, 247–257.
——— & Staton, M. C. The fate of untreated alcoholics. *Quarterly Journal of Studies on Alcohol,* 1966, 27, 30–41.
Knupfer, G. The epidemiology of problem drinking. *American Journal of Public Health,* 1967, 57, 973–986.
——— & Room, R. Abstainers in a metropolitan community. *Quarterly Journal of Studies on Alcohol,* 1970, 31, 105–131.
Mendelson, J. (Ed.) Experimentally induced intoxication and withdrawal in alcoholics. *Quarterly Journal of Studies on Alcohol,* 1962, Suppl. 2, 188ff.
Mukasa, H. A new treatment of alcoholism with cyanamide (H_2NCN). Presented at the joint meeting of the Japanese Society of Psychiatry and Neurology and the American Psychiatric Association, Tokyo, May 1963.
Myers, I. Briggs. *The Myers-Briggs type indicator manual.* Princeton, N.J.: Educational Testing Service, 1962.
Norvig, J., & Nielsen, B. A. Follow-up study of 221 alcohol addicts in Denmark. *Quarterly Journal of Studies on Alcohol,* 1956, 17, 633–642.
Pattison, E. M., Headley, E. B., Gleser, G. C., & Gottschalk, L. A. The relation of drinking patterns to overall health in successfully treated alcoholics. Presented at meeting of the American Psychiatric Association, New York, May 1965. (Published in revised version, *Quarterly Journal of Studies on Alcohol,* 1968, 29, 610–633.)
Pfeffer, A. Z., & Berger, S. A follow-up study of treated alcoholics. *Quarterly Journal of Studies on Alcohol,* 1957, 18, 624–648.
Rakkolainen, V., & Turunen, S. From unrestrained to moderate drinking. *Acta Psychiatrica Scandinavica,* 1969, 45, 47–52.
Robins, L. N. *Deviant children grown up: A psychiatric and sociological study of sociopathic personality.* Baltimore: Williams & Wilkins, 1966.
Room, R. Assumptions and implications of disease concepts of alcoholism. Paper presented at the 29th International Congress on Alcoholism and Drug Dependence, Sydney, N.S.W., Australia, February 1970.
Rossi, J. J., Stach, A., & Bradley, N. J. Effects of treatment of male alcoholics in a mental hospital: A follow-up study. *Quarterly Journal of Studies on Alcohol,* 1963, 24, 91–108.
Selzer, M. L., & Holloway, W. H. A follow-up of alcoholics committed to a state hospital. *Quarterly Journal of Studies on Alcohol,* 1957, 18, 98–120.

Shea, J. E. Psychoanalytic therapy and alcoholism. *Quarterly Journal of Studies on Alcohol*, 1954, 15, 595–605.
Thimann, J. Who is qualified to treat the alcoholic. Comment on Krystal Moore discussion. *Quarterly Journal of Studies on Alcohol*, 1965, 26, 310–311.
Thorpe, J. J., & Perret, J. T. Problem drinking: A follow-up study. *American Medical Association Archives of Industrial Health*, 1959, 19, 24–32.
Wing, J. K. A 4-year follow-up of 50 alcohol addicts after treatment in hospital. Ph.D. thesis, London University, 1956.

LIST OF CONTRIBUTORS AND PARTICIPANTS

List of Contributors and Participants

Haroutun M. Babigian, Strong Memorial Hospital, 260 Crittenden Boulevard, Rochester, New York 14642

Remi J. Cadoret, Department of Psychiatry, Washington University, 4940 Audubon Avenue, St. Louis, Missouri 63110

Stella Chess, Department of Psychiatry, New York University Medical Center, 550 First Avenue, New York, New York 10016

James K. Dent, Adult Psychiatry Branch, National Institute of Mental Health, 9000 Rockville Pike, Bethesda, Maryland 20014

Barbara Snell Dohrenwend, Department of Psychology, City College, CUNY, New York, New York 10031

Bruce P. Dohrenwend, Research Unit, College of Physicians & Surgeons of Columbia University, 128 Ft. Washington Avenue, New York, New York 10031

L. Erlenmeyer-Kimling, Department of Medical Genetics, New York State Psychiatric Institute, 722 West 168th Street, New York, New York 10032

Patricia Fleming, Counseling Center, Queens College, Flushing, New York 11367

Norman Garmezy, Department of Psychology, University of Minnesota, Minneapolis, Minnesota 55455

Donald W. Goodwin, Department of Psychiatry, Washington University, 4940 Audubon Avenue, St. Louis, Missouri 63110

Samuel B. Guze, Department of Psychiatry, Washington University, 4940 Audubon Avenue, St. Louis, Missouri 63110

Anna C. Hampton, Hamm Memorial Psychiatric Clinic, 940 Blair Avenue, St. Paul, Minnesota 55104

Richard W. Hudgens, Department of Psychiatry, Washington University, 4940 Audubon Avenue, St. Louis, Missouri 63110

Donald F. Klein, Hillside Hospital, 75-59 263rd Street, Glen Oaks, New York 11004

Genevieve Knupfer, 740 Menlo Oaks Drive, Menlo Park, California 94025

Gary Kulak, Department of Psychiatry, Washington University, St. Louis, Missouri 63110

Jon Tek Lum, Department of Psychiatry, Washington University, St. Louis, Missouri 63110

Charles C. McArthur, University Health Services, Harvard University, 75 Mount Auburn Street, Cambridge, Massachusetts 02138

William McCord, Department of Sociology, Syracuse University, Syracuse, New York 13210

Sue Marten, Renard Hospital, St. Louis, Missouri 63110

Sarnoff Mednick, New School for Social Research, 66 West 12th Street, New York, New York 10011

Charles H. Merideth, Department of Psychiatry, Washington University, St. Louis, Missouri 63110

Rodrigo A. Munoz, 417 Security First National Bank Building, Sheboygan, Wisconsin 53081

George E. Murphy, School of Medicine, Washington University, 4940 Audubon Avenue, St. Louis, Missouri 63110

Jerome K. Myers, Department of Sociology, Yale University, New Haven, Connecticut 06520

John A. O'Donnell, Department of Sociology, University of Kentucky, Lexington, Kentucky 40506

Max Pollack, Department of Psychology, Queens College, Flushing, New York 11367

Yvette Pollack, Bank Street College, New York, New York 10014

John D. Rainer, Department of Medical Genetics, New York State Psychiatric Institute, 722 West 168th Street, New York, New York 10032

Eli Robins, Department of Psychiatry, Washington University, 4940 Audubon Avenue, St. Louis, Missouri 63110

Lee N. Robins, Department of Psychiatry, Washington University, 4940 Audubon Avenue, St. Louis, Missouri 63110

Merrill Roff, Institute of Child Development, University of Minnesota, Minneapolis, Minnesota 55455

Carol Rogalski, Hillside Hospital, 75-59 263rd Street, Glen Oaks, New York 11004

Marc Schuckit, 7945 Delmar, St. Louis, Missouri 63130

Fini Schulsinger, Psychological Institute and Department of Psychiatry, Kommunehospitalet, Copenhagen, Denmark

Philip D. Seat, Graduate Education in Clinical Psychology, University of Minnesota, Minneapolis, Minnesota 55455

Denis Stott, Centre for Educational Disabilities, University of Guelph, Guelph, Ontario, Canada

John S. Strauss, Psychiatric Assessment Section, National Institute of Mental Health, 9000 Rockville Pike, Bethesda, Maryland 20014

Alexander Thomas, Department of Psychiatry, New York University Medical Center, 550 First Avenue, New York, New York 10016

Vicente B. Tuason, 1420 Grattan Street, St. Louis, Missouri 63104

George E. Vaillant, University Health Services, Harvard University, 75 Mount Auburn Street, Cambridge, Massachusetts 02138

George Winokur, Department of Psychiatry, University of Iowa, Iowa City, Iowa 52240

Robert D. Wirt, Division of Clinical Psychology and Coordinator of Education in Psychiatry, University of Minnesota Health Sciences Center, Minneapolis, Minnesota 55455

Margaret G. Woerner, Hillside Hospital, 75-59 263rd Street, Glen Oaks, New York 11004

INDEX

INDEX

Index

Actuarial analysis: methods of, 143, 145–146, 152; results of, 146–151. *See also* Causal analysis
Addiction, *see* Narcotics addiction
Adolescents: rates of schizophrenia in, 162
Adult unsoundness: defined, 201; correlates of, 206
Affective disorder: defined, 128; diagnostic terms, 128; bipolar and unipolar, 128–135; sex differences in, 129–132; morbid risk for, 129–133; genetic transmission of, 130–132, 132–134; and suicide, 211, 214, 216, 220, 222, 224, 225, 226
Age factor: 162; temporal order of life events, 141; in suicidal communication, 221
Alcohol problems: 203; as antecedents of deviant behavior, 140, 141, 142, 146, 147, 148, 149, 150, 151, 152, 152–153, 153, 154; effects of, 152, 219, 221, 224, 275, 277–278; in preaddiction, 241, 248; distinguished from alcoholism, 257–258; treatment of, 260–276 *passim*, 277, 278; rates of, 275. *See also* Alcoholism
Alcoholics: half-siblings of, 120–127; rehabilitation of, 260–276 *passim*, 277, 278
Alcoholics Anonymous, 256, 269, 272. *See also* Ex–problem drinkers
Alcoholism: study of, 120–126 *passim*, 256; related to alcoholic parent, 121, 122, 123, 124, 125, 126, 127, 261, 262; related to suicide, 211, 214, 216, 218, 220, 222, 224, 225; diagnosis of, 226; distinguished from problem drinking, 257–258. *See also* Alcohol problems
American Psychiatric Association: 19; classification of personality disorders by, 61–62
Anterospective studies: 35–46; advantages and disadvantages of, 190
Arrest: as predictor of deviant behavior, 151

Behavior disorders: 14, 197; and family life, 21–23; and communicative incompetencies, 22–23; development of, 36, 40–41, 42, 187, 188, 195; determination of, 37; etiology of, 188–189; manifestations of, 192; and chronic morbidity, 194; genetic cause of, 195–196; as a population control, 196
Bipolar affective illness, 128–132
Birth complications, *see* Pregnancy
Brain damage: 106; in etiology of psychopathy, 116–117, 118; inhibitional failure and, 187
Breech delivery: and later defects, 187
Bristol Social Adjustment Guide, 7, 66, 192, 193, 194

California Personality Inventory (CPI): in studying preadolescents, 70
Case registers, psychiatric, *see* Psychiatric case registers
Causal analysis: temporal order of events, 137–142, 152; direction of, 140, 141, 142; actuarial approach to, 142–146
Character disorders: distinguished from psychopaths, 108–109; suicide attempts of, 226–227. *See also* Alcoholism
Child guidance clinics: 14, 78; as data source, 10, 21, 48, 75
Chronic morbidity: and behavior disturbance, 194
Cleft lip and palate, 195

Confidentiality: in psychiatric research, 167–168
Confinement, *see* Jail; Training schools
Conformist orientation: in lower classes, 26–27
Congenital factors, 194, 195
Criminality: and associated events, 237–252; and narcotics addiction, 243–244, 248, 249, 253; and alcoholism in Denmark, 277–278. *See also* Jail
Cyclothymic temperament, 132–133
Cytogenetics, 106

Death rate: among narcotics addicts, 243, 251, 252. *See also* Suicide
Delinquency: 12; prevention of, 11, 68; and socioeconomic status, 11, 88–111; defined, 66, 67, 78–79, 90; prediction of, 66, 68–69, 70–71, 74, 262; adjudication of, 77, 79; and record in the service, 77–78, 80–81, 82, 85, 86, 87–88; and education, 80–88, 89, 262; and early peer relations, 88–101 *passim*; theories of, 98–99, 188; in lower-class culture, 99–101; two-factor explanation of among boys, 100–101; and narcotics addiction, 253; as antecedent of alcoholism, 262. *See also* Dropout
Delinquency Prediction Scale (Hampton): development of, 71; described, 73–74
Delinquency Scale (Nye & Short), 67, 70
Denmark: psychiatric case registers in, 18–19, 20, 107–108, 226; treatment of alcoholism in, 277–278
Depression: 134–135; defined, 192
Deprivation: in etiology of psychopathy, 106, 115–116, 118, 186–187; pre- and neonatal, 164; neo-Freudian work on, 186–187
Distractibility: as temperament trait, 41
Divorce: as antecedent of deviant behavior, 140, 141, 142, 146, 147, 149, 150, 151, 152, 153, 154; parental, 148, 154, 263, 276; relation of to stress, 206–207; among addicts, 246. *See also* Parents
Dropout, school: subsequent deviant behavior of, 138, 140, 141, 142, 143, 146, 147, 148, 149, 150, 151, 152, 152–153, 154
Drug use, 112. *See also* Heroin use; Narcotics addiction

Ebbinghaus study of memory, 13
Education: and later adjustment of juvenile delinquents, 80, 84–88. *See also* Dropout; School
Emotional stress: relation of symptoms of in college and adult life, 199–208
Employment: and ex-convicts, 237–238; and narcotics addiction, 240, 242, 244–246, 248–249; and alcoholism, 275
Environmental factors: 37, 39; school as, 38, 43, 44, 45, 261, 262; related to social stressors, 181. *See also* Socioeconomic class
Etiology: of psychopathy, 9, 10, 11, 16–29, 105–106, 113, 114, 115–116, 116–117, 118, 186; biogenesis versus psychogenesis, 10; psychogenic model of, 21–24; and deprivation, 106, 115–116, 118, 186–187; of alcoholism, 121–126
Ex-convicts: unemployment among, 137–138
Ex-problem drinkers: categories of, 260; normal drinking among, 268–269. *See also* Alcohol problems; Alcoholism
Extrafamilial influences: in behavior disorders, 38, 39, 44

Familial disorganization: and schizophrenia, 18–31
Family history studies: uses and limitations of, 120
Family size: of schizophrenics, 19–20; related to gains and losses, 183; of narcotics addicts, 246
Fathers, *see* Parents
Fertility rates: 186; of schizophrenics, 19–20; of narcotics addicts, 246
Follow-back investigation, 48
Follow-up studies: uses of, 138–140, 141
Freud, Sigmund, 5, 9, 10–11

Gains and losses in life events: 172–182; higher rate of losses in lower classes, 172, 177, 179–180, 182, 182–183, 183, 183–184; checklist of, 173–174; relation to social class and income level, 177–180
Genetics: and schizophrenia, 16, 18–21, 24, 25, 162; in etiology of psychopathy, 16–25, 105–106, 107, 113–115, 117–118, 175–176; and alcoholism, 120–127; of bipolar affective illness, 132; prenatal, 195–196

INDEX

Glueck Social Prediction Table: 67, 68–69; shortcomings of, 69–70
Guidance, parental: in treatment of children with character disorders, 39, 41, 42

Half-sibling method: in study of alcoholism, 120–127. *See also* Sibling research
Harrison Narcotic Act (*1914*), 236
Health: relation of physical and psychological, 199–207
Healy, Dr. William, 11
Hebephrenic schizophrenia: diagnosis of, 228; study of, 228–233, 234, 235
Heroin use: defined, 140; in relation to other deviant events, 140, 141, 142, 146, 147, 148, 149, 150, 151, 152, 153, 154. *See also* Narcotics addiction
Heterotypic continuity, 192
High-risk populations, *see* Vulnerability research
Hypomania, 132, 134
Hysteria: and suicide, 226–227

Imprinting: and affectionless character, 187
Inconsequence: 197; defined, 188, 192–193; described, 192–193; related to prenatal stress, 194
Individual Delinquent, The, 11
Inhibitional failure: behavioral and social consequences of, 187
Insomnia: relation of to emotional stress, 202, 203, 204, 205–206
Intervention: in children with character disorders, 39, 41, 42; in remedying alcohol problems, 138
Intrafamilial influences: in behavior disorders, 38, 39, 42, 43
IQ: 139, 186; of pre-schizophrenics and their sibs, 48, 64; stability of over time, 63; of narcotics addicts, 239

Jail: relation of to prior stay in training schools, 78, 79; in relation to other deviant events, 140, 141, 142, 146, 147, 149, 150, 151, 152, 153, 154
James, William: quoted, 273
Juvenile delinquency, *see* Delinquency

KD Proneness Scale and Check List, 67, 69, 70

Leaving home early: as predictor of life events, 147

Leonhard, K.: on relation of personality type to family type, 132–133
Life history research: defined, 3
Longitudinal studies: of psychopathy, 14–15, 107–118; of children, 18, 35–46; central registers as aid to, 18, 107–108, 155–161, 162, 162–163, 163, 164–165; of high-risk populations, 18–20, 21, 22–31, 163–165; of schizophrenia, 18–20, 30, 48, 229–233; of delinquency, 77–78, 79–88, 88–92; of alcoholics, 120–127, 258–262, 275–276, 277–278; of gains and losses, 172, 174–175, 183; of somatic symptoms, 199–207, 208, 209; of suicidal communication, 211–222; of narcotics addiction, 236, 238–239, 239–241, 248–250, 250–251, 252, 253
Lower-class culture: relation of to psychopathy, 24, 25–27, 162, 170, 172, 182; and juvenile delinquency, 99–101; higher rate of events involving loss in, 172, 177, 179–180, 182, 182–183, 183, 183–184

Manic-depressives: personalities of children of, 132. *See also* Affective disorder
Marihuana, use of: as predictor of later deviance, 151, 241
Marriage: 249; fertility of among schizophrenics, 19–20; early as predictor of later deviance, 147, 148; as stressful transition state, 170, 171; unstable under stress, 204, 207; multiple by addicts, 246; effect of unhappy on children, 261, 276. *See also* Divorce
Mental subnormality: prenatal events and, 189
Methadone: in treatment of addiction, 251
Military service: former delinquents in, 77–78, 80–81, 82, 85, 86, 87–88; future narcotics addicts in, 240
MMPI: 67, 68, 73; used in studying delinquency, 68, 70, 71, 100; criticism of, 70, 74–75
Monroe County (N.Y.) Psychiatric Case Register: described, 155–160; as aid to other longitudinal studies, 155–161, 162, 162–163, 163, 164–165
Morbidity: and pregnancy complications, 189; chronic, 194; for nonepidemic diseases, 195
Mothers, *see* Parents
Mulligan Scale, 66, 70

Multiple impairment: law of, 194–195

Narcotics addiction: antecedents of, 140–154 *passim*, 240, 241, 250, 253; longitudinal studies of, 236, 238–239, 239–241, 248–250, 250–251, 252, 253; and IQ, 239; and employment, 240, 242, 244–246, 248–249; self-concept in, 242, 247–248, 249; and drug subculture, 242–243, 247, 251; correlates of career of, 242–250 *passim*, 252; death rate in, 243, 251, 252; and criminality, 243–244, 248, 249, 253; changing patterns of, 249–251. See also Causal analysis; Heroin use

Narcotics addicts: defined, 236; pre-addiction charactistics of, 239–241, 248, 250, 253

Neo-Freudians: work on early deprivation, 186–187

Nervous system: maturation of, 209

Neurological dysfunction: and behavior disturbance, 197

New York Longitudinal Study, 35

Nye and Short Delinquency Scale, 67, 70

Parental guidance: as therapeutic procedure, 39, 41, 42

Parents: as informants in research, 12, 14, 57–58, 70–71, 189, 191–192; schizophrenic, 18, 19–20, 20, 22, 24, 29; fertility of, 19–20, 186, 246; effects of early separation from, 20, 29, 179–180, 240, 261, 276; relations of with child, 36–37, 38, 38–39, 42–46, 187–188; effects of alcoholic on children, 121, 122, 123, 124, 125, 126, 261, 262; manic-depressive, 132; divorce of, 148, 154

Peer group: importance of, 38; schizophrenics in, 53–54, 55, 56–57, 59; delinquents in, 88–92, 99–101; in drug subculture, 242–243, 247, 251

Penitentiary, *see* Jail

Persistence: as temperament trait, 41, 44

Personality: normal and abnormal compared, 47, 52–64; in elementary school, 52–54; in junior high, 54–55

Personality disorders: antisocial, 47; siblings of, 52–64 *passim*, 110–112, 112–114; sex differences in, 53–54, 55; compared with schizophrenics, 53–54, 59–61

Personality Inventory for Children

(PIC): used to predict delinquency, 71; described, 71–73

Pinel, Philippe: quoted, 102

Postnatal stress: vulnerability to related to congenital insult, 194

Pregnancy: neglect in, 27, 28, 164; results of complications of, 28–29, 187, 189, 193, 194, 195, 196, 197

Prematurity, *see* Pregnancy

Pre-schizophrenics: siblings of, 48, 58; IQ of, 48, 64; sex differences among, 58–59, 64. *See also* Schizophrenia; Schizophrenics

Probation: value of, 78

Problem drinkers, *see* Alcohol problems; Alcoholism

Problem-drinking score, 249–260

Process-reaction dimensions, 63

Psychiatric case registers: in Denmark, 18–19, 20, 107–108, 226; as base for high-risk populations, 18–20, 107–108, 163–165; in Monroe County (N.Y.), 155–156; uses for, 156, 161–163, 166

Psychogenic model, 16, 21–24

Psychological soundness, 200–201

Psychological unsoundness: defined, 201; relation of in college and adult years, 202–203

Psychopaths: distinguished from character neurotics, 108–109

Psychopathy: 108; classification of, 102–105

Psychoses: incidence of, 129

Psychosomatic symptoms, *see* Somatic symptoms

Psychotherapy: in guidance of character disorders, 39, 41, 46

Retardation, mental, 189, 235

Retrospective studies: 137; reliability of data in, 12, 14, 57–58, 70–71, 189, 191–192; follow-back, 48; value of, 189–192; and etiology of behavior disturbance, 192; of alcoholism, 256

Risk research: future of, 29–31. *See also* Vulnerability research

Rubella: effects of, 189–190

Schizophrenia: 10; antecedents of, 5, 12, 21, 47; etiology of, 12, 25, 30, 47, 59; high-risk samples for, 14, 18–20, 22–31, 48, 162, 164–165; rates of, 18, 20, 24–25, 26; defined, 27; and personality disorders, 53, 54, 55, 59–61; sex differences in, 53, 54, 57, 58–59, 64;

INDEX

hyperactive, 62; and socioeconomic class, 62, 162; hebephrenic, 228, 229, 230, 231–232, 232–233, 234, 235; simple, 228, 232–233, 234–235

Schizophrenics: parents of, 18, 19–20, 20, 22, 24, 29; siblings of, 20, 38, 47–61, 62–64, 108; ages of, 21, 63, 162; adjustment of, 58; IQ of, 64

Schneider, K.: classification of psychopathy, 103–104

School: records of, 35, 48, 49–52, 57, 63, 79, 139; as environmental factor, 38, 43, 44, 45, 261, 262; extracurricular activities in, 50–51, 56–57; poor work in and neurological symptoms, 187. *See also* Dropout; Education

Scottish Mental Survey, 186

Self-concept: and socioeconomic class, 25, 26, 26–27; in narcotics addiction, 242, 247–248, 249

Self-Concept Scale, 66

Sexual activity: precocious as a predictor, 147, 151

Sibling research: in studying schizophrenia, 20, 28, 47–61, 108; in studying psychopathy, 107–118; in studying alcoholism, 120–127

Social apprehensiveness, 193

Social Prediction Table (Glueck & Glueck), 67, 68–69, 70

Socioeconomic class: 62, 161; and schizophrenia, 24–25, 26, 27, 162; and self-concept, 26; and juvenile delinquency, 89–101 *passim*; and frequency of stressors, 170, 171, 172, 176–177, 180, 181, 182, 183–184; lower, psychiatric symptoms in, 170, 172, 183; middle, somatic symptoms in, 199–207, 208–209. *See also* Lower-class culture

Sociogenic model, 11, 16, 24–27

Sociopathic personality: 105; suicidal attempts of, 226–227

Somatic symptoms: listed, 200, 201, 202, 204, 205, 206; medical evaluation of, 200, 205, 206; changes in over time, 201, 201–202, 203, 204–205, 206, 209–210; relation of to functioning, 207–208; nature of, 208–209

Statistical association, 140–141. *See also* Causal analysis

Status deprivation: related to juvenile delinquency, 98–99

Stress: susceptibility to, 36–37, 39, 41, 42; relation of social class to frequency of, 171, 172, 176–177, 180, 181, 182, 183–184; differences in response to, 204–205

Subdepressives, 132

Suicide: and psychiatric illnesses, 211, 212, 214, 216, 218, 220, 222, 224, 225, 226–227; and alcoholism, 211, 214, 216, 219, 220, 221, 222, 224, 225; communication about, 211–225 *passim*; of narcotics addicts, 243, 251, 252

Teachers: as informants, 70

Temperament: 6; and behavior disorders, 5, 38, 188; defined, 36–37, 38; interaction of with environment, 37, 39; and behavior disorders, 40–41

Therapeutic intervention: in psychoanalysis, 10, 39, 41, 46; through parental guidance, 39, 41, 42

Training schools: relation of stay in to later offenses, 78, 79; relation of to military service, 83–86

Transition states: examples of, 170; effects of, 170–171

Twins, monozygotic: schizophrenia in, 28. *See also* Sibling research

Unforthcomingness: defined, 188, 192; and pregnancy stresses, 193, 196

Unipolar affective illness, *see* Affective disorder

Vulnerability research: 18–20, 21, 22–31, 163–165; methods for studying, 12–16; genetic model, 18; psychogenic model, 21; sociogenic model, 24; early neglect model, 27; half-sibling method, 120–127

Young adults: rates of schizophrenia in, 162

RC
454
L5
1970
v.2

APR 8 1975

AUG 8 1974